To John and Cindy,
with my best
regards,
Dan Caldwell

The Dynamics of Domestic Politics
and Arms Control

THE DYNAMICS
of
DOMESTIC POLITICS
and ARMS CONTROL

The SALT II Treaty Ratification Debate

Dan Caldwell

University of South Carolina Press

Copyright © 1991 University of South Carolina

Published in Columbia, South Carolina, by the
University of South Carolina Press

Manufactured in the United States of America

Library of Congress Cataloging-in-Publication Data

Caldwell, Dan.
    The dynamics of domestic politics and arms control : the SALT II
Treaty ratification debate / Dan Caldwell.
        p.   cm.
    Includes bibliographical references (p.   ) and index.
    ISBN 0-87249-747-X (alk. paper)
    1. Strategic Arms Limitation Talks   II. 2. Nuclear arms control
United States.   3. United States—Politics and
government—1977–1981.   I. Title.
JX1974.75.C35   1991
327.73—dc20   90-23923

To my sister, Bo Caldwell,
and my friend, Edward J. Laurance

Contents

Figures and Tables

Acknowledgments

Writing a book is in many ways like trying to solve a jigsaw puzzle. At the beginning, there are many, many pieces of the puzzle, and they do not appear to be related in any way. After much work, however, the puzzle solver is able to make some order out of chaos. An author trying to create order out of a complex policy issue such as arms control is faced with analogous chaos at the beginning of the project. With help from a number of people—other analysts, former policymakers, librarians, archivists, and colleagues—and some luck, the contours of the policy puzzle become evident after concerted work. With a puzzle, one never knows whether all of the pieces were packed with the puzzle until it is done. I leave it to the reader to decide whether all of the pieces of the puzzle of the SALT II Treaty ratification debate are contained in this account.

I have had substantial help from a number of individuals and institutions on this project. I gratefully thank those who took time out of their schedules to grant me interviews for this book; they provided many of the pieces of the puzzle that would have been left as gaping holes without their help. I would like to thank President Jimmy Carter, President Gerald R. Ford, Secretary of State Cyrus Vance, Adm. Stansfield Turner, Sen. Mark O. Hatfield, Sen. John Culver, Sen. Alan Cranston, Sen. Jake Garn, Sen. William Proxmire, and Sen. Richard Stone.

Other former executive branch officials who generously granted me interviews were: David Aaron, J. Brian Atwood, Barry Blechman, Landon Butler, Michael Chanin, Warren Christopher, Lloyd Cutler, Ralph Earle II, Mark Garrison, William Hyland, Curtis Kammen, Spurgeon Keeny, Michael Krepon, Joseph Kruzel, Ray McCrory, Edward Meyer, Roger Molander, Matthew Nimetz, William Perry, Alan Platt, Gerald Rafshoon, Edward Rowny, George Seignious II, Walter Slocombe, Peter Tarnoff, James Timbie, Victor Utgoff, Paul Warnke, and Anne Wexler.

The former congressional staff members I interviewed were: William Bader, Hans Binnendijk, Alton Frye, Karl Inderfurth, Bruce Jentleson, William Miller, Eric Newsom, Richard Perle, Larry Smith, Charles Stevenson, Ronald Tammen, and Roy Werner.

I also interviewed a number of staff members from public interest groups including: J. Brian Hehir, John Isaacs, William Kincade, Charles Kupperman, Nancy Ramsey, and Eugene Rostow.

I interviewed a total of seventy-two individuals for this book; fifteen chose to remain anonymous. Of the fifty-seven who allowed me to identify them, almost all agreed to be interviewed on the record. I have therefore been able to indicate the sources of most of the direct quotations throughout the text. I believe that this adds significantly to the historical record, and I appreciate the candor of my sources and their willingness to be interviewed for the record.

Much of the information contained in this book has come from several archives. The staff at the Jimmy Carter Library was most helpful, and I would particularly like to thank Martin I. Elzy, Keith Shuher, and James Yancey for their help. In addition, Linda Brady and Steve Hochman of the Carter Center helped me to arrange my interview with President Carter, and I appreciate their help. The staff at the University of Washington Library helped me find my way through the Henry M. Jackson Papers, and thanks to their assistance, I was able to locate many important documents.

I supplemented the information from interviews and archives with a number of formerly classified papers, and I would like to thank the staff members of the Freedom of Information units at the Department of Defense, the Department of State, and the National Security Council for their help.

Finally, I would be remiss if I did not acknowledge the substantial debt that I owe to analysts and scholars who have previously written about arms control, the Carter administration, and SALT II. In particular, I have learned much from the writings of Strobe Talbott, Gaddis Smith, Steven Miller, Thomas Graham, Gloria Duffy, and David Kurkowski. Ralph Earle II allowed me to read and quote from an unpublished manuscript concerning SALT II, and I appreciate his generosity.

Writing a book is often a lonely experience; it becomes bearable, and sometimes even exhilarating, when others read and comment on work in progress. I am fortunate to have a number of friends and colleagues who were willing to read and make comments on all or part of the manuscript, and I deeply appreciate the suggestions of the following: Robert Art, Lora Caldwell, Lloyd Jensen, Neil Joeck, Michael Krepon, Joseph Kruzel, Edward Laurance, Roger Molander, Barry Pavel, Bennett Ramberg, Larry Smith, B. Thomas Trout, and Eugene Wittkopf.

Several institutions have provided support for this study, and I would like to acknowledge and express my deep appreciation for that support. The University Research Council and the Sabbatical Leave Committee of Pepperdine University provided me with both time and money, the two essential prerequisites for doing research. In addition, David Davenport, the president of Pepperdine, helped arrange my interview with President Ford, and I appreciate his help. The United States Institute of Peace awarded me a research grant to complete this study. The opinions, findings, and conclusions or recommendations expressed in this book are mine and do not necessarily reflect the views of the United States Institute of Peace. Thomas F. Collins tutored me in the arcane world of computers, and his help was invaluable. I am grateful for the support of all of these individuals and organizations.

I have dedicated this book to my sister and friend, Bo Caldwell, and to my professional colleague, Edward J. Laurance, who over the years has become like a brother to me.

The Dynamics of Domestic Politics and Arms Control

Domestic Politics and Arms Control

A treaty entering the Senate is like a bull going into the arena:
no one can say just when or how the blow will fall—
but one thing is certain—it will never leave the arena alive.

John Hay

Jimmy Carter and Leonid Brezhnev signed the SALT II Treaty on June 18, 1979, and four days later President Carter submitted it to the Senate for its "advice and consent," as required by the Constitution. The formal debate on treaty lasted for a period of seven and a half months, from June 18 until January 3, 1980. But the informal debate on SALT II and its objectives had begun much earlier, soon after the SALT I agreements were signed in May 1972.

The debate over the SALT II Treaty involved the American public, a number of diverse interest groups, the Congress, the executive branch, the media, U.S. allies, and, of course, the Soviet Union. In the past, analysts have tended toward a "billiard ball" explanation of negotiations between or among states. According to this view, the United States and the Soviet Union negotiate and conclude agreements like separate billiard balls colliding on a table; each country is characterized as an anthropomorphized, unitary, national actor.[1] But such a view does not allow for the role that individuals and groups within each country may play in the process of treaty negotiation and ratification. Few analysts have focused on domestic politics as an explanation of treaty success or failure;[2] however, in recent years, several analysts have called attention to the importance of domestic factors in accounting for the successes and failures of modern arms control.[3]

This book focuses on the role of domestic factors in arms control in general and the influence of domestic factors in the SALT II Treaty ratification debate in particular. While it is difficult to generalize on the basis of one case, crucial cases such as SALT II can provide the scholar and the policymaker valuable lessons about the processes of treaty formulation and ratification.

A number of journalists, scholars, and former policymakers, including Strobe Talbott, Henry Kissinger, Jimmy Carter, Cyrus Vance, and Zbigniew

Brzezinski, have focused in their writings about SALT II on the negotiation of the treaty. Despite the attention given to the negotiation of SALT II, scholars and policymakers have devoted relatively little attention to the attempt to gain ratification of the treaty.[4] This book attempts to fill this gap in the existing literature.

It is also a case study of the role that domestic politics plays in arms control within the United States. Despite the general lack of attention to this subject, domestic politics have played a role in the past. For example, in the late 1950s and the early 1960s, many Americans became concerned about the increasing amounts of a radioactive isotope, strontium 90, found in the bone marrow of children. The presence of this isotope was related to the incidence of leukemia among children, and many believed that the increased levels of strontium 90 were due to nuclear tests conducted in the atmosphere. Consequently, many people called for the halting of such tests, a goal that was translated into policy with the Limited Nuclear Test Ban Treaty of 1963.[5]

In another example, toward the end of the 1960s, many Americans became concerned about the development and potential deployment of anti-ballistic missile (ABM) defense systems. To the surprise of government officials who thought that Americans would want ABM systems to protect their cities, many citizens opposed the building and deployment of ABMs. This factor was important in convincing President Nixon to seek stringent limits on anti-ballistic missile deployments. Then, in the early 1980s, many Americans became concerned about the threat posed by a nuclear arms race and campaigned for an immediate, bilateral freeze on the production and deployment of nuclear weapons. The nuclear freeze campaign was a grassroots movement and demonstrated the power of public involvement in a public policy issue.

The principal question this book addresses is why the SALT II Treaty faced such strong opposition and in the end failed to win ratification. The analyses published to date offer three answers to this question. First, critics of SALT II argued that the treaty was substantively flawed, and that it was therefore unacceptable to the American people and to the U.S. Congress.[6] Second, some, including most prominently Zbigniew Brzezinski, contended that Soviet international behavior doomed the treaty. In Brzezinski's words, "SALT II was buried in the sands of the Ogaden."[7] Third, some observers believe that SALT II was not ratified because of the ineptness of the Carter administration; these analysts focus on the executive branch in explaining the SALT II failure. The analysis contained in this book addresses these three explanations and supplements them by considering the roles of public opinion, interest groups, and the U.S. Senate in the SALT II Treaty ratification debate.

This book examines several central propositions. First, domestic politics matter in arms control, and a president ignores domestic political factors in formulating arms control policy at his peril. Second, an administration's strategy and tactics for winning approval of an arms control agreement must be carefully tailored to the international and domestic political environments. Third, it is clear that domestic political factors do not always determine the outcome of arms control treaty-ratification debates; in the SALT II case several external events unrelated to the treaty played a crucial role in determining the outcome of the ratification debate.

PLAN OF THE BOOK

President Carter entered office having criticized the Republican administrations of Richard Nixon and Gerald Ford for having neglected what he saw as the major historical strength and distinguishing feature of American foreign policy, its emphasis on morality and humanitarianism. Because Carter's approach to international relations differed significantly from that of his predecessors, it is described in chapter 1.

Whereas the first chapter reviews the Carter administration's approach to foreign policy in general, chapter 2 reviews its approach to arms control. President Carter wanted to achieve meaningful limits on nuclear weapons in particular and wanted to do so quickly. Consequently, he and his advisers developed a "comprehensive proposal" for achieving deep cuts in the strategic arsenals of the United States and the Soviet Union which Secretary of State Vance presented to the Soviets during his visit to Moscow in March 1977. Rather than achieving the rapid progress for which Carter had hoped, this proposal and the way in which it was presented infuriated the Soviets, and they immediately rejected it and the American fallback proposal. Thus, the March 1977 proposal is an important part of the SALT II story.

Chapter 3 focuses on the Carter administration's strategy and tactics for winning the ratification of the SALT II agreement. By the time that SALT II was signed, the administration had achieved a significant foreign policy victory with the ratification of the Panama Canal treaties. Using their Panama ratification strategy as a model, members of the Carter administration fashioned a new ratification strategy for the SALT II Treaty. This strategy was described by high-level advisers in a number of confidential memos to the president. Although these memos were highly sensitive at the time (a number are marked "For the President's Eyes Only"), they were not given national security classifications because they did not concern intelligence sources and methods or American negotiating positions. Therefore, these memos were available to me at the Carter Library. The information gained from these sources was supplemented with interviews with senior members of the Carter administration.

Public opinion is the foundation of democratic government, and in the contemporary era, public and private pollsters gauge the state of public opinion on a wide variety of subjects. Chapter 4 reviews the polls that were taken on arms control, SALT II, defense spending, and the fears of the American people. Different polls sponsored by diverse organizations have found that approximately 75 percent of Americans consistently support "generic" arms control. At the beginning of the SALT II ratification debate, some Carter administration officials assumed that the same percentage would support the SALT II Treaty. This was not the case. In addition, the polls specifically focusing on SALT II had widely divergent results. Although the Department of State tracked all of the major polls on SALT II, President Carter depended primarily on the results of polls conducted by Patrick Caddell, and these findings differed significantly from those of other polls.

The SALT II Treaty became the target of a number of conservative interest groups, and the campaign against the ratification of the treaty represented, according to former deputy national security adviser David Aaron, "the revenge of the hawks over Vietnam and the Carter administration's defense program."[8] In chapter 5 the principal interest groups that were involved in the SALT II debate are described and their effectiveness assessed. The principal arguments for and against the treaty are also briefly presented in this chapter.

Charles Kegley and Eugene Wittkopf have pointed out that "During the past decade, American foreign policy has become increasingly politicized, to the point that the old aphorism 'politics stops at the water's edge' now seems little more than a quaint historical cliché."[9] This observation is particularly relevant to the debate over the SALT II Treaty within the Senate, the topic addressed in chapter 6. Four major groups of senators are identified: the treaty supporters, the conservative opponents, the liberal critics, and the undecided senators. In addition, the roles of the relevant committees and influential staff members are considered. Various estimates of the likely vote of the Senate on SALT II are presented.

Several decades ago, events could be neatly categorized as either "domestic" or "international"; those days are now long gone. Domestic events are internationalized and international events are domesticated. During the debate over SALT II, as chapter 7 recounts, three events outside the boundaries of the United States had a profound influence on the fate of the treaty within the United States: the "discovery" of a Soviet combat brigade in Cuba at the end of August 1979, the takeover of the American embassy in Tehran by a group Iranian "students" in November, and the Soviet invasion of Afghanistan at the end of December. Although none of these events was directly related to the SALT II Treaty, a number of politicians and treaty critics were quick to link them to SALT II. Thus, these three international events became part of the political debate within the United States over the fate of the SALT II Treaty.

In chapter 8, I consider the questions of whether the SALT II Treaty could have been ratified and why it was not ratified. Following the failure of the SALT II Treaty to win ratification, a number of scholars and former policymakers (some of whom had been involved in the SALT II debate) called for amending the constitutional requirement for a two-thirds majority vote in the Senate to ratify treaties. Several alternatives to the status quo are considered in the concluding chapter. Finally, the lessons of the SALT II Treaty ratification debate are presented.

Dan Caldwell
Pacific Palisades, California

NOTES

1. Graham T. Allison, *Essence of Decision: Explaining the Cuban Missile Crisis* (Boston: Little, Brown, 1971), 10–38.

2. The defeat of the Treaty of Versailles by the U.S. Senate stimulated some interest in the role of domestic politics in the treaty ratification process; see Alan Cranston, *The Killing of the Peace* (New York: Viking Press, 1960); Royden J. Dangerfield, *In Defense of the Senate: A Study in Treaty Making* (Norman: University of Oklahoma Press, 1933); and William C. Widenor, *Henry Cabot Lodge and the Search for an American Foreign Policy* (Berkeley: University of California Press, 1980).

3. Duncan L. Clarke, *Politics of Arms Control: The Role and Effectiveness of the U.S. Arms Control and Disarmament Agency* (New York: The Free Press, 1979) and Steven E. Miller, "Politics over Promise: Domestic Impediments to Arms Control," *International Security* 8, no. 4 (Spring 1984): 67–90.

4. Strobe Talbott added a chapter focusing on the ratification debate to the paperback version of his excellent book, *Endgame: The Inside Story of SALT II* (New York: Harper and Row, 1979).

5. Mary Lepper, *Foreign Policy Formulation: A Case Study of the Nuclear Test Ban Treaty of 1963* (Columbus, Ohio: Bobbs Merrill, 1971).

6. This is the view of former staff member of the Committee on the Present Danger, Charles Kupperman, "The SALT II Debate" (Ph.D. diss., University of Southern California, 1980).

7. Zbigniew Brzezinski, *Power and Principle: Memoirs of the National Security Adviser 1977–1981* (New York: Farrar, Straus and Giroux, 1983), 189.

8. David Aaron, interview with author, San Francisco, January 16, 1988.

9. Charles W. Kegley, Jr., and Eugene R. Wittkopf, eds., *The Domestic Sources of American Foreign Policy: Insights and Evidence* (New York: St. Martin's Press, 1988), 9.

CHAPTER ONE

The Carter Administration's Foreign Policy

After he had been in office a little more than six months, President Jimmy Carter was asked, "Has running our foreign policy been tougher than you expected?" He answered, "The extreme complexity of it has exceeded anything that I could have envisioned."[1]

There were good reasons why President Carter seemed almost overwhelmed by the demands of making foreign policy. He had served one four-year term as governor of Georgia from 1971 through 1974 and had little practical experience in the field of foreign policy. This lack of experience undoubtedly made the job difficult. In addition, Vietnam and Watergate had a twofold effect on public opinion: they shattered the consensus that had characterized American foreign policy since the late 1940s and reduced the confidence of the public in American politicians and political institutions. In addition, the international system of the mid–1970s was characterized by complexity and growing interdependence. Indeed, whether states cooperated with one another in the solution of worldwide problems or whether they confronted one another, for better or worse, they were growing increasingly dependent upon one another.

Thus, in the latter half of the 1970s, the task of directing the American ship of state in the waters of international relations would have been a difficult one for the most experienced captain; for President Carter, who lacked significant foreign policy experience, it proved to be exceedingly difficult. He at least had the wisdom to recognize that it was a complicated job and to try to meet its demands by choosing experienced advisers and by devoting long hours to learning about the problems the United States faced.

This chapter focuses on the domestic and international contexts in which the Carter administration operated; Carter's approach to dealing with international relations in general and the Soviet Union in particular; Carter's foreign policy advisers; the substantive issues faced by the administration; and the eventual division in opinion in the administration concerning the proper way of dealing with several important foreign policy issues. This chapter describes the environment in which the SALT II ratification debate was conducted.

THE DOMESTIC AND INTERNATIONAL CONTEXTS

Presidents enter office with a substantial amount of foreign policy "baggage" from previous administrations; they are not free to make the policies that they would like without regard to what has gone on before. Executive agreements and treaties, for example, are binding on the United States and not simply on the particular president who negotiates and signs them. In addition to negotiating international agreements, presidents develop approaches for managing the United States' relations with the rest of the world. Since the end of World War II, American presidents have been particularly concerned with U.S. objectives toward the Soviet Union.

During the acute cold war period—from 1947 through 1962—three presidents pursued approximately the same policy toward the USSR: the containment of the Soviet Union. This posture, initially described by George Kennan and implemented by President Truman and Secretary of State Dean Acheson, was followed by presidents Eisenhower and Kennedy. There were, of course, differences in the ways that each of these presidents implemented the doctrine of containment, but the overriding objective of containing Soviet expansion and the general strategy of employing primarily military means in order to achieve this goal remained the same from 1947 through 1962.

The Soviet attempt to install missiles in Cuba led to one of the most serious crises of the entire cold war (the other two were the Berlin crises of 1948 and 1961). Following the resolution of the Cuban missile crisis, Kennedy and Khrushchev moved to reduce tensions between their two countries.

Increasing American involvement in Vietnam from the mid–1960s on and the Soviet invasion of Czechoslovakia in August 1968 precluded the continued lessening of tensions and improvement of relations between the United States and USSR during the Johnson administration.

President Nixon and his assistant for national security affairs, Henry Kissinger, wanted to go beyond simply reducing tensions to dramatically improving relations between the United States and the Soviet Union and between the United States and the People's Republic of China.[2] They sought to do this in order to maintain the United States' international commitments (including, most importantly, an orderly withdrawal from Vietnam) with reduced public and congressional support. Reflecting the European tradition in international relations, Nixon and Kissinger sought to create a tripolar balance of power and emphasized the pursuit of American national interests even at the cost of peace. As Kissinger wrote in his first book, "Whenever the international order has acknowledged that certain principles could not be compromised even for the sake of peace, stability based on an equilibrium of forces was at least conceivable."[3] The foreign policy of the Nixon administration and the Ford administration that followed was based on realpolitik and was inconsistent with a characteristic American orientation to foreign policy that emphasized ideals rather than simply national interests.

While Metternich and Bismarck were the exemplars of diplomacy for Kissinger, Woodrow Wilson was Jimmy Carter's paragon. According to Carter, as he read the inaugural addresses of his predecessors in preparing his own inaugural address, he was "touched most of all by Wilson's. Like him, I felt that I was taking office at a time when Americans desired a return to first principles by their government. His call for national repentance also seemed appropriate."[4] To Wilson and Carter, nations and individuals should follow the same moral codes; to proponents of realpolitik, such a notion was foolhardy, if not dangerous.

The Vietnam War was the first war that the United States had lost, and that experience had a profound effect on Americans and their beliefs about foreign policy. The final fall of South Vietnam occurred in April 1975, less than two years before the inauguration of Jimmy Carter. The images of the final days of twenty-five years of American involvement in Vietnam were simultaneously tragic and humiliating: U.S. Marines using rifle butts to keep Vietnamese from climbing aboard already overloaded helicopters; South Vietnamese soldiers firing at the departing aircraft. "No more Vietnams" had become the rallying cry of many Americans, and the slogan raised the danger of being as misapplied as the central lesson of the previous generation: "No more Munichs!" The war had divided both the American foreign policy establishment and the public, and this division had a profound impact on the foreign policy of the Carter administration.

The United States' failure in Vietnam not only affected the nation as a whole; it had a dramatic effect on the Democratic party. Many Democrats who might have been attracted to foreign policy in earlier years were not interested in pursuing graduate studies or careers in international affairs, a field that was tainted in the minds of many young Americans by Vietnam. During the Vietnam War and for several years afterwards, enrollments in international relations courses at American colleges and universities plummeted. As a result of the disillusionment that resulted from the war, some of the most talented thinkers in the Democratic party turned their attention to domestic issues. Another result, according to a former senior congressional aide, was that when the Carter administration entered office, within the Democratic party "there was a conceptual vacuum; there were not even the building blocks of a well thought-out security policy."[5]

Vietnam was not the only demon that Jimmy Carter sought to exorcise from the American body politic; he also had to deal with widespread public disillusionment and disgust resulting from the scandal that was caused by the illegal break-in at the Democratic party's offices in the Watergate office and apartment complex. In fact, Carter probably owed his election to Watergate; many Americans voted against Gerald Ford simply because he had pardoned Nixon of all charges and alleged crimes relating to the Watergate break-in and cover-up. Once elected, however, Carter had to increase public confidence in the office of the presidency in order to implement effectively domestic and foreign policies.

CARTER'S APPROACH TO U.S. FOREIGN POLICY

During the 1976 presidential campaign, Jimmy Carter emphasized several aspects of his personal philosophy and background. First, he said that he wanted the United States to follow the same moral code that individuals were supposed to follow; he would not lie to the American people, nor would the United States government lie to the rest of the world. In addition, Carter sought to make a virtue out of his lack of national-level governmental experience. In his memoirs, Carter readily admitted that, "having run deliberately and profitably as one who had never been part of the Washington scene, I was not particularly eager to change my attitude after becoming President."[6]

In some ways, Carter's background provided insight into the issues he would face as president. Following graduation from the United States Naval Academy, he spent eleven years as a professional naval officer, including service on a nuclear submarine. As a result, he was the first president with a firsthand knowledge of at least part of the spectrum of nuclear issues. Carter had four years of experience as chief executive of a state government. In addition to his backgound and experience, Carter had a widely noted penchant for detail. According to those who worked for him, Carter would carefully read and comment on papers on a variety of specialized subjects. Former National Security Council staff member Gary Sick noted:

President Carter was totally absorbed by the *substance* of policy. On an important issue he would immerse himself in the facts, drawing on the best expertise he could find, and would very quickly make himself into something of an expert on the subject. He made a decision only after he was confident that he had mastered the complexities of the issue, and once he made a decision he pursued it with single-minded intensity.[7]

According to a former Department of Defense official: "We would send over a number of papers to the White House on SALT, and the next day they would come back with Carter's notes and questions noted in the margins. It was unbelievable."[8]

Although Carter's penchant for detail meant that he was well informed about a number of issues, this characteristic had a negative effect. As former NSC staff member William Hyland noted, Carter "demonstrated an incredible capacity for hard work and an insatiable appetite for details . . . to the point [where] he began to lose sight of the forest."[9] Curiously, even though Carter served in the navy at the height of the cold war, there is no mention of the events of the cold war in either his preelection autobiography, *Why Not the Best?*, or in his presidential memoirs. Carter's advisers noted his "odd lack of a sense of history" and "his view of problems as technical, not historical, his lack of curiosity about how the story turned out before."[10]

Even though Carter lacked a sense of history, he perceptively sensed what the voters were seeking in 1976. During the campaign, in speech after speech, Carter emphasized that he would tell the truth and pursue a foreign policy that was "worthy of the American people." Carter was clearly addressing his comments to the most obvious constituents of U.S. foreign policy: the American people. But there is another, often unnoticed, constituency of U.S. foreign policy: the leaders of foreign states. Nixon and Kissinger were very successful in winning support for their foreign policy initiatives from foreign leaders. Indeed, the Nixon-Kissinger policies of détente toward the Soviet Union and rapprochement toward the People's Republic of China would have been impossible without the support of Leonid Brezhnev and Mao Zedong.

But Nixon's and Kissinger's policies were not as popular with the Congress and the American people. The 1972 Jackson amendment concerning the SALT I agreements, the 1972 Jackson-Vanik amendment concerning most favored nation status for the Soviet Union, and the 1973 Stevenson amendment severely limiting credits from the Export-Import Bank for the Soviet Union were significant, congressionally imposed obstacles to the implementation of the Nixon-Kissinger policy of détente. Despite the attempts by the Nixon and Ford administrations to inform the U.S. public about their foreign policy initiatives in annual foreign policy reports, speeches, and interviews, the public neither fully understood nor supported what Nixon, Ford, and Kissinger were attempting to do and thus remained skeptical of their policy toward the USSR. Ironically, détente—like the policies of Metternich and Bismarck that were analyzed and admired by *Professor* Kissinger—failed for primarily domestic political reasons.

Carter and his advisers realized that the American people did not support the Nixon-Ford-Kissinger policies and sought to develop an approach that would command broad-based public and congressional support. They returned to a traditional focal point for American foreign policy, human rights. According to Carter: "Our policy is based on a historical vision of America's role. Our policy is derived from a large view of global change. Our policy is rooted in our moral values, which never change. Our policy is reinforced by our material wealth and by our military power. Our policy is designed to serve mankind."[11] One can almost see the direct lineage of this passage from Woodrow Wilson to Jimmy Carter. Furthermore, the emphasis on human rights was characteristic of the American moralistic approach to international relations, and it commanded the respect of a wide spectrum of Democrats; everyone from Sen. Russell Long on the right to Sen. Edward Kennedy on the left supported Carter's call for increased observation of basic human rights throughout the world. Given the democratic values of the United States, it would be hard to imagine any politician who would not publicly support human rights. Thus, through the vehicle of human rights, Carter was able to win the unified support of members of his party. That was the good news.

The bad news was that foreign leaders, particularly those of left- and right-wing dictatorships, were unenthusiastic about Carter's "new" approach. Brezhnev called Carter's campaign for human rights "psychological warfare" and said that "a normal development of relations on such a basis is, of course, unthinkable."[12]

Carter's emphasis on human rights was later roundly criticized; however, this criticism should not obscure the fact that most Democrats strongly supported this approach during the first two years of the Carter administration, and this support enabled Carter to patch together the fabric of the Democratic party that had been torn asunder by the Vietnam War.

When Carter took the oath of office, his only significant experience in international relations stemmed from his membership on the Trilateral Commission, a group formed in 1973 at the instigation of David Rockefeller by prominent business, political, and academic leaders from North America, Western Europe, and Japan to foster closer cooperation among these three regions on common economic, political, and social problems. Carter was the first governor and one of only six southerners among the sixty-five North Americans appointed to the commission. Zbigniew Brzezinski, then a professor of political science at Columbia University, was the executive director of the commission whose membership included a number of individuals who later joined the Carter administration. Nineteen of the sixty-five North American members were appointed to high-level postions or served as official advisers during the first month of the Carter administration.[13] Carter described the value of his participation in this group to Hamilton Jordan. "Those Trilateral Commission meetings for me were like classes in foreign policy—reading papers produced on every conceivable subject, hearing experienced leaders debate international issues and problems, and meeting the big names like Cy Vance and Harold Brown and Zbig."[14]

CARTER'S FOREIGN POLICY ADVISERS

In addition to the "big names"—Vance, Brown, and Brzezinski—Carter named a number of other Trilateral Commission members to his foreign policy team, including Vice President Walter Mondale, Secretary of the Treasury W. Michael Blumenthal, Director of the Arms Control and Disarmament Agency Paul C. Warnke, Deputy Secretary of State Warren Christopher, Under-Secretary of State Richard N. Cooper, Panama Canal treaties negotiator Sol Linowitz, and U.S. representative to the People's Republic of China Leonard Woodcock. Also influential in Carter's thinking about foreign policy was his wife, Rosalynn, whom Yale historian Gaddis Smith contends "was more involved with foreign policy than any Presidential spouse since Eleanor Roosevelt."[15]

Individuals and personalities can make a difference in politics, and they had an important influence on the foreign policy of the Carter administration.

Cyrus Vance, Carter's secretary of state, was the quintessential "in-and-outer," an individual who combined a successful nongovernmental career (in Vance's case a Wall Street law practice) with periodic service in government. He was appointed general counsel to the Department of Defense under Robert McNamara in 1961 and named secretary of the army in 1962. President Johnson utilized Vance's talents as a negotiator and troubleshooter on a number of occasions: in Panama (1964), the Dominican Republic (1965), Vietnam (1966), Detroit (after the race riots of 1967), Korea (following the takeover of the American naval vessel, the USS *Pueblo*, in 1968), and Paris for peace talks with the North Vietnamese (1968–69). Vance and Carter became good friends; in fact, in his memoirs, Carter notes, "Among all the members of my official Cabinet, Cy Vance and his wife, Gay, became the closest personal friends to Rosalynn and me."[16]

Because of his training in law, his successful negotiation of a number of conflict-prone crises, and his involvement with Vietnam, Vance believed strongly in the efficacy of negotiations over the use of force in international relations. Perhaps related to his negotiating experience both in government and outside of it, Vance sought to understand how other statesmen perceived reality rather than automatically assuming certain intentions on their part. The dominant element in Vance's outlook, according to his biographer, David McLellan, was the threat of nuclear war.[17]

For his national security affairs adviser, President Carter selected Zbigniew Brzezinski, the son of a Polish diplomat whose family immigrated to Canada following the Communist takeover of Poland. Brzezinski attended McGill

University in Montreal and then went on to Harvard for his doctorate in government. While teaching at Harvard from 1953 to 1960, Brzezinski focused his attention on the Soviet Union and Eastern Europe and wrote several books that reflected a hard-line view of Soviet foreign policy intentions.[18] In 1960 Brzezinski moved to Columbia University in New York, and in 1965 he authored a book in which he advocated the "building of bridges" between the United States and the Eastern European states.[19] This book caught the attention of several prominent members of the Johnson administration, and in 1966 Brzezinski went to Washington to serve on the Policy Planning Council of the Department of State. After two years, Brzezinski returned to Columbia and in 1970 wrote a book focusing on the effects of modern communications and technology on domestic political systems and international relations.[20]

In his academic writings, Brzezinski offered broad—and sometimes contradictory—conceptual approaches, combining elements of the belief systems of the cold war internationalists and the post–cold war internationalists.[21] For example, in his earlier writings, he portrayed the world as bipolar. However, in his later writings, he focused on the converging effects of technology and communications. Throughout his work, however, runs a consistently critical view of the Soviet Union. The following quotation from *Between Two Ages* is typical of his view: "The Communist Party of the Soviet Union has a unique achievement to its credit: it has succeeded in transforming the most important revolutionary doctrine of our age into dull social and political orthodoxy. That orthodoxy is revolutionary in rhetoric but conservative in practice."[22] Given his background, his hostility toward the USSR was not surprising. As one former senior member of the Carter administration put it, only partly facetiously, "Brzezinski was the first Pole in 400 years to be able to stick it to the Russians, and he was not about to pass up the opportunity."[23]

Rivalry between the secretary of state and the president's assistant for national security affairs had characterized the relationship between William Rogers and Henry Kissinger during the Nixon administration. In a number of articles, Brzezinski had criticized Kissinger's conduct of U.S. foreign relations as a one-man show, and at the beginning of the Carter administration, he, Vance, and President Carter agreed that they wanted to avoid a repetition of that pattern.[24] All three thought that conflict between Vance and Brzezinski would not be a problem; the two men had worked together in several organizations including the Trilateral Commission and the Council on Foreign Relations, and both had worked hard for the election of Carter. In fact, the two men and their wives dined and watched the returns together on election night. Ironically, given the conflict that later developed between the two men, Vance had recommended Brzezinski to Carter to serve as the president's assistant for national security, and Brzezinski recommended that Vance be named secretary of state.[25]

According to Hamilton Jordan: "The President-elect was not worried about conflicts, and relished their different ideas and lively debate. The roles were clear to him: Zbig would be the thinker, Cy would be the doer, and Jimmy Carter would be the decider."[26] For his part, Vance supported a "collegial approach [to decision making] with one critical reservation. Only the president and his secretary of state were to have the responsibility for defining the administration's foreign policy publicly."[27] Initially, Brzezinski accepted his role as the administration's foreign policy "thinker," but over time, he became increasingly interested in becoming a "doer" and not just providing staff advice. There were also differences in personality between Vance and Brzezinski; a former NSC staff member observed, "If Vance was the steady, patient negotiator, Brzezinski was the theoretician and the manipulator."[28] Hamilton Jordan noted: "Vance didn't have an ounce of the self-promoter in him. He wasn't concerned with his image: he was there to serve his President and his country. And if Cy Vance didn't have an ounce of the self-promoter in him, then Zbig had several pounds."[29]

President Carter's closest personal advisers—Hamilton Jordan and Jody Powell—knew little about foreign policy, and Brzezinski took it upon himself to tutor them and to bring them around to his view. In his memoirs, Brzezinski recalls, "I found them to be useful allies, who often shared my feeling that the Carter Administration needed to project a tougher profile on the central issue of the American-Soviet relationship."[30] In their efforts to influence Jimmy Carter's thinking about various issues, these three advisers—Jordan, Powell, and Brzezinski—in contrast to non–White House advisers such as Vance and Harold Brown, had the advantage of being able to confer with the president frequently and to "walk their memos" directly into the Oval Office, "circumventing the prescribed system for the circulation of memorandums going to the President."[31]

Carter's other foreign and defense policy advisers each had significant background and experience in the foreign policy field. Vice President Walter Mondale had served in the Senate and had closely followed defense and arms control issues. Secretary of Defense Harold Brown had previously served in the Department of Defense under Kennedy and Johnson, as a member of the U.S. delegation to the SALT I negotiations, and as president of the California Institute of Technology. According to SALT chronicler Strobe Talbott, Brown was Carter's "single most trusted adviser on SALT."[32] Although Brown initially saw no need to increase defense expenditures or military programs significantly, by 1979 he had become a bureaucratic ally of Brzezinski's and called for substantial increases in the U.S. defense effort.

Carter selected a former U.S. Naval Academy classmate, Adm. Stansfield Turner, to direct the Central Intelligence Agency. In a deft bureaucratic move designed to cut Turner out of policy-making, Brzezinski took over the duty of giving Carter the daily intelligence briefing from the first day of the administration. When Turner complained, Brzezinski simply changed the name of the daily "intelligence briefing" to the daily "national security briefing."[33] From that time on, Turner was effectively out of the policy loop, although he did play a role in the development of selected elements of SALT II policy including, importantly, the encryption and telemetry issues.

In retrospect, it seems surprising that Carter and his advisers did not recognize the possibility that problems could develop between Brzezinski and Vance. Brzezinski had favored Henry Jackson for president "on substantive grounds" prior to the formal 1976 Democratic primaries. For his part, Brzezinski was critical of the other foreign policy advisers in the administration. He considered Vance, Brown, and Gen. David Jones, chairman of the Joint Chiefs of Staff, "to be badly bitten by the Vietnam bug," and criticized Vance as "not an effective communicator" and "overly concerned with the UN and with U.S.-Soviet accommodation, and . . . not enough of a conceptualizer."[34] Brzezinski recognized that his position and power within the administration depended entirely on his relationship with Jimmy Carter, and he worked hard to cultivate and nurture his friendship with the president and Mrs. Carter.

THE CARTER ADMINISTRATION'S APPROACHES TO INTERNATIONAL RELATIONS

When they assumed office in January 1977, Carter, Vance, and Brzezinski agreed that the United States should move away from the Nixon-Ford-Kissinger balance of power-oriented approach to international relations toward a "world order" approach. In contrast to the balance of power policy, the new approach placed greater emphasis on the role of economics and on nonsuperpower states. According to this view, particularly popular in academic circles in the mid–1970s, Japan and Western Europe had recovered from World War II and, as former colonial areas had become independent, the world had grown more complex, pluralistic, and interdependent. Many of the ideas Brzezinski presented in *Between Two Ages* and his published articles in the early 1970s were based on this approach.[35]

At their first meeting, the members of Carter's National Security Council reached two important decisions that indicated that Soviet-American relations would not receive the highest priority of the new administration. First, the NSC decided to conclude the Panama Canal negotiations as quickly as possible, and second, it decided to send Secretary Vance to the Middle East as early as the following month.[36] During the Carter administration, Presidential Review Memoranda were the means by which the White House tasked the agencies and departments within the executive branch to study and offer policy recommendations. A list of the subjects of the first fifteen Presidential Review Memoranda provides an overview of the administration's priorities during its first months: (1) Panama Canal treaties, (2) SALT, (3) the Middle East, (4) South Africa, (5) Cyprus, (6) mutual and balanced force reduction arms control negotiations, (7) the economic summit, (8) north-south strategy, (9) Europe, (10) U.S. force posture, (11) U.S. intelligence, (12) conventional arms sales, (13) Korea, (14) the Philippines, and (15) nuclear proliferation.[37]

Despite the new administration's avowed interest in moving away from a preoccupation with U.S.-Soviet relations, it did have to develop an approach for dealing with the world's other most powerful state. President Carter emphasized four concepts in his early thinking about American-Soviet relations. First, Carter stressed the need for arms control; in his inaugural address he expressed his hope of achieving the "ultimate goal—the elimination of all nuclear weapons from this earth." In saying this, Carter became the first president to declare publicly complete nuclear *disarmament* (in contrast to *arms control*) as a goal for U.S. policy. In his first letter to Brezhnev, Carter assured the Soviet leader that there were three areas where progress in U.S.-Soviet relations could be made: SALT, the comprehensive test ban negotiations, and the mutual and balanced force reduction talks.[38] Two months after writing this letter, the president sent Secretary Vance to Moscow to present a new arms control proposal calling for large cuts in Soviet and American nuclear arsenals.

The second element of Carter's early approach to the Soviet Union was an emphasis on human rights. In mid-February, Carter received a letter from the eminent Soviet physicist and human rights activist Andrei Sakharov. Having criticized Gerald Ford during the presidential campaign for failing to receive Alexander Solzhenitsyn, the noted Russian author and dissident, in the White House, and as a dramatic way of signaling his emphasis on human rights, Carter replied to Sakharov's letter saying: "I am always glad to hear from you. . . . You may rest assured that the American people and our government will continue our firm commitment to promote respect for human rights not only in our country but also abroad."[39] In March, the president received Soviet human rights activist Vladimir Bukovsky in the Oval Office, a dramatic gesture that underscored his emphasis on human rights. These actions disturbed Soviet leaders a great deal; they considered them to be "interference in the internal affairs of the USSR," which, as the Soviets pointed out, was prohibited by the United Nations Charter.

The third element of President Carter's approach to the Soviet Union concerned "linkage," a means of gaining diplomatic leverage that has existed since states were formed, and an approach that Nixon and Kissinger employed extensively. For example, Nixon and Kissinger would not agree to the opening of the SALT I negotiations until the Soviet Union agreed to work for the resolution of the conflicts in Vietnam and the Middle East. In contrast to Nixon and Kissinger, President Carter believed that arms control was so important that it should not be linked to other issues.[40]

A fourth element of Carter's approach to dealing with the Soviet Union was to de-emphasize anticommunism. In what many consider to be the most important of his early speeches describing his approach to international relations—his commencement address at the University of Notre Dame in May 1977—Carter said: "We are now free of that inordinate fear of communism which once led us to embrace any dictator in that fear. . . . For too many years, we've been willing to adopt the flawed and erroneous principles and tactics of our adversaries, sometimes abandoning our values for theirs."[41]

Jimmy Carter was the first American president in twenty-five years who was not forced to confront the dilemmas that the United States faced in Vietnam; his was the "first post-Vietnam presidency."[42] Carter chose to emphasize the importance of north-south relations in the Western Hemisphere even before he was inaugurated president, and the conclusion of the Panama Canal treaties became a symbol of Carter's new "world order" approach to international relations. There were several reasons for Carter's emphasis on developing states in general and Latin America in particular. The Commission on United States–Latin American Relations was founded in 1973 by David Rockefeller and in several respects was similar to the Trilateral Commission: both had been founded by Rockefeller and both involved a number of the same people—prominent scholars, businessmen, and government officials. Unlike the Trilateral Commission, however, the Commission on United States–Latin American Relations focused on developing nations in the Western Hemisphere rather than the advanced industrialized states of North America, Europe, and Japan.

The commission issued two reports in 1974 and 1976 and a third in mid-December 1976, just a month before President Carter assumed office.[43] All three reports emphasized the importance of concluding the long-running Panama Canal negotiations. Secretary of State–designate Vance received a copy of the third report soon after it was released, and he sent it to the president-elect. In keeping with his penchant for detail and learning as much as he could about the issues he would face as president, Carter read the report over the Christmas holidays. When he met with his foreign policy advisers two days after Christmas, he announced that he was going to give high priority to the Panama Canal negotiations, which he thought "ought to be resolved quite rapidly."[44] Carter believed that concluding the Panama Canal treaties was the right thing to do and "despite the opposition of Congress and the public, . . . if the facts could be presented clearly," approval of the agreements could be achieved. All of Carter's foreign policy advisers supported the Panama negotiations. According to Vance, "The Panama situation was pressing, the negotiations were far advanced, and we could not shape a more realistic and lasting hemispheric policy until this obstacle was removed."[45] Carter's Panama Canal negotiator, Sol Linowitz, believed that this issue was "the most explosive and urgent problem in the hemisphere."[46] Apparently, there was no extended discussion within the administration of the potential domestic political implications of signing the Panama Canal treaties prior to SALT II.

Once in office, the members of the Carter administration continued to show great interest in Latin America. During the first year and a half of the administration, the president and Mrs. Carter, the vice president, the secretary of state and his deputy, the secretary of the treasury, and the U.S. ambassador to the United Nations all visited the region. Carter delivered his second major speech as president to the Organization of American States, and the first state visit to the United States by a foreign chief of state after Carter became president was from Mexico's president, Jose Lopez Portillo. In the view of Professor Abraham Lowenthal, who had served on the Commission on United States–Latin American Relations, "Neglect, benign or otherwise, is no longer Washington's approach to the nations of the Western Hemisphere."[47]

The administration moved rapidly to conclude the Panama Canal negotiations, and in September 1977 a dramatic signing ceremony was held in Washington, D.C. The heads of seventeen Latin American states attended the ceremonies and had individual meetings with President Carter. The Panama Canal treaties were the key to the administration's new approach to foreign policy; as one White House lobbyist put it, "Nothing would have worked without it."[48]

Another part of Carter's approach to foreign policy was his emphasis on arms control, and a number of Carter's early speeches and decisions on this issue irked American conservatives. In a meeting with the Joint Chiefs of Staff soon after taking office, Carter deeply disturbed them by indicating that he would like to see the total number of nuclear missiles reduced to several hundred.[49] Conservatives were further concerned by the appointment of Paul Warnke as director of the Arms Control and Disarmament Agency and as chief SALT negotiator. Warnke was a Washington attorney, a close friend of Cyrus Vance, and a former Department of Defense official in the Johnson administration. Like Vance, Vietnam had caused Warnke to question the efficacy of military force in general and of nuclear weapons in particular. In a widely quoted article in the influential quarterly *Foreign Policy*, Warnke had written that the United States and the Soviet Union were "like apes on a treadmill" in their attempts to achieve greater security by continually adding to their arsenals.[50]

Warnke's conservative critics vociferously opposed his appointment and bought full-page advertisements in the leading newspapers in the United States opposing his nomination. Readers could not fail to notice the half-inch type in these ads.[51] In a highly personal attack, Paul Nitze, a long-time foreign and defense policy adviser to the U.S. government, wrote a letter to the Senate Foreign Relations Committee to oppose Warnke's appointment. Nitze wrote:

> I am concerned that Mr. Warnke, who has spoken with such certainty on matters of military requirements, weapons capabilities, and strategy, may nevertheless not be a qualified student or competent judge of any of these matters. It is claimed that he is a superb negotiator. I am unfamiliar with his successes in this area. I recognize that he has certain abilities as an advocate, but at least with respect to defense matters, these do not include clarity or consistency of logic.[52]

Nitze testified to both the Senate Foreign Relations and Armed Services committees opposing the Warnke nomination. Sen. Thomas McIntyre asked Nitze whether he thought that he was "a better American" than Warnke, and he responded, "I really do."[53] Senator Jackson questioned Warnke's veracity during his confirmation hearings, writing, "Sitting through the hearings was like watching a statue perform somersaults. . . . I cannot vote to confirm as our Chief Negotiator a man who has shattered my confidence that I know where he stands, that I know what he believes."[54] Despite these criticisms, after contentious confirmation hearings, Warnke was approved by a vote of seventy to twenty-nine as director of ACDA and by the narrower margin of fifty-eight to forty as chief SALT negotiator. Although the administration "won" this battle, the latter vote served as a powerful signal that Carter could face a difficult time in obtaining the Senate's approval of any future arms control treaty since a two-thirds majority would be required. Warnke's opponents had mustered four more votes against his appointment than would be needed to block approval of a treaty.

THE MIDDLE EAST AND THE HORN OF AFRICA

The Arab-Israeli War of October 1973 and the ensuing oil-export boycott by Arab oil-producing states were still in the minds of President Carter and his advisers when they took office in January 1977, just a little more than three years after the war. The Middle East was the subject of Presidential Review Memorandum 3, indicating the high priority that Carter attached to this issue. Nixon, Ford, and Kissinger had sought to force the Soviets out of the Middle East through Kissinger's "step-by-step" shuttle diplomacy and were successful in playing the role of "honest broker" between Israel and the Arab states, particularly Egypt.

Members of the Carter administration had criticized the Kissinger approach. In a preelection memorandum to Jimmy Carter in October 1976, Cyrus Vance wrote that he favored security guarantees to Israel and enlisting Soviet cooperation "at an appropriate time."[55] Brzezinski believed that the Arab-Israeli dispute and the energy issue were inextricably linked. According to Brzezinski, the United States would have to maintain closer relations with Saudi Arabia in order to retain access to the vast oil reserves that the Saudis possessed.[56] In his preelection writings about the Middle East, Brzezinski stressed the importance of including the Soviets in the peace process so that they would not upset any solution that was worked out. In one article (coauthored with a Japanese and a European, in good trilateral fashion), Brzezinski advocated American and Soviet "participation in an international force patrolling safety zones on either side of the agreed frontiers."[57]

Soviet leaders viewed the "détente agreements" (the SALT I agreements and the Basic Principles of Relations) signed at the 1972 Moscow summit as granting the Soviet Union coequal status with the United States in international relations, and they were furious that they had been effectively closed out of the Middle East by Kissinger's diplomatic maneuvers following the October war. They were anxious to play a role in one of the world's most important regions. Several members of the Carter administration, most notably Cyrus Vance, recognized Soviet anxiety and proposed to include the Soviets in a comprehensive conference concerning the Middle East to be held in Geneva. According to the principal NSC aide for the Middle East, William Quandt, "Although on the whole there was a rare degree of congruence in the views of all the top officials and their staffs, Brzezinski was more skeptical of Geneva and of the Soviet role than Vance was."[58] During the week of activities associated with the signing of the Panama Canal treaties in September 1977, Secretary Vance obtained President Carter's approval of a comprehensive conference concerning the Middle East, and the Geneva conference was publicly announced on October 1. In order to be included in the conference, the Soviet Union agreed to seek a resolution of the conflict between the Arabs and Israel and promised not to refer to Soviet support for the establishment of an independent Palestinian state. This was the not insignificant price of admission that the Soviets paid to attend the Geneva conference.

Everything was set for the conference to convene, but in November President Anwar Sadat of Egypt seized the initiative and announced that he would go to Jerusalem. With this dramatic move, Sadat torpedoed the Geneva conference and left the Soviet Union out in the cold. In the ensuing months, Carter and Vance met with the principal leaders of the Middle East to work out a settlement that would be mutually acceptable. These meetings culminated in the dramatic summit meeting at Camp David on September 5–19, 1978. After taking great political risks, the leaders involved in the Camp David negotiations—Carter, Sadat, and Prime Minister Menachem Begin of Israel—were able to lay the groundwork for the first-ever peace treaty between Israel and an Arab state. In his memoirs, Carter noted, "Looking back on the four years of my Presidency, I realize that I spent more of my time working for possible solutions to the riddle of Middle East peace than on any other international problem."[59]

Following the Camp David agreement, Carter told his advisers that he wanted to "convert the force for peace-making we've unleashed here into something that will finally give us SALT."[60] But standing in the way of achieving progress on SALT were several other important issues: most notably, Soviet and Cuban activities in the Horn of Africa and the normalization of relations with China.

In 1974, following the overthrow and death of Emperor Haile Selassie, a Marxist group gained control of the Ethiopian government and in December 1976 signed an arms-supply agreement with the Soviet Union. The Carter administration suspended U.S. aid to Ethiopia, objecting to Ethiopia's attacks on the province of Eritrea. At this time the Soviets had a "treaty of friendship" with Ethiopia's hostile neighbor, Somalia, which was planning an attack on the Ethiopian province of Ogaden. The Soviets objected to this operation, but the Somalis went ahead with the atttack in July 1977. As a result, Somalia abrogated its treaty with the Soviets in November, and the Soviets responded by sending weapons and an estimated twenty thousand Cuban troops to Ethiopia.[61]

Although Vance and Brzezinski had disagreed about other policies, it was their disagreement over the significance of and ways to deal with Soviet and Cuban actions in the Horn of Africa that caused their disagreement to become public by the beginning of 1978.[62] Brzezinski believed that the Cubans were acting merely as "surrogates" for the Soviets and that Soviet and Cuban actions had international significance; if the United States did not stop Soviet-Cuban adventurism in the Horn, then Soviet aggression throughout the Third World would continue and perhaps even increase. In Brzezinski's mind, Soviet and Cuban activities in the Horn of Africa and the Middle East were dangerously linked. "For Vance, a succcessful conclusion to the SALT talks was the overriding priority. But although I shared the Secretary's concern, I had by then become quite preoccupied with Moscow's misuse of détente to improve the Soviet geopolitical and strategic position around Saudi Arabia, especially through the Cuban military presence in Ethiopia."[63] In contrast to Brzezinski, Vance viewed the Ogaden war as a regional conflict that should be dealt with as a regional, rather than a global, problem.

The key point of disagreement between Vance and Brzezinski was the degree to which Soviet and Cuban actions in the Horn should be linked to other Soviet-American issues and negotiations. On March 1, 1978, Brzezinski publicly warned that Soviet actions in the Horn would affect the SALT negotiations and that "linkages may be imposed by unwarranted exploitation of local conflicts for larger international purposes." The Soviets wasted no time in responding to Brzezinski's statement; on March 2, *Pravda* called Brzezinski's warning "unsavory and dangerous" and said that he was "playing with the main problems of international security and détente" and that his statement "smacks of crude blackmail which is impermissible in international relations."[64] President Carter tried to clarify the administration's position by noting that Soviet actions in the Horn could "make it more difficult to ratify a SALT agreement or comprehensive test ban treaty. . . . We [the administration] don't initiate the linkage."[65] Vance was clearly opposed to linking Soviet and Cuban actions to SALT and thought that the president "simply described political reality," in contrast to Brzezinski's attempts to link the two publicly. Vance believed that such a linkage had two serious drawbacks: it adversely affected American interests, and it would "probably have little or no effect on Soviet actions in the Horn."[66]

The second major issue over which Vance and Brzezinski seriously disagreed was China. In 1972, Nixon and Kissinger had dramatically opened a new chapter in Sino-American relations with their trip to China and the signing of the Shanghai communiqué. Little had been done to further improve Sino-American relations since 1972. Brzezinski was anxious to complete the normalization of relations with China as a means of placing greater pressure on the Soviet Union. From a bureaucratic perspective, Brzezinski was closed out of dealing with other major issues of foreign policy. Indeed, at the beginning of the administration, he had been assigned the role of the foreign policy "thinker," but he was anxious to make foreign policy and not simply to think about it. But Vance had firm control over U.S.-Soviet relations, and the president himself chose to oversee American policy toward the Middle East. China was the only other major issue left for Brzezinski to manage.[67]

Throughout his memoirs, Brzezinski emphasizes the importance of the normalization of Sino-American relations and the central role that he (according to himself) played in this process. For example, in a chronology of "major turning points" in the normalization process, Brzezinski lists the "Vance trip to Beijing and Chinese rebuff" (August 23–26, 1977), the "Brzezinski trip to Beijing [that] reaches secret understanding" (May 21–23, 1978), and "secret negotiations by Leonard Woodcock in Beijing and Brzezinski at the White House" (October–November 1978).[68] According to this summary account, Brzezinski succeeded where Vance failed.

When asked about the purpose of Brzezinski's May 1978 trip to China on "Face the Nation," Vance responded: "Now, Zbig is not going to negotiate anything about normalization. . . . [His trip] is part of this continuing global exchange with them."[69] In fact, Brzezinski was working hard to normalize relations between the United States and the People's Republic of China, and in December 1978, when Vance was in the Middle East, Brzezinski was able to arrange for the announcement of the formal normalization. Until he was informed of the signing ceremony, Secretary of State Vance did not know that the decision to conclude the normalization agreement had been made.[70] The announcement of normalization of Sino-American relations was made on December 15, 1978, just one week prior to a meeting scheduled between Vance and Soviet Foreign Minister Andrei Gromyko to discuss SALT.

Carter believed that, as 1978 came to an end, "we were almost at the end of our SALT discussions with the Soviets."[71] In his memoirs, Brzezinski argues that the normalization decision regarding China did not affect Soviet thinking and actions on SALT; he recounts, with some pleasure, informing an "absolutely stunned" Soviet Ambassador Dobrynin of the decision. President Carter, however, noted that Brezhnev sent him a letter on December 27 warning that unless the United States pressured its allies not to sell military equipment to China, there would be no progress on SALT II. According to Carter, "It was obvious that the Soviet leaders were more concerned about our new relations with China than we had supposed."[72]

CONCLUSION

Jimmy Carter entered office under the clouds of Vietnam and Watergate, and he sought to forge a new American foreign policy that contrasted with Nixon and Kissinger's realpolitik approach. His emphasis on north-south relations in the Western Hemisphere was clear during the first months of the administration, and the Panama Canal treaties became a symbol of this new approach. After a tough fight, the president and his advisers concluded the negotiations on the treaties and were then able to win ratification with only one vote to spare. With the treaties behind them, the president and his advisers moved on to other pressing issues. The president was able to play a key role in forging a new chapter in the history of the Middle East by concluding the Camp David agreements. But the unanimity that had characterized the administration's Panama and Middle East policies began to break down in the face of the continued Soviet military buildup at home and abroad, Soviet and Cuban actions in Africa, and the normalization of Sino-American relations.

Dissension is, to a greater or lesser extent, present in all administrations, and the Carter administration was no different. Dissension within the Carter administration grew in prominence given the high priority that Carter placed on achieving "real" arms control.

NOTES

1. *Time,* August 8, 1977, 25.

2. Dan Caldwell, *American-Soviet Relations: From 1947 to the Nixon-Kissinger Grand Design and Grand Strategy* (Westport, Conn.: Greenwood Press, 1981).

3. Henry A. Kissinger, *A World Restored: The Politics of Conservatism in a Revolutionary Age* (Boston: Houghton Mifflin, 1957), 1.

4. Jimmy Carter, *Keeping Faith: Memoirs of a President* (New York: Bantam, 1982), 19.

5. Larry Smith, interview with author, Washington, DC, October 20, 1987.

6. Carter, *Keeping Faith,* 126.

7. Gary Sick, *All Fall Down: America's Tragic Encounter with Iran* (New York: Penguin Books, 1986), 262.

8. Walter Slocombe, interview with author, Washington, DC, June 3, 1987.

9. William Hyland, *Mortal Rivals: Superpower Relations from Nixon to Reagan* (New York: Random House, 1987), 209.

10. Hedley Donovan, *Roosevelt to Reagan: A Reporter's Encounters with Nine Presidents* (New York: Harper and Row, 1985), 233; James Fallows, "The Passionless Presidency," *Atlantic Monthly,* May 1979, 44.

11. Jimmy Carter, Commencement Address at University of Notre Dame, *New York Times,* May 23, 1977.

12. *Time,* August 8, 1977, 8.

13. *Washington Post,* January 16, 1977.

14. Carter, quoted in Hamilton Jordan, *Crisis: The Last Year of the Carter Presidency* (New York: G. P. Putnam's Sons, 1982), 45.

15. Gaddis Smith, *Morality, Reason and Power: American Diplomacy in the Carter Years* (New York: Hill and Wang, 1986), 34.

16. Carter, *Keeping Faith,* 51.

17. David S. McLellan, *Cyrus Vance* (Totowa, N.J.· Rowman and Allanheld, 1985), 41.

18. Zbigniew Brzezinski, *The Permanent Purge* (Cambridge: Harvard University Press, 1956); Carl J. Friedrich and Zbigniew Brzezinski, *Totalitarian Dictatorship and Autocracy* (Cambridge: Harvard University Press, 1956).

19. Zbigniew Brzezinski, *Alternative to Partition: For a Broader Conception of America's Role in Europe* (New York: McGraw-Hill, 1965).

20. Zbigniew Brzezinski, *Between Two Ages: America's Role in the Technetronic Era* (New York: Viking Press, 1970).

21. Ole R. Holsti and James N. Rosenau, *American Leadership in World Affairs: Vietnam and the Breakdown of Consensus* (Boston: Allen and Unwin, 1984).

22. Brzezinski, *Between Two Ages*, 138.

23. Author's confidential interview.

24. Zbigniew Brzezinski, "The Balance of Power Delusion," *Foreign Policy* 7 (Summer 1972): 54–59; Zbigniew Brzezinski, "U.S. Foreign Policy: The Search for Focus," *Foreign Affairs* 51, no. 4 (July 1973): 708–27.

25. Carter, *Keeping Faith*, 52.

26. Jordan, *Crisis*, 47.

27. Cyrus Vance, *Hard Choices: Critical Years in America's Foreign Policy* (New York: Simon and Schuster, 1983), 35.

28. William B. Quandt, *Camp David: Peacemaking and Politics* (Washington: The Brookings Institution, 1986), 35.

29. Jordan, *Crisis*, 49.

30. Zbigniew Brzezinski, *Power and Principle: Memoirs of the National Security Adviser, 1977–1981* (New York: Farrar, Straus and Giroux, 1983), 73.

31. Jordan, *Crisis*, 42.

32. Strobe Talbott, *Endgame: The Inside Story of SALT II* (New York: Harper and Row, 1979), 50, 193.

33. Brzezinski, *Power and Principle*, 64.

34. Ibid., 11, 29.

35. Brzezinski, "U.S. Foreign Policy."

36. Brzezinski, *Power and Principle*, 51.

37. Ibid., 51–52.

38. Jimmy Carter to Leonid Brezhnev, 26 January 1977, quoted in ibid., 151–52.

39. Jimmy Carter to Andrei Sakharov, 17 February 1977, quoted in Sandy Vogelsang, *American Dream, Global Nightmare: The Dilemma of U.S. Human Rights Policy* (New York: W. W. Norton, 1980), 103–4.

40. Edward Walsh, "Carter Stresses Arms and Rights in Policy Speech," *Washington Post*, March 18, 1977.

41. *New York Times*, May 23, 1977. According to the author's interviews, Brzezinski was the principal author of this speech, including the "inordinate fear of communism" phrase.

42. George D. Moffett III, *The Limits of Victory: The Ratification of the Panama Canal Treaties* (Ithaca, N.Y.: Cornell University Press, 1985), 58.

43. *The Americas in a Changing World: A Report of the Commission on United States–Latin American Relations* (New York: Quadrangle, 1974); *The United States and Latin America: Next Steps. A Second Report by the Commission on United States–Latin American Relations* (New York: Center for Inter-American Relations, 1976).

44. William J. Jorden, *Panama Odyssey* (Austin: University of Texas Press, 1984), 341; also see Brzezinski, *Power and Principle*, 134.

45. Vance, *Hard Choices*, 33.

46. Interview with Sol Linowitz, cited in Moffett, *The Limits of Victory*, 69.

47. Abraham F. Lowenthal, "Jimmy Carter and Latin America: A New Era or Small Change?" in *Eagle Entangled: U.S. Foreign Policy in a Complex World*, eds. Kenneth A. Oye, Donald Rothchild, and Robert J. Lieber (New York: Longman, 1979), 291.

48. Interview with Robert Beckel in Moffett, *The Limits of Victory*, 69.

49. Brzezinski, *Power and Principle*, 152.

50. Paul C. Warnke, "Apes on a Treadmill," *Foreign Policy* 18 (Spring 1975): 12–29.

51. Emergency Coalition Against Unilateral Disarmament, "Why Paul Warnke should NOT be confirmed as Director of the *Arms Control and Disarmament Agency* and Chief Negotiator for the *Strategic Arms Limitations Treaties* . . . an Open Letter to the United States Senate," *Washington Post*, February 22, 1977 (emphasis in original).

52. Paul H. Nitze to Sen. John J. Sparkman, February 7, 1977, Henry M. Jackson Papers, Accession no. 3560–6, Box 61, Folder 14, University of Washington Libraries.

53. In his memoirs Nitze indicates that what he meant to say was, "I really do take exception to what I believe to be inconsistent and misleading testimony by Mr. Warnke." But that is not how the press interpreted Nitze's comment. See Paul H. Nitze, with Ann M. Smith and Steven L. Rearden, *From Hiroshima to Glasnost: At the Center of Decision* (New York: Grove Weidenfeld, 1989), 355.

54. "Statement by Senator Henry M. Jackson on the Nomination of Paul C. Warnke," March 4, 1977, Henry M. Jackson Papers, Accession no. 3560–6, Box 12, Folder 116, University of Washington Libraries.

55. Vance, *Hard Choices*, 32, 447–48.

56. Zbigniew Brzezinski, "Recognizing the Crisis," *Foreign Policy* 17 (Winter 1974–75): 16–17.

57. Zbigniew Brzezinski, Francois Duçhêne, and Kiichi Saeki, "Peace in an International Framework," *Foreign Policy* 19 (Summer 1975): 3–17.

58. Quandt, *Camp David*, 61.

59. Carter, *Keeping Faith*, 429.

60. Talbott, *Endgame*, 205.

61. Larry C. Napper, "The Ogaden War: Some Implications for Crisis Prevention," in *Managing U.S.-Soviet Rivalry: Problems of Crisis Prevention*, ed. Alexander L. George (Boulder, Colo.: Westview Press, 1983), 225–54.

62. Brzezinski, *Power and Principle*, 178; Vance, *Hard Choices*, 84.

63. Brzezinski, ibid., 203–4.

64. Quoted in Talbott, *Endgame*, 147.

65. Carter quoted in Vance, *Hard Choices*, 87.

66. Vance, *Hard Choices*, 85.

67. Author's confidential interview with an official who served in the Department of State during the Carter administration.

68. Brzezinski, *Power and Principle*, 194.

69. Interview with Cyrus Vance, "Face the Nation," CBS, 30 April 1978, U.S. Department of State, press release no. 196, May 1, 1978, transcript.

70. Vance, *Hard Choices*, 118–19.

71. Carter, *Keeping Faith*, 411.

72. Ibid., 234.

CHAPTER TWO

Arms Control, SALT, and the Carter Administration

*All of the glib talk about ICBM's, MIRV's, SLCM's
and GLCM's . . . tended to lull some people into indifference
or resignation about the unbelievable destruction they represented.
That horror was constantly on my mind.*

Jimmy Carter

On January 20, 1977, Jimmy Carter delivered his inaugural address; in it he said that it was his hope to move toward the elimination of nuclear weapons from the face of the earth. Many people, both in the United States and abroad, were deeply moved and encouraged by Carter's address. The eminent British statesman and winner of the 1959 Nobel Peace Prize, Philip Noel-Baker, wrote the new president a long personal letter offering his "deeply-felt and ardent gratitude for your magnificent inaugural Speech . . . and for your equally magnificent message to the world."[1]

Others were not as laudatory; indeed, conservatives were shocked at Carter's speech and at his appointments in the foreign policy and national security fields. In a memo, a member of Senator Jackson's staff wrote to the senator:

> Like children who have pooled their resources to buy a single admission ticket to the circus so that the kid with the ticket can raise the corner of the tent and let the others sneak in, Carter is rapidly getting around him a group of new left doves whose loyalty is to their conception of what foreign policy ought to be and not to the new administration or to what we believe Carter wants for the U.S. It is almost certain that he does not know the full extent of the penetration of his operation. The Whizz [sic] kids are back, worse than before, because they are overcome with guilt over Vietnam. Here are a few names of people who are in positions of authority in connection with the transition: John Newhouse at ACDA, Dick Steadman at DOD, Walt Slocombe at DOD, Tony Lake at State, Dick Moose (former Fulbright) at State, etc.
>
> We should aim at getting someone into the transition before it is too late.[2]

A month after the inauguration, Eugene Rostow, a member of the Executive Committee of the Committee on the Present Danger, sent a handwritten letter, labeled "a very personal note," to Zbigniew Brzezinski saying: "I hope the hobbledy-hoy period ends soon. The confusion, Andy Young, conflicting signals, the prevalence of Tony Lakes, is causing deep concern."[3]

Carter clearly wanted to achieve significant progress in the field of arms control and disarmament, and he and his advisers wanted to begin right away. But public policy is not written on a blank slate; there is always a history to any public policy issue, and very often that history is contentious. In this chapter, the history of nuclear arms control, the SALT negotiations, and the Carter administration's approach to arms control are described and analyzed.

THE DEVELOPMENT OF ARMS CONTROL

Military strategy is an ancient field of study. The advent of nuclear weapons in 1945 caused modern strategists to reevaluate their field in order to ascertain the extent to which the old principles of military strategy still applied in the nuclear world. Recognizing the destructiveness of nuclear weapons, strategists thought about ways that the new weapons could be controlled, and in 1961, the first four books focusing exclusively on nuclear arms control and disarmament were published.[4] In their book, Thomas Schelling and Morton Halperin wrote that there were three objectives of arms control: (1) to reduce the probability of war occurring, (2) to reduce the destructiveness of war should it occur, and (3) to reduce the economic cost of preparing for war. Over time, these became the canonical objectives of arms control.

Nuclear war was primarily a hypothetical possibility in the minds of nuclear strategists until the Cuban missile crisis of October 1962 took the United States and the Soviet Union to the brink. After the crisis had ended, President Kennedy estimated that the probability of a Soviet-American war had been between one out of three and even. The crisis brought President Kennedy and Chairman Khrushchev to the realization that nuclear war could actually occur. Following the resolution of the crisis, the two leaders quickly moved to conclude two agreements to reduce the risk of nuclear war. The Hot Line Agreement, signed in June 1963, called for the installation of a direct communications link between Washington, D.C., and Moscow so that leaders in the two capitals could communicate with one another quickly, secretly, and securely. The Limited Nuclear Test Ban Treaty, signed in August 1963, prohibited nuclear testing in outer space, under water, and in the atmosphere. Extensive committee hearings were held on the treaty, followed by three weeks of floor debate, and approval (by a vote of eighty to nineteen) came only after President Kennedy gave assurances to the Joint Chiefs of Staff, Sen. Henry Jackson, and other Senate leaders that the United States would maintain an extensive standby capability for atmospheric testing and would pursue a rigorous underground nuclear testing program. So despite the fact that the treaty was a good environmental protection measure, it neither reduced the number of nuclear test explosions nor slowed the development of new nuclear weapons.

A number of other arms control agreements were signed in the 1960s, including the Outer Space Treaty, the Latin American Nuclear Free Zone Treaty, and the Nuclear Non-Proliferation Treaty. From the mid–1960s on, however, Vietnam increasingly dominated the attention of the president and other members of his administration. By 1968, with more than half a million Americans in Vietnam and mounting casualties, Lyndon Johnson announced that he would not seek a second term of office. He did not want to leave office as a president remembered for war, but as a leader remembered for peace.

As early as 1964, Johnson had proposed a verified freeze on the number and characteristics of strategic nuclear offensive and defensive delivery vehicles.[5] Johnson made several other arms control overtures to the Soviets in 1965 and 1966, but they did not respond. However, in 1967 Soviet Premier Alexei Kosygin visited the United States. Kosygin listened to Secretary of Defense Robert McNamara describe the destabilizing characteristics of defensive, anti-ballistic missile systems. Finally, unable to continue passively listening to McNamara's lecture, Kosygin interrupted him, saying, "Defensive weapons are moral; offensive weapons are immoral!"[6] In the months following the Glassboro summit meeting, members of the Johnson administration and the Soviets met to discuss the possibility of opening negotiations to limit nuclear weapons, and on August 19, 1968, Soviet Ambassador Dobrynin informed the United States that his government had agreed to open such negotiations on September 30. However, on August 20, just one day after Dobrynin's message, the Soviet Union invaded Czechoslovakia, and the Johnson administration announced that, because of the invasion, the meeting was canceled.

THE FIRST STRATEGIC ARMS LIMITATION TALKS

Following his hard-fought, narrow victory in the 1968 presidential election, people did not know what to expect from Richard Nixon. To the surprise of many, Nixon appointed former Rockefeller foreign policy adviser and Harvard government professor Henry Kissinger as his national security affairs adviser. Despite their differences in background and education, Nixon and Kissinger thought in similar terms about international relations and the tasks facing the United States in the late 1960s and beyond.[7] After a nine-month review of U.S. strategic programs and policies, Nixon and Kissinger agreed to open the Strategic Arms Limitation Talks, which quickly came to be known by the acronym SALT.

The SALT negotiations took place on several different levels. The American and Soviet delegations met alternately in Vienna and Helsinki and traded proposals and counterproposals.[8] Often unbeknownst to the U.S. delegation, Kissinger and Dobrynin conducted extensive "back-channel" negotiations in Washington.[9] After seven formal negotiating sessions over a two-and-a-half-year period, the United States and the Soviet Union concluded two agreements: a five-year executive Interim Agreement on Offensive Forces limiting offensive, long-range ballistic missiles, and a permanent treaty limiting each side to deploying no more than two hundred antiballistic missiles, the ABM Treaty (see Table 2–1 for a complete summary of the terms of these two agreements).

In May 1972 Nixon and Kissinger traveled to Moscow to sign these agreements, and on their return to Washington, Nixon flew directly from An-

Table 2-1: Summary of Major SALT Agreements and Proposals

	SALT I Interim Agreement (May 1972) U.S./USSR	VLADIVOSTOK ACCORDS (November 1974)	MOSCOW COMPREHENSIVE PROPOSAL (March 1977)	SALT II Agreement (June 1979)
ICBM's	1000 1409			2,400–2,250
SLBM's	710 950	2400 (total Strategic Nuclear Launch Vehicles, SNLV)	1,800–2,000	(by 12/31/81)
Long-Range Bombers	•			
MIRVed Launchers	•	1320	1,100–1,200	1,200 for ICBM and SLBM, 1,320 including ALCM
MIRVed ICBM's	•	•	550	820
MLBM's†	308	308	150	308
ACLM	•	[dispute over whether included under SNLV ceiling]	2,500 km range limit	2,500 km range limit during 3-yr. protocol <500 km range not to count as MIRVed launchers

(*continued*)

Table 2-1 (*Continued*)

	SALT I Interim Agreement (May 1972) U.S./USSR	VLADIVOSTOK ACCORDS (November 1974)	MOSCOW COMPREHENSIVE PROPOSAL (March 1977)	SALT II Agreement (June 1979)
GLCM/ SLCM	*	*	2,500 km range limit	600 km range limit
Backfire Bomber	*	[dispute over whether included under SNLV ceiling]	"strict limit" on deployment to intercontinental range	statement to accompany agreement
Land- Mobile ICBM's	U.S. Unilateral Statement Favoring Ban	*	0	protocol includes prohibition on testing
"New" ICBM's and SLBM's	*	*	ban on new ICBM's only	one new ICBM allowed
Ballistic- Missile Flight- Test	*	*	6 per year for ICBM's 6 per year for SLBM's	
Limits on MIRV's				10 for ICBM's/ASBM's 14 for SLBM's

*not included
†USSR only
Source: Dan Caldwell, "SALT: An Introduction and Simulation," *Learning Materials in National Security Education*, no. 4 (Columbus, Ohio: Consortium for International Studies Education, Ohio State University, 1980), 44.

drews Air Force Base to the Capitol to deliver a report on the Moscow summit to a joint session of Congress. The American public, as well as members of the U.S. Congress, acclaimed the agreements.

Despite public and congressional support of the SALT I agreements, there were several cautionary notes. First, Senator Jackson, widely known in the Senate as an expert on defense issues, was bothered by the numerical asymmetries contained in the Interim Agreement; the Soviet Union was allowed 40 percent more land- and sea-based missiles than the United States. Consequently, Jackson introduced an amendment to the legislation approving the Interim Agreement stipulating that any subsequent agreement should "not limit the United States to levels of intercontinental strategic forces inferior to the limits provided for the Soviet Union."[10] The Jackson amendment was popular in the Senate and was approved by a vote of 56 to 35. Following the adoption of the amendment, the Senate approved the ABM Treaty by a vote of 88 to 2. At the insistence of conservatives, the 1961 law that established the Arms Control and Disarmament Agency had required that all arms control agreements be approved by a simple majority of both houses of Congress. Therefore, President Nixon submitted the Interim Agreement to the House, where it was approved by a vote of 307 to 4 and to the Senate where it was approved by a margin of 88 to 2. In all subsequent negotiations, American negotiators would have to keep in mind the terms of the Jackson amendment, for if future agreements did not provide for equal aggregates for U.S. and Soviet forces, it was very unlikely that they would be ratified. In essence, the Jackson amendment put the executive branch on notice: the Interim Agreement would be the first and the last agreement that the Senate would approve that gave the Soviet Union the right to have more weapons than the United States.

A second development following the conclusion of SALT I that reflected the power of Senator Jackson and his dissatisfaction with the SALT I agreements was the replacement of virtually all of the senior officials of the Arms Control and Disarmament Agency. Of the seventeen top ACDA officials who were in office in 1972, only three remained in office by 1974. Gerard Smith resigned as ACDA director and U.S. SALT negotiator because he felt that he had been "persistently denied the responsibility he thought he should have had."[11] As part of the "ACDA purge," the Joint Chiefs of Staff's representative to the SALT negotiations, Air Force Lt. Gen. Royal B. Allison, was replaced by Army Lt. Gen. Edward L. Rowny. Senator Jackson had a long-standing friendship with General Rowny; in fact, in 1961 he had recommended that Rowny be appointed as a "politico-military assistant" in the Kennedy White House or as director of politico-military affairs in the State Department.[12] According to a member (and later chairman) of the U.S. SALT delegation, Ralph Earle II: "Rowny was an old friend of Dorothy Fosdick, Senator Jackson's principal foreign policy adviser, as well as a friend of Senator Jackson. One could only infer that Rowny had been in effect nominated by Jackson, and subsequent events were to make this very evident."[13] In an interview with the author, General Rowny confirmed that he was originally appointed to the SALT delegation because Senator Jackson "believed that Allison was not faithfully carrying out—representing—the security interests of the United States, largely over the ABM Treaty issue. . . . Jackson felt that he [Allison] was not representing the Chiefs, and the Chiefs did not like the way that Allison was operating."[14] General Rowny remained a member of the U.S. SALT delegation until days before the signing of the SALT II Treaty.

THE SALT II NEGOTIATIONS, 1972–76

Nixon and Kissinger portrayed the 1972 Moscow summit as an event that marked the end of the cold war and the beginning of a new era of peace in Soviet-American relations. Many members of the public and the Congress believed Nixon's and Kissinger's rhetoric concerning this new era, and this public perception contributed to Nixon's landslide victory over George McGovern in the 1972 presidential election. By late 1973, many people felt that Nixon and Kissinger had oversold the dividends of both the "new era of negotiations" and arms control.

Despite some public disillusionment over arms control, the new round of negotiations (referred to as SALT II), designed to result in a follow-up agreement to SALT I, opened in Geneva on November 21, 1973. The expectation was that the United States and the USSR would complete a SALT II agreement in a relatively short period of time. In fact, it took almost seven years for the two sides to conclude the SALT II Treaty. There were a number of political and technical reasons why SALT II took four years longer to complete than SALT I. Whereas the Interim Agreement and the ABM Treaty primarily concerned quantitative limitations, the SALT II Treaty contained both quantitative and qualitative limitations; the latter were far more complex than the earlier controls. In addition, qualitative limitations were more difficult to verify, so the issue of verification became more important. Several new weapons systems also complicated the negotiations; it was as if technological developments and diplomacy were in a race.

The SALT I agreements were the capstone of the Moscow summit and, more broadly, of the Nixon-Kissinger détente policy. Within a year and a half, however, the Egyptian-Syrian attack on Israel in October 1973 raised questions about Soviet commitment to the "new era of peace" supposedly ushered in by détente. In the aftermath of the October War, in which both the United States and the Soviet Union resupplied their respective client states with military matériel, one French observer, rephrasing the respected nineteenth-century military strategist, Karl von Clausewitz, asked, "Is détente simply the cold war carried on by other means?" The October War was followed by other crises in American-Soviet relations; for example, the two nations supported opposite sides in Angola, and the Soviets supported the

Communist party in Portugal following the death of dictator Antonio de Oliveira Salazar.

The Nixon administration's attention was increasingly dominated by a domestic crisis, which became more pressing than any international matter. In June 1972, four men paid by Nixon's Committee to Re-Elect the President were arrested for breaking into the offices of the Democratic National Committee in the Watergate apartment complex in Washington, D.C. This event and the attempted cover-up by the Nixon administration led to the "Watergate" crisis and ultimately to the resignation of President Nixon in August 1974.

In foreign policy, President Ford continued the policies of the Nixon administration and retained the same advisers. In fact, one of the first things that Ford did following Nixon's resignation was to call Henry Kissinger and ask him to stay on as secretary of state, a position to which he had been appointed by Nixon in September 1973.[15] President Ford was anxious to reestablish the credibility of the presidency both domestically and internationally, and consequently he agreed to meet Leonid Brezhnev at Vladivostok in November 1974 to discuss U.S.-Soviet relations and SALT.

At Vladivostok, Ford and Brezhnev signed what in diplomatic parlance is called an *aide-mémoire*, a statement of agreed intentions, which called for each of the two sides to have in its arsenal: (1) a total of no more than 2,400 strategic nuclear-launch vehicles (ICBMs plus SLBMs plus long-range bombers); (2) no more than 1,320 of these to be launchers carrying multiple independently targetable (MIRV) warheads; and (3) 308 large ICBMs for the Soviet Union.[16] Two issues were not defined at Vladivostok and would bedevil the SALT negotiators until the conclusion of the negotiations: the Soviet Backfire bomber and cruise missiles.

The Backfire bomber, or Tupolov–26 as it was known in the USSR, was first observed by the West in 1969; it was larger and generally viewed as more capable than the FB–111, the largest American bomber based in Europe and not covered by SALT. However, the Backfire was less capable than the planned new U.S. bomber, the B–1. So the Backfire's characteristics placed it in a gray area between a medium-range and a long-range bomber. Within the United States, there was a great deal of controversy about whether to consider the Backfire a medium or a strategic bomber. If it was categorized as the former, it would not be covered by SALT; if it was categorized as strategic, it would be.

The situation was confused almost from the day the Vladivostok summit ended. Following the summit, Secretary Kissinger flew to Tokyo and then to China for meetings with the Chinese. On the flight to China, Kissinger conducted a press conference "on background," which meant that it was "official" but that information and quotations could not be attributed to a named individual. Asked if the Backfire was to be included as a heavy bomber in the Vladivostok Accord, Kissinger replied, "No, it's an entirely different kind of airplane."[17] These remarks were transcribed verbatim and placed in the State Department's pressroom where they were available to all reporters, including those from the Soviet Union. Eventually, the United States withdrew this transcript from circulation and classified it "confidential," but not until it had been widely distributed. According to former SALT II negotiator Ralph Earle II:

> There can be no doubt that they [the transcripts] were seen and noted by Soviet representatives who surely reported to their authorities that the Secretary of State had stated flatly that the Backfire was not a heavy bomber and therefore did not count against the overall limitation of 2,400 agreed to at Vladivostok by the two presidents. One can hardly blame the Soviets for maintaining the same position![18]

Backfire was not yet a problem, but it became one two months later at a meeting of the Verification Panel, the National Security Council committee chaired by Kissinger with responsibility for overseeing the SALT negotiations. At the end of a meeting in the White House situation room attended by the members of the panel and the SALT delegation, Gen. George Brown, chairman of the Joint Chiefs of Staff, asked, "What about Backfire?" As he stood up from the table to leave the room, Kissinger said, "Why not throw it in? Let's see what we can get for it."[19] Thus emerged one of the most contentious issues of the SALT II negotiations.

A second weapon that caused great controversy in the SALT II negotiations was the cruise missile. Neither Ford nor Brezhnev mentioned the words "cruise missile" at Vladivostok or in the *aide-mémoire*; however, the United States agreed to count air-to-surface missiles with a range greater than six hundred kilometers against the overall ceiling of twenty-four hundred.[20] The United States later "clarified" this to mean *ballistic* air-to-surface missiles, while the Soviets insisted that all air-to-surface missiles, including cruise missiles, be included in the count. The second issue that would cause endless debates in Geneva, Washington, and Moscow had been born.

The United States and the Soviet Union did not conduct the SALT negotiations in a vacuum; rather, they were carried on within the context of the domestic politics of each country. In the United States, both SALT and détente became central issues in the 1976 presidential campaign. Ronald Reagan, Henry "Scoop" Jackson, George Wallace, and, to a lesser extent, Jimmy Carter criticized the Nixon-Ford-Kissinger détente policy on a number of grounds. Reagan attacked Ford and Kissinger for "giving away everything and getting nothing in return from the Soviet Union."[21] Jackson was more specific in his criticism; he believed that the SALT I agreements favored the USSR by allowing it a greater number of missiles and that Nixon, Ford, and Kissinger placed too little emphasis on human rights. Carter argued that the United States must "try to make détente broader and more reciprocal."[22] Ford responded to these criticisms by moving to the right and in March 1976 even banned the use of the word "détente" by members of his staff.

Despite these actions, Ford still almost lost the Republican nomination to Reagan, a surprising development since Ford was an incumbent president. Following his near defeat at the Republican convention, Ford accepted the Republican party's platform, which in many respects represented a rejection of his administration's foreign policy. Clearly, the 1976 presidential campaign had the effect of suspending progress at the SALT negotiations until the election's outcome was determined.

SALT II AND THE CARTER ADMINISTRATION

During his tenure in office, Jimmy Carter hoped to make dramatic progress in controlling nuclear weapons. But arms control negotiations, as Carter learned early in his administration, involved at least four sets of interactions: between the United States and the USSR, within the executive branch, between the White House and the Congress, and between the United States and its allies. This multidimensional character of arms control negotiations complicates the process and at times makes the signing and ratification of an agreement close to impossible.

President Carter thought that many arms control treaties were "cosmetic" agreements that had little effect on reducing the risk of nuclear war, and he wanted to conclude "real" arms control agreements. In addition, Carter, like the predecessor he greatly admired, Woodrow Wilson, believed in "open covenants openly arrived at." Carter wanted international negotiations to be open to public scrutiny because he believed that secrecy in general and the secretive manner of the Nixon and Ford administrations in particular were antithetical to democratic practice.

Carter wanted to achieve quick and significant progress on controlling nuclear arms. Just four days after his inauguration, Carter called for a halt to nuclear testing.[23] He also wanted to achieve rapid progress in the SALT negotiations. In September 1976 during the presidential campaign, Carter authorized W. Averell Harriman, former U.S. ambassador to the USSR and a long-time Democratic foreign policy adviser, to tell Brezhnev that, if elected, Carter would move rapidly to conclude a SALT agreement based on the Vladivostok Accord.[24] Soon after his inauguration, Carter told Dobrynin that he would like to conclude an agreement along the lines of the Vladivostok Accord.[25] But following his election, according to former NSC aide William Hyland, "Completing the Vladivostok accords seemed to Carter to be an admission of failure."[26] Within the administration, the proposal to complete the Vladivostok Accord was known as the "if Ford had won" option.[27] Consequently, Carter pressed his advisers to develop an approach that would achieve both substantial progress on arms control and bipartisan support in the Congress. Meanwhile, based on Carter's earlier assurances, Brezhnev gave a speech in which he indicated that he expected to conclude an agreement based on Vladivostok.

President Carter was aware that any arms control agreement that he signed would have to be approved by the Congress; if it were an executive agreement, it would have to be approved by both houses of Congress because of the provisions of the 1961 law that established the Arms Control and Disarmament Agency. If it were a treaty, according to the Constitution, the agreement would have to be ratified by two-thirds of the Senate. Carter knew that he would have to negotiate with the Congress if he were successful in negotiating an agreement with the Soviets, and he therefore wanted to enlist the support of the Senate's recognized expert in defense policy, Henry Jackson, in his endeavor to control nuclear weapons. Jackson had played a central role in the debates over the most important previous arms control agreements, the Limited Nuclear Test Ban Treaty and SALT I.

Relations between Carter and Jackson were mixed. In 1972, Carter had made one of the presidential nominating speeches for Jackson at the Democratic convention. Four years later, however, Carter defeated Jackson in the Pennsylvania primary, knocking him out of the race. Following his nomination, President Carter recalled: "I wound up the '76 campaign on fairly good terms with him [Jackson]. He was one of the six I seriously considered as a vice president."[28] Following his election, Carter asked Jackson to come to his home in Plains, Georgia, in order to consult with him about SALT.[29] It was known that Jackson closely followed four major issues in the Senate: SALT, energy, human rights, and U.S.-Israeli relations. These were also important issues to the president, and once in office, Carter made a concerted effort to maintain communication with Jackson on these issues. Carter frequently sent notes of thanks to Jackson for his support of the administration's programs; on one occasion Carter noted, "Your advice is always helpful and welcome."[30]

Senator Jackson and many other conservatives as well as liberals applauded President Carter's foreign policy emphasis on human rights. The Soviets, however, were deeply disturbed. According to Georgi Arbatov, the director of the Soviet Institute for the Study of the United States and Canada: "The American Government, including all its agencies—I think they have gone too far. It [human rights] has become a very exciting and funny game, and they forget sometimes what is at stake."[31]

In a further effort to gain Senator Jackson's support, President Carter met with him on February 4, 1977, to discuss SALT. Following this meeting, Jackson and his foreign policy aide, Richard Perle, prepared a twenty-three-page, single-spaced memo concerning SALT and sent it to the president on February 15.[32] In the memo, they criticized the Nixon and Ford administrations for creating a "climate of urgency that made it difficult to think carefully about these complex issues" and noted that "it is essential to remember that not all negotiable agreements are in our interest; that some agreements may be worse than none; that the failure to obtain an agreement does not necessarily foreclose the possibility of doing so in the future; and that an unsound agreement now could make it difficult or impossible to obtain a sound one later."[33] According to reports, Paul Warnke dismissed the memo as a "first-class polemic."[34] President Carter, however, took the memo very seriously and sent it to Secretary of Defense Harold Brown and Secretary of State Cyrus Vance, who distributed it within their respective departments. In an interview with me, President Carter recalled: "Scoop came and met with me one time fairly early in my term . . . and brought me a long document that I kept in my private safe near the Oval Office outlining his draft of what a SALT II Treaty should be. I referred to that every now and then just to see if there were ways that I could accommodate Scoop's very ambitious demands, and sometimes I was able to."[35]

Jackson gave his memo to Carter at a crucial time, for the administration was working on the proposals that Secretary Vance would present when he visited Moscow in late March. Vance's own preference was to "take advantage of the political strength of a new administration, and the traditional honeymoon with the Congress, to attempt to conclude an agreement based essentially on Vladivostok, which would postpone the cruise missile and Backfire issues until SALT III."[36] But Carter was anxious to make progress on "real" arms control and to gain the support of conservatives such as Henry Jackson. Consequently, two of Carter's principal national security advisers, David Aaron and William Hyland, formulated a "comprehensive proposal" for making deep reductions in the Vladivostok levels. Specifically, the proposal called for: (1) a reduction in the total number of strategic launchers from 2,400 to a level between 1,800 and 2,000; (2) a reduction from 1,320 multiple warhead launchers to a level between 1,100 and 1,200; (3) a new sublimit of 550 on the number of MIRVed ICBMs; (4) a cut in Soviet large ICBMs from 308 to 150; and (5) a range limit of 2,500 kilometers on all cruise missiles and mobile ICBMs; new types of ICBMs were banned completely. At the urging of Harold Brown, there was a limitation on the number of missile test flights that were allowed (see Table 2–1 for a summary of the provisions of the proposal).

Although Senator Jackson and Richard Perle did not work on the drafting of the March proposal, they nevertheless were pleased with it and were instrumental in convincing President Carter to accept it;[37] Jackson called it "eminently reasonable and sensible" and issued a statement to the press praising it as a step in the right direction, away from what he characterized as the "folly of the Kissinger-Nixon-Ford approach."[38]

While Jackson and Perle were pleased, the Soviets were outraged. Soviet Foreign Minister Andrei Gromyko called a press conference (the first of its kind in twenty years) to publicly denounce the U.S. proposal, branding it "a cheap and shoddy maneuver."[39] The Soviets were angry for four major reasons. First, they were angered by the Carter administration's human rights campaign, and Carter's and Mondale's meeting with Vladimir Bukovsky at the White House in early March did nothing to create a positive atmosphere for the Moscow meeting. Second, the Soviets were taken by surprise by the comprehensive proposal. Brezhnev had expected Carter to conclude the Vladivostok Accord, as Averell Harriman had assured him Carter would do. When Carter decided to present a new proposal, he did not, as had been the case under Kissinger, have the secretary of state go over the proposal privately with Ambassador Dobrynin in Washington before presenting it in Moscow. Third, the March proposal called for reductions that fell almost entirely on the Soviet side. Fourth, in keeping with his campaign pledge to open up government, Carter had publicly described the proposal even before it was presented to the Soviets.[40] In short, the Soviets saw the March comprehensive proposal as sabotaging plans for quickly concluding a SALT II agreement and moving on to SALT III. According to Georgi Arbatov: "The proposals were extremely one-sided and in fact amounted to a suggestion that the negotiations should start again from scratch. This confirmed the impression in Moscow that Carter was not serious."[41]

President Carter had authorized Secretary Vance to present a backup proposal if the Soviets rejected the comprehensive proposal. Within the bureaucracy, the backup was known as Vladivostok Plus because it was so similar to the Vladivostok *aide-mémoire*. However, the Soviets were so angered by both the public presentation and the content of the comprehensive proposal that they were not interested in even discussing the American fallback proposal.

The March 1977 imbroglio had a number of repercussions in the United States as well. Vance's trip to Moscow had been the Carter administration's first high-level contact with the Soviet politburo, and the encounter had obviously not gone well; achieving "real" arms control was going to be harder than many in the administration had thought, and the flap that resulted from the comprehensive proposal caused a slowing in the negotiations. The administration's acceptance of the comprehensive proposal showed that Carter could "bargain with the Pentagon and 'Scoop' Jackson—but not with the Russians."[42] In retrospect, a staff member of the National Security Council characterized the March proposal as Jackson's "honey trap," inviting Carter to "'come on in; this is great.'. . . Carter was set up for a fall."[43]

In the months and years that followed, the March proposal became the standard by which subsequent proposals were measured, an irreducible minimum that had to be achieved in order to obtain conservatives' support rather than simply an opening negotiating position.[44] In a private memo to Senator Jackson summarizing Vance's Moscow meeting, Richard Perle noted: "The Soviet reaction was predictable. The Soviets never make concessions until the last possible moment. . . . It is essential that Mr. Carter stand firm. He is being tested. The U.S. proposal is not one-sided or unfair. . . . We ought to stand firm. After eight years in which we made all the concessions it is time for the Soviets to make their fair share to the reaching of an equitable agreement."[45] Importantly, the March proposal illustrated Carter's desire to achieve an arms control agreement that was acceptable to conservatives such as Senator Jackson.

After the fact, Carter recognized that Jackson and Perle would be difficult to convince to support SALT II:

> One of the things that Scoop insisted on was the total elimination of the extra large missiles that the Soviets had. Well, there was no way that I could meet Scoop's demands which were obviously unilateral in nature. I could have written a SALT II Treaty much more credible to us than the final result if I did not have to consult with the Soviets on it. . . . I never did have much hope that I could convince Richard Perle that we needed the SALT II Treaty or [that we] ought to negotiate any treaty with the Soviet Union. I never was able to meet Scoop's demands.[46]

After the recriminations issued by both Soviets and Americans in the aftermath of Vance's trip to Moscow, Carter and Brezhnev each publicly expressed a desire to get the negotiations back on track.[47] In May, three months after the debacle in Moscow, Secretary Vance met Soviet Foreign Minister Gromyko in Geneva where they signed an agreement banning "environmental modification," the use of climate modification techniques for hostile purposes. In addition, the two leaders discussed ways to make progress in the stalled SALT negotiations.

In the months following the resumption of the SALT talks, Carter appeared to vacillate in his policy toward the Soviet Union, and for good reason: his two principal foreign policy aides were divided on what they thought should be the policy of the United States toward the Soviet Union. As Zbigniew Brzezinski recalled in his memoirs, "In time, the debate divided the Administration, at first ideologically and eventually personally."[48] In his commencement address at the University of Notre Dame in May 1977, Carter noted that détente with the Soviet Union must be "both comprehensive and reciprocal. We cannot have accommodation in one part of the world and the aggravation of conflicts in another." This was Brzezinski's view.

Zbigniew Brzezinski had always been skeptical of arms control; he had made his academic reputation criticizing the Soviet Union. In his memoirs, Brzezinski revealed his skepticism concerning arms control by entitling the chapter dealing with strategic arms control "SALT *cum grano salis*" which literally translated from Latin means "with a grain of salt." More figuratively, this means "with allowances or reservations," which accurately summarized Brzezinski's view of arms control. In an illuminating footnote in his memoirs, Brzezinski wrote: "Actually, I had relatively little confidence that we would make any progress in MBFR [Mutual Balanced Force Reduction talks] and CTB [Comprehensive Test Ban negotiations], and throughout the Carter years I was not very interested in these subjects. I saw them as nonstarters, but out of deference to the President's zeal for them, I went through the motions of holding meetings, discussing options, and developing negotiating positions."[49] To Brzezinski, achieving arms control agreements was at best a secondary objective; the principal goal of the administration in his view should be the containment of Soviet power. Supporting his views on the NSC staff were several aides Brzezinski had appointed, including Harvard professor Samuel Huntington and army officer William Odom.

In contrast to Brzezinski, Cyrus Vance was a strong advocate for arms control. He had served on a number of commissions and study groups and was well informed and very interested in the subject. To Vance, the threat of nuclear weapons was the preeminent threat in the modern era, and the United States and the USSR should cooperate to control their nuclear arsenals even if they could not reach agreements in other areas.[50] In short, arms control was so important, it should be delinked from other aspects of American-Soviet relations. Brzezinski was not reassured: "I had profound reservations about both the tactics and the substance of Vance's, and to some extent also the President's, approach to the Soviets."[51]

Carter had a difficult problem that stemmed from the complexity of foreign policy and from having two strong-willed foreign policy advisers with conflicting views. Unfortunately, Carter did not have the knowledge or the background in foreign policy to be able to evaluate adequately the positions of Brzezinski and Vance. Instead of choosing to follow the recommendations of one adviser or the other, Carter tried to split the difference and to integrate the often mutually exclusive views of his two senior foreign policy advisers. As a result, observers were quick to note that Carter's speeches sounded as if they were simply amalgams of drafts from the NSC and the

State Department. The *Washington Post* characterized a July 1977 speech by the president as "conciliatory in some places and tough in others."[52]

Carter's policy toward the Soviet Union was based on the premise that Soviet-American relations were characterized by conflict and cooperation, the degree of each depending on the time and the issue. In fact, this was the major theme of the writings of Marshall Shulman, a Columbia University professor who served as Vance's principal adviser on the Soviet Union.[53] The two men's views of the Soviet Union and U.S.-Soviet relations were very similar. The tension between cooperation and conflict was evident in a number of areas of U.S.-Soviet relations, including weapons decisions by each country. Carter's decision to move ahead with the development and deployment of the highly accurate Mark 12–A warhead for the Minuteman III ICBM caused much controversy. *Pravda* said that this new weapon "moved the nuclear arms race to a new stage."[54] Underscoring the conflictual nature of U.S.-Soviet relations, Carter decided to speed up the development of the cruise missile, saying that it was "aimed at compensating for the growing threat presented by a buildup of Soviet offensive strategic weapons."[55]

While these weapons programs were applauded by conservatives, Carter's decision to cancel the B–1 bomber, announced on June 30, 1977, caused great concern. Carter made the decision primarily on economic grounds; both he and Secretary of Defense Brown concluded that the missions assigned to the B–1 could be achieved at lower cost by B–52s equipped with long-range, standoff cruise missiles. Carter's political opponents strongly criticized him for "unilateral disarmament" and noted that many B–52s were "older than the pilots who fly them." Carter was also criticized for "giving away the B–1 and getting nothing in return." Vance noted the impact of the B–1 decision in his memoirs: "Regrettably, this correct and courageous decision became a millstone around the administration's neck and hurt us in the [SALT II] ratification debate."[56]

During his first year in office, Jimmy Carter attempted both to make dramatic progress on arms control and to convince conservatives such as Henry Jackson to support his policies. By the end of 1977, Carter found that these two goals were very difficult to achieve, and the two groups with which he had been negotiating—one domestic and the other foreign—were growing restive. The March comprehensive proposal that Vance had presented in Moscow had incensed Soviet leaders, and by the end of the year, despite the resumption of the SALT negotiations, Ambassador Dobrynin expressed concern to Brzezinski that the U.S. Senate would not ratify a SALT agreement.[57] In contrast to the Soviets, American conservatives had strongly supported the March proposal, and they tenaciously clung to it even after the vociferous Soviet rejection of it. Indeed, the fact that the Soviets had rejected it so quickly and completely may have even increased the attractiveness of the March proposal to conservatives. In April and December, Richard Perle sent Senator Jackson summary reports of the degree to which the administration was failing to observe the criteria for a SALT agreement that Jackson had sent to President Carter in February 1977. In December, Perle concluded, "In reviewing that [February 15] memorandum in light of the administration's current approach to an agreement it is striking how virtually all of the criteria have been violated."[58]

Carter had hoped in 1977 to win over arms control skeptics such as Jackson, but by the end of the year, the skeptics were all but lost. Despite these setbacks, Carter remained optimistic, and at the end of December remarked: "I would be disappointed if we don't have a SALT agreement this year [1978]. . .my guess is that 1978 will see us successful. And my guess is that when we present it to the Congress, the SALT agreements will be approved."[59]

1978: PANAMA, THE HORN OF AFRICA, CAMP DAVID, CHINA, AND A NEAR MISS ON SALT

Four foreign policy events dominated the Carter administration's agenda for 1978: the campaign for the ratification of the Panama Canal treaties, Soviet and Cuban intervention in the Horn of Africa, the American sponsorship of the Egyptian-Israeli summit at Camp David, and the normalization of relations with China. Although none of these events was directly related to SALT, each had a significant impact on the negotiation of and debate over the SALT II Treaty.

The Panama Canal treaties, negotiated under four different presidents, were finally concluded and signed in September 1977. The treaties were then forwarded to the Senate for ratification. At the end of January 1978, the Senate Foreign Relations Committee reported on the treaties and recommended by a vote of fourteen to one that they be ratified. Six weeks later in mid-March, the first of the treaties, called the Panama Canal Treaty, which gave the United States the primary responsibility for operating and defending the canal through December 1999, was ratified by a vote of sixty-eight to thirty-two. After more debate and lobbying by the administration, the second treaty, called the Treaty Concerning the Permanent Neutrality and Operation of the Panama Canal, which gave complete control for the operation and maintenance of the canal to Panama after 1999, was passed by the same vote in mid-April.

The Carter administration viewed the approval of the two treaties as a great victory; however, the administration had expended a great deal of political capital in order to gain the Senate's approval, and the margin of victory had been slight. If just two of the senators who voted in favor of the treaties had reversed their votes, the treaties would not have been ratified. The administration had pressured a number of moderate Republican senators to vote for the treaties, but there was a limit to the number of times these senators could vote with the administration without alienating their conservative constituents. As Howard Baker told President Carter, "If I vote right many more times, I'm going to lose the next election!"[60] The canal treaty "exercise" (as some in the administration referred to the ratification effort) was also significant in that it served as a precursor to the SALT ratification campaign. President Carter noted that he modeled the SALT ratification campaign "to a substantial degree" on the effort to achieve ratification of the Panama Canal treaties.[61]

The intervention of Soviet and Cuban troops in the Horn of Africa was the second issue that came to the fore in 1978. In July 1977, the first deployment of Cuban troops to the Horn was reported. Within the administration, Brzezinski was the most concerned and vocal about the Soviet-Cuban intervention into the Ethiopian-Somalian conflict. In his view: "More was at stake than a disputed piece of desert. To a great extent our credibility was under scrutiny by new, relatively skeptical allies in a region strategically important to us. I believed that if Soviet-sponsored Cubans determined the outcome of an Ethiopian-Somalian conflict, there could be wider regional and international consequences."[62] Brzezinski believed therefore that this issue should be linked to other issues of Soviet-American relations. This view contrasted markedly with that of Vance, who believed that SALT should not be linked to human rights, trade, or Soviet and Cuban actions in the Horn of Africa. According to Vance: "I think it is in the interests of both nations and in the interest of world peace for us to reach a satisfactory, negotiated settlement with them. So I think it [SALT] stands on its own two feet."[63]

Policy disagreements between the secretary of state and the president's assistant for national security affairs have been common since the establishment of the NSC in 1947; at times these disagreements have remained private and at other times they have become public. In the Vance-Brzezinski case, their disagreements over the Horn and linkage became intense and were leaked to the press. In addition, at this time Brzezinski assumed a greater public role. Brzezinski did not give his first television interview until October 1977, ten months into the new administration. But from that time on, he frequently acted as spokesman on foreign policy issues for the administration. In March 1978, he gave a series of background briefings concerning the Soviet-Cuban intervention in Ethiopia. Conservatives generally agreed with

Brzezinski and applauded his effort to link SALT and Soviet-Cuban actions in the Horn.[64] Meanwhile, President Carter continued to vacillate between his two principal foreign policy advisers. In June, he went to his alma mater, the U.S. Naval Academy, to deliver the commencement address, which appeared to be a combination of the Brzezinski and Vance drafts.[65] One columnist noted that you could almost see the cut and paste marks where Carter's aides cut up the two drafts to combine them into a single speech.

One area on which Carter, Brzezinski, and Vance agreed was the Middle East, and in September, Carter hosted Israeli Prime Minister Begin and Egyptian President Sadat at Camp David for fourteen days of intense talks.[66] At the end of these negotiations, the three parties had achieved an unprecedented breakthrough in Middle Eastern politics: an Arab state recognized Israel, and the two states agreed to work on a peace treaty. Following the Camp David agreement, President Carter enjoyed the highest popularity rating of his presidency.

Nixon and Kissinger had improved relations with the People's Republic of China primarily to gain leverage with the Soviet Union. During his 1972 visit to China, Nixon signed the Shanghai communiqué, in which the two sides promised to improve relations; however, relations remained stalemated. Within the Carter administration, Brzezinski was the most enthusiastic about resuscitating the effort to normalize relations with China, and he arranged a trip to China in May. During his visit, Brzezinski made a number of anti-Soviet remarks, called the Soviets "international marauders" for their policy in Africa, and assured his Chinese hosts that the Carter administration "had made up its mind" on full normalization of relations with China.[67] In the communiqué that was signed at the end of Brzezinski's visit, there was a reference to mutual Sino-American opposition to "hegemony," a Chinese code word describing Soviet global ambitions; this reference particularly angered Soviet leaders.[68] Brzezinski's visit and undiplomatic comments came just prior to a meeting between Vance and Gromyko concerning SALT and had a pronounced negative effect on the meeting.

Brzezinski's view was clear: "excessively assertive [Soviet] behavior" in the Horn of Africa and elsewhere demanded that the administration link SALT to other issues and that the United States normalize its relations with China, and Brzezinski saw himself as the president's agent for achieving this objective. In December 1978, Brzezinski was able to convince Carter that the time was right to conclude the normalization agreement, and without the knowledge of Vance (who was out of town), this decision was reached. Carter announced the full normalization of relations with China on December 15.

The normalization announcement was made days before Vance went to Geneva to meet with Gromyko to resolve the few remaining issues in the

SALT negotiations. In Washington, Brzezinski said that Carter and Brezhnev might hold a summit meeting as soon as mid-January, but on his arrival in Geneva, Gromyko commented: "I do not foresee the conclusion of an accord at this time. That would be too much to hope for."[69]

In fact, in their negotiations, Vance and Gromyko came very close to reaching an agreement. At a crucial point on Friday evening, December 22, Vance sent a cable to Washington reporting on the status of the negotiations.[70] He indicated that the United States and the USSR were very close to agreement and that the main obstacle concerned the encryption of information during missile tests. Vance explained that he and Gromyko had worked out language that prohibited encryption "whenever it impeded" verification and permitted it whenever it did not impede verification. Brzezinski called a meeting in his office, and David Aaron, Harold Brown, Stansfield Turner, Warren Christopher, and Spurgeon Keeny attended. After a long, contentious discussion, Brzezinski called President Carter, who had gone to his home in Plains, Georgia, for Christmas, and said that it was the consensus of the group in his office that the Vance-Gromyko position on encryption should not be accepted. Carter authorized Brzezinski to send Vance a cable indicating that he should discuss the encryption issue further.

It was midnight in Washington when the cable was sent to Vance in Geneva, where it was 6 A.M. Vance read the cable just after he woke up and immediately called Brzezinski. According to a senior NSC aide who heard the conversation between Vance and Brzezinski: "Cy Vance is ready to kill. He is so angry and is telling Zbig, 'This is unacceptable! Gromyko is certain to reject it!' The issue was whether they should wake up the president to give him the opportunity to review the decision."[71] A decision was made to call Jody Powell, who was with the president in Plains. The question then became who would call Powell, and Brzezinski volunteered to make the call. Vance thereby lost his best opportunity to present his case directly to the president and, not surprisingly, Carter reaffirmed the decision that Brzezinski had recommended the previous evening.

The foreign policy events of 1978 illustrated both the strengths and the weaknesses of the Carter administration's foreign policy team. In the two major cases about which Vance and Brzezinski agreed—the Panama Canal treaties and Camp David—the administration was able to achieve two of its most impressive accomplishments, but in the cases where there was substantial disagreement—SALT and the Horn of Africa and linkage—there was a stalemate that led to the paralysis of policy.

Although the bureaucratic politics approach can be overemphasized, it may provide insights as to why the events of 1978 developed as they did. President Carter had little background or experience in foreign policy prior to becoming president. He therefore depended heavily on the advice of his principal foreign and defense policy advisers, Cyrus Vance, Zbigniew Brzezinski, and Harold Brown. He depended on Brown and Vance for advice on SALT and on Vance on Middle Eastern issues. It may well be that Brzezinski saw the Horn and China as opportunities to influence policy and to become a major player.

THE FINAL SALT II NEGOTIATIONS

In retrospect, it appears that the normalization of relations with China delayed the conclusion of the SALT II negotiations by a matter of four to six months.[72] The new Sino-American relationship was underscored at the end of January when Deng Xiaoping visited Washington. Meanwhile, American and Soviet negotiators continued to work on the draft of the SALT II Treaty. Finally, after six and a half years of negotiations, the SALT II Treaty was initialed on April 18, 1979. Vance had met with Gromyko nine times since the March 1977 fiasco. Because of Brezhnev's frail health, the summit was scheduled to be held relatively close to the USSR in Vienna from June 15 to June 18.

The night before the president left for Vienna, in a speech to the conservative Coalition for a Democratic Majority, Henry Jackson delivered a broadside attack on the as yet unreleased SALT II Treaty and on the three administrations responsible for it. Jackson compared the policies of the Nixon, Ford, and Carter administrations to the appeasement policy of Neville Chamberlain in the 1930s:

> To enter a treaty which favors the Soviets as this one does on the ground that we will be in a worse position without it, is appeasement in its purest form. . . . It is all ominously reminiscent of Great Britain in the 1930s, when one government pronouncement after another was issued to assure the British public that Hitler's Germany would never achieve military equality—let alone superiority. The failure to face reality today, like the failure to do so then—that is the mark of appeasement.[73]

Vance responded by calling Jackson's remarks "misguided and simply wrong." Carter was so sensitive to Jackson's criticism that he ordered his staff not to use umbrellas upon their arrival in Vienna, even if it was raining, lest the umbrellas remind people of the famous picture of Chamberlain returning from the Munich meeting.[74] The administration received some more bad news before leaving for Vienna: Gen. Edward Rowny, Jackson's protégé who had served as the Joint Chiefs of Staff representative to the SALT negotiations since 1974, announced that he was resigning from the army, creating the impression that he was doing so as a matter of principle because he opposed the SALT II Treaty.

Before he left for Vienna, President Carter told his aides that he looked forward to the summit more than almost anything else during his presidency, and he told those who saw him off in Washington that the goals of the summit "transcend all other issues that I will face during my life in public office."[75] Carter and Brezhnev had several meetings to discuss last-minute details of the agreement, and at one point Brezhnev surprised Carter by telling him, "God will not forgive us if we fail."[76] On June 18, the two leaders signed the SALT II Treaty, which was far more comprehensive and complex than the first strategic arms limitation agreements.

The treaty consisted of three parts: a treaty, a protocol, and a statement of principles.[77] (The provisions of the treaty are summarized in Table 2–1.) The treaty, scheduled to remain in effect from the time it entered into force until December 31, 1985, contained nineteen articles and was seventy-eight pages long. It placed a limit of 2,400 (to be lowered to 2,250 by the end of 1981) on the number of "strategic nuclear launch vehicles" (ICBMs plus SLBMs plus air-to-surface ballistic missiles [ASBMs] plus long-range bombers) held by each side. Within this ceiling, no more than 1,320 ICBMs, SLBMs, and heavy bombers could be equipped with multiple independently targetable reentry vehicles (MIRVs) or long-range cruise missiles. Within this sublimit, no more than 1,200 ICBMs, SLBMs, or ASBMs could be MIRVed, and within that sublimit, no more than 820 ICBMs could be MIRVed. In addition to these overall limits, the treaty contained the following additional limitations:

- Ceilings on the throw weight and launch weight of light and heavy ICBMs
- A limit on the testing and deployment of one new type of ICBM
- A freeze on the number of reentry vehicles on certain types of ICBMs: a limit of ten reentry vehicles on the one new type ICBM permitted for each side, a limit of fourteen reentry vehicles on SLBMs, and a limit of ten reentry vehicles on ASBMs
- A ban on the testing and deployment of air-launched cruise missiles with ranges greater than six hundred kilometers on aircraft other than those counted as heavy bombers
- A ban on the construction of additional fixed ICBM launchers and on any increase in the number of fixed heavy ICBM launchers, which limited the USSR to 308 modern large ballistic missiles and the United States to zero
- A ban on heavy mobile ICBMs, heavy SLBMs, and heavy ASBMs
- A ban on certain types of strategic offensive weapons not yet deployed by either side, such as ballistic missiles with ranges greater than six hundred kilometers on surface ships
- An agreement to exchange data on a regular basis on the numbers of weapons deployed and limited by the treaty
- Advance notification of certain ICBM test launches
- A ban on ICBM systems with a capacity to reload quickly

The second part of the SALT II agreement consisted of a protocol, scheduled to remain in effect until the end of 1981, that banned the flight testing and deployment of ICBMs from mobile launch platforms; prohibited the deployment of land-based or sea-based cruise missiles with a range of greater than six hundred kilometers; and banned the testing and deployment of air-to-surface ballistic missiles. The third part of the agreement was a joint statement of principles concerning the next round of SALT negotiations.

The Soviet Backfire bomber was one of the major points of contention in the SALT II negotiations. Although limitations on the Backfire were not formally part of the SALT II agreement, in a letter to President Carter accompanying the agreement, Brezhnev committed his country to produce no more than thirty planes per year and to limit the upgrading of the capabilities of the Backfire. The State Department noted that these commitments had the same legal force as the rest of the SALT II agreement and if the Soviet Union were to violate these commitments, the United States could withdraw from the treaty.[78]

Attempting to re-create the atmosphere of 1972 when Nixon had flown directly to the Capitol from Andrews Air Force Base upon his return from the Moscow summit, President Carter flew directly to the Capitol upon his return from Vienna, and in less than two hours after his landing in the United States, Carter delivered a report on the Vienna summit to a joint session of Congress. Carter told the legislators: "SALT is not a favor we are doing for the Soviet Union. It is a deliberate, calculated move we are making as a matter of self-interest—a move that happens to serve the goals both of security and of survival, that strengthens both the military position of the United States and the cause of world peace."[79]

Although the opponents had been campaigning for two years against SALT II, the administration began its campaign to gain public and congressional support in earnest only after the agreement was signed, and the administration had a very important asset. As one member of the Carter administration recalled, "We had one resource they [SALT II opponents] didn't have; we had the president of the United States and, therefore we could pay—endlessly. . . . You want a big MX program; we'll give you a big MX. You want five percent real growth in the defense budget; we'll give you five percent real growth. You want a new ambassador in Moscow; we'll give you a new ambassador. . . ."[80] Once the treaty was signed, the full-fledged ratification battle began.

NOTES

1. Letter from the Right Honorable Philip Noel-Baker to President Jimmy Carter, January 26, 1977, "Executive, ND 18, 4/1/77–4/30/77," Box ND–49, WHCF–Subject File, National Security–Defense, Jimmy Carter Library, p. 1.

2. "Memorandum on SALT for Senator Jackson," no date, but apparently written during the Carter transition period, in Henry M. Jackson Papers, Accession no. 3560–6, Box 50, Folder 17, University of Washington Libraries.

3. Letter from Eugene V. Rostow to Zbigniew Brzezinski, February 21, 1977, "FG 6–1–1/Brzezinski, Zbigniew 2/16/77–3/7/77," Box FG–25, WHCF–Subject File, Federal Government–Organizations, Jimmy Carter Library.

4. Donald G. Brennan, ed., *Arms Control, Disarmament, and National Security* (New York: George Braziller, 1961); Hedley Bull, *The Control of the Arms Race* (New York: Praeger, 1961); Arthur T. Hadley, *The Nation's Safety and Arms Control* (New York: Viking Press, 1961); and Thomas C. Schelling and Morton H. Halperin, *Strategy and Arms Control* (New York: Twentieth Century Fund, 1961).

5. For the events leading up to the SALT negotiations, see John Newhouse, *Cold Dawn: The Story of SALT* (New York: Holt, Rinehart and Winston, 1973).

6. Lecture by Robert McNamara, Harvard University, September 28, 1983.

7. Dan Caldwell, ed., *Henry Kissinger: His Personality and Policies* (Durham, N.C.: Duke University Press, 1983).

8. The history of the delegations' negotiations is well told by the chief American negotiator Gerard Smith, *Doubletalk: The Story of SALT I* (Garden City, N.Y.: Doubleday, 1980).

9. See Henry Kissinger, *White House Years* (Boston: Little, Brown, 1979).

10. Office of Senator Henry M. Jackson, *Strategic Arms Limitation Talks (SALT): Legislative History of the Jackson Amendment 1972*, unpublished document, n.d., ii.

11. Gerard Smith quoted by Newhouse, *Cold Dawn*, 44.

12. Résumé of Edward L. Rowny and List of Recommended Appointees, in Henry M. Jackson Papers, Accession no. 3560–6, Box 83, Folder 19, University of Washington Libraries.

13. Ralph Earle II, "Chapter III," unpublished manuscript on SALT II, February 28, 1983, 14. I am indebted to Ambassador Earle for allowing me to quote from this manuscript.

14. Gen. Edward L. Rowny, interview with author, Washington, DC, June 3, 1987.

15. Gerald R. Ford, *A Time to Heal* (New York: Berkley Books, 1979), 126.

16. For the best history of SALT II, see Strobe Talbott, *Endgame: The Inside Story of SALT II* (New York: Harper and Row, 1979); also see Thomas W. Wolfe, *The SALT Experience* (Cambridge: Ballinger, 1979).

17. Henry Kissinger, quoted in Ralph Earle II, "Back Channel and Backfire," unpublished manuscript, August 18, 1982, 9–10.

18. Earle, ibid., 11–12.

19. Ibid.

20. Talbott, *Endgame*, 35.

21. *Washington Post*, February 24, 1976.

22. Quoted in Leslie Gelb, "Carter, Ford May Differ Widely on Foreign Policy," *New York Times*, August 1, 1976; Robert Shogan, "Carter Seeks to Prove He's Not 'Fuzzy on Issues,'" *Los Angeles Times*, May 9, 1976.

23. "Carter Is Calling for a Prompt Halt to All Atom Tests," *New York Times*, January 25, 1977.

24. Talbott, *Endgame*, 39.

25. Richard E. Neustadt and Ernest R. May, *Thinking in Time: The Uses of History for Decision Makers* (New York: Free Press, 1986), 116.

26. William G. Hyland, *Mortal Rivals: Superpower Relations from Nixon to Reagan* (New York: Random House, 1987), 208.

27. Walter Slocombe, interview with author, Washington, DC, June 3, 1987.

28. Jimmy Carter, telephone interview with author, April 12, 1988, transcript, 2.

29. Jimmy Carter, *Keeping Faith: Memoirs of a President* (New York: Bantam, 1982), 36, 67.

30. See, for example, Letter from Jimmy Carter to Henry M. Jackson, April 5, 1977, in Henry M. Jackson Papers, Accession no. 3560–6, Box 36, Folder 17, University of Washington Libraries; Letter from Jimmy Carter to Henry M. Jackson, August 22, 1977, "Henry Jackson (Presidential)," WHCF–Name File, Jimmy Carter Library.

31. "Soviet Expert on U.S. Asserts Rights Issue May Cloud Arms Talk," *New York Times*, March 17, 1977.

32. "Memorandum for the President on SALT," Henry M. Jackson to Jimmy Carter, February 15, 1977, in Henry M. Jackson Papers, Accession no. 3560–5, Box 315, Folder 35, University of Washington Libraries.

33. Ibid., i.

34. Talbott, *Endgame*, 53.

35. Jimmy Carter, interview with author, 2.

36. Cyrus Vance, *Hard Choices: Critical Years in America's Foreign Policy* (New York: Simon and Schuster, 1983), 48.

37. William Perry, interview with author, Menlo Park, California, January 15, 1988.

38. Quoted in I. M. Destler, "Treaty Troubles: Versailles in Reverse," *Foreign Policy* 33 (Winter 1978–79): 55; Talbott, *Endgame*, 66.

39. David K. Shipler, "Gromyko Charges U.S. Seeks Own Gain in Arms Proposals," *New York Times*, April 1, 1977.

40. Bernard Gwertzman, "Carter Says Vance, in Soviet, Will Seek Deep Weapons Cuts," *New York Times*, March 25, 1977. In his memoirs, Vance recognized this as a mistake; see Vance, *Hard Choices*, 53.

41. Georgi Arbatov, interview with Paul Brill, "Détente Is Not Dead," *De Volkskant* (Amsterdam), March 16, 1981, quoted by Garthoff, *Détente and Confrontation: American-Soviet Relations from Nixon to Reagan* (Washington: Brookings Institution, 1985), 566.

42. Murrey Marder, "The Arms Muddle: Some Aides Feel U.S. Miscalculated," *Washington Post*, April 2, 1977.

43. Former National Security Council staff member, confidential interview with author.

44. After SALT II was signed, Richard Perle wrote, "What we are left with is a nearly complete treaty in which virtually nothing remains of the American position as it was tabled in Moscow in March 1977." Richard Perle, "Echoes of the 1930s," *Strategic Review* 7 (Winter 1979): 14.

45. "Memorandum for Senator Jackson, April 29, 1977," from Richard Perle, in Henry M. Jackson Papers, Accession no. 3560–5, Box 315, Folder 36, University of Washington Libraries.

46. Jimmy Carter, interview with author, 2.

47. David K. Shipler, "Brezhnev Bids U.S. Seek Arms Control 'In Deeds, Not Words,'" *New York Times*, April 6, 1977; James R. Wooten, "Carter Says Soviet Is Serious on Arms," *New York Times*, April 9, 1977.

48. Zbigniew Brzezinski, *Power and Principle: Memoirs of the National Security Adviser, 1977–1981* (New York: Farrar, Straus and Giroux, 1983), 146.

49. Ibid., 172.

50. Cyrus Vance, interview with author, New York, July 14, 1988.

51. Brzezinski, *Power and Principle*, 317.

52. Austin Scott, "Carter Lays Out Goals for Soviet Talks," *Washington Post*, July 22, 1977.

53. Marshall Shulman, *Beyond the Cold War* (New Haven: Yale University Press, 1965).

54. "Pravda Sees Warhead Deployment Threatening a New Arms Accord," *New York Times*, June 6, 1977.

55. Scott, "Carter Lays Out Goals."

56. Vance, *Hard Choices*, 58.

57. Brzezinski, *Power and Principle*, 179–80.

58. "The Emerging SALT II Agreement and the Jackson Memorandum of February," Memo from Richard Perle to Henry Jackson, December 5, 1977, in Henry M. Jackson Papers, Accession no. 3560–5, Box 315, Folder 37, University of Washington Libraries, 1.

59. "Interview with President Carter," December 28, 1977, News Release, Bureau of Public Affairs, Office of Media Services, Department of State, 4.

60. Howard Baker, quoted in Carter, *Keeping Faith*, 88.

61. Jimmy Carter, interview with author, 4.

62. Brzezinski, *Power and Principle*, 182–83.

63. "Interview with Cyrus Vance," February 3, 1977, Bureau of Public Affairs, Office of Media Services, Department of State, 5.

64. See, for example, Rowland Evans and Robert Novak, "Tougher Policy Toward Russia, Africa," *Washington Post*, May 24, 1978.

65. Jimmy Carter, "The United States and the Soviet Union" (Commencement address delivered at the U.S. Naval Academy, June 7, 1978), Department of State Publication 8948, General Foreign Policy Series 307, Bureau of Public Affairs, Office of Public Communication.

66. For the most detailed account of these negotiations, see William Quandt, *Camp David: Peacemaking and Politics* (Washington: Brookings Institution, 1986).

67. "Full Ties with Peking," *Baltimore Sun*, June 12, 1978.

68. Vance, *Hard Choices*, 110–11.

69. Don Cook, "Soviets Rule Out Quick Arms Pact," *Los Angeles Times*, December 21, 1978.

70. For the published accounts of this incident, see Brzezinski, *Power and Principle*, 329–30; Vance, *Hard Choices*, 111–12; and Talbott, *Endgame*, 240–44.

71. Roger Molander, interview with author, Washington, DC, October 22, 1987.

72. Author's interviews.

73. Speech by Henry Jackson to the Coalition for a Democratic Majority, quoted in Talbott, *Endgame*, 5.

74. James Reston, "The Vienna Waltz," *New York Times*, June 17, 1979.

75. "'Khorosho,' Said Brezhnev," *Time*, June 25, 1979, 11; Jack Nelson, "Carter Confident Pact Will Reduce Nuclear Dangers," *Los Angeles Times*, June 15, 1979.

76. "The SALT Summit," *Newsweek*, June 25, 1979, 26.

77. U.S. Department of State, "SALT II Agreement," Selected Documents no. 12A (Washington: Bureau of Public Affairs, 1979).

78. U.S. Department of State, "SALT II Treaty," 50.

79. Rudy Abramson, "Carter Hails SALT II as a Pact for Peace," *Los Angeles Times*, June 19, 1979.

80. Walter Slocombe, interview with author

CHAPTER THREE

The Carter Administration's SALT Ratification Strategy

Following the announcement at the end of April 1979 that the United States and the Soviet Union had initialed the SALT II Treaty, President Carter sent a handwritten note to "Top Administration Officials:"

> No issue facing our administration, our nation or the world is more important than SALT. I want you personally to study these materials [on SALT] and to become thoroughly familiar with the subject. Please rely on this information and on my speech emphases in any public presentations of SALT issues.[1]

This letter began the Carter administration's formal effort to win the ratification of the SALT II Treaty. The administration had already won another contentious battle for the ratification of the Panama Canal treaties. That effort, in fact, served as the model for the SALT II ratification effort. This chapter focuses on the administration's experience with the Panama Canal treaties, the organization and strategy developed for the SALT II ratification debate, and the administration's presentation of the treaty.

THE PANAMA CANAL TREATIES RATIFICATION CAMPAIGN

President Johnson began negotiations to turn over control of the Panama Canal to the Panamanian government. Presidents Nixon, Ford, and Carter continued these negotiations, and in September 1977 two treaties were signed.[2] The Panama Canal treaties were very controversial; just prior to the signing of the treaties, NBC polled the general public about whether the United States should sign a treaty that would eventually return control of the Panama Canal to the government of Panama. Some 55 percent replied that the United States should not do so, and only 27 percent supported such a treaty. When the Associated Press asked whether the Senate should ratify the treaties a week after they were signed, 50 percent replied negatively and 29 percent affirmatively.[3] It was quite clear that the administration had an uphill battle to fight and that it would have to expend substantial political capital in order to win the Senate's approval of the treaties.

President Carter had a limited amount of political capital to expend on the ratification of treaties that he would conclude during his tenure in office. Did he and his advisers consider the advisability of concluding the Panama Canal treaties prior to the SALT II Treaty? Was it wise to "lead" with the Panama treaties? Curiously, President Carter and members of his administration do not discuss these questions in their memoirs. Landon Butler, deputy to Chief of Staff Hamilton Jordan and one of those responsible for developing the administration's ratification strategy, explained:

> We were totally surprised that the Panama Canal treaties fell into our laps. . . . Sol Linowitz went down to negotiate; we took strong positions, and the Panamanians agreed to them. I don't think anyone expected the Panamanians to suddenly agree to the positions that we took as quickly as they did. . . . Suddenly we had this treaty in our lap. These guys had agreed to our negotiating position and he [President Carter] couldn't very well not sign it. . . . There was not much serious consideration given to dragging out the Panama Canal treaties for two or three years longer and do SALT first. There was just no way to know when or how we were going to get either one of them.[4]

The Carter administration developed a ratification strategy for the Panama Canal treaties that focused on influencing public opinion and undecided senators. In his memoirs, President Carter noted that the task force he appointed under the chairmanship of Hamilton Jordan "developed a somewhat limited objective: not to build an absolute majority of support among all citizens, but to convince an acceptable number of key political leaders in each important state to give their senators some 'running room.'"[5]

Four types of events were used to support this strategy. First, the White House organized briefings for prominent labor, business, civic, academic, and religious leaders from states with undecided senators. These briefings were held at the White House and typically included a briefing by a high-level administration official such as Cyrus Vance, Harold Brown, or Zbigniew Brzezinski. Second, cabinet-level members of the administration appeared on television programs in order to explain and defend the treaties. These appearances included network news broadcasts, specials, and the Sunday news programs. Third, members of the administration made more than fifteen hundred public speaking appearances around the country describing and defending the treaties. Typically, these appearances included speeches and interviews with newspaper editors and local radio and television stations. Fourth, the administration supported and nurtured grassroots campaigns through an umbrella support organization, the Committee of Americans for the Canal Treaties.

The debate over the Panama Canal treaties was viewed by both proponents and opponents as extremely important. It was seen as a prelude to other significant foreign policy debates, including those over China and SALT II. Brzezinski believed, "If we had lost [the Panama Canal treaties], there is no doubt that our policy on SALT and most importantly the Middle East would have been dead ducks."[6] The Senate Foreign Relations Committee recommended the approval of the treaties by a vote of fourteen to one, and once the treaties were reported out of committee, they went to the Senate floor where they were debated for twenty-two days, the longest foreign policy debate since the Versailles Treaty of 1919–20. The length of the debate indicated the contentiousness of the treaties. On April 18, 1978, the first Panama Canal Treaty was approved by a vote of sixty-eight to thirty-two, barely enough for approval.

Brzezinski characterized the campaign for the ratification of the Panama Canal treaties as "difficult and personally draining, an uphill fight all the way to the end."[7] In the end, the support of moderate Republicans had been crucial. Former President Ford not only publicly supported the ratification of the treaties, but also actively lobbied a number of Republican senators to vote for them.[8] Vance noted that Senate Minority Leader Howard Baker's "leadership was indispensable, and it was an act of statesmanship."[9] Former Secretary of State Henry Kissinger had also supported the treaties, and after they were ratified, President Carter sent a handwritten letter to Kissinger, thanking him for his support and noting, "Your help was crucial."[10]

The Carter administration's victory on the Panama Canal treaties was won at great cost. The administration had pressured moderate Republicans to vote in favor of the treaties, which went against the grain of many of their conservative constituents. Senator Baker and other moderates believed that they could not continue to support President Carter's foreign policy initiatives without losing the support of some of their important constituents.[11] President Carter believed that "a large number of members of the Congress were later defeated for reelection because they voted for the Panama treaties."[12] Of the twenty senators who voted for the treaties and who were scheduled to run for reelection in 1978, six did not run, seven won, and seven were defeated. In 1980, eleven more senators who had voted for the treaties were defeated.

In an excellent book about the ratification of the Panama Canal treaties, George Moffett III concludes: "In the end, of course, the administration did win in the Senate. Still, what the administration gained was in nearly every respect a Pyrrhic victory. In exhausting its political capital, it was forced to relinquish its leverage on other issues."[13] This critical view was not recognized at the time that the treaties were ratified; instead, members of the administration believed they had won a major foreign policy victory that cleared the way for further foreign policy breakthroughs.

THE ADMINISTRATION'S APPROACH TO THE RATIFICATION OF SALT II

The Carter administration's campaign to win Senate ratification of the SALT II Treaty proved to be far more difficult than gaining approval of the

Panama Canal treaties. One administration official remarked, "Compared with SALT II, passing the Panama Canal treaties was playing tiddlywinks."[14] In his memoirs, President Carter recalled, "The lobbying campaign we mounted throughout the nation [for SALT II] . . . made the Panama Canal treaties pale into relative insignificance."[15]

One of the major problems was timing; it took Carter and the members of his administration longer than they expected to conclude the SALT II Treaty. Cyrus Vance, in particular, was frustrated by the length of the negotiations:

> The fact that the negotiations have dragged on and on has inhibited us from laying out the strengths of our position and from answering misleading or false statements that are being made by those who oppose SALT. This has given an impetus to the anti-SALT movement that it's going to take us a while to push back. If we'd been free to lay it all out to our critics as we went along, it would have been a lot better, but you have to deal with the realities of your negotiating parameters. God knows, it's been frustrating to read some of these stories and not be able to say, 'That's untrue! Here's what the actual facts are . . .' It's just been frustrating the hell out of me.[16]

In addition to the timing of the SALT II debate, the Carter administration officials who worked on the ratification campaign proved to be very important. For the most part, those members of the administration who worked on the ratification strategy for the Panama Canal treaties were the same ones who worked on the ratification campaign for SALT II. For example, Hamilton Jordan developed the ratification plan for the Panama treaties and then developed the ratification plan for SALT II. He was also the chairman of the task forces established within the administration for the ratification of the treaties. Robert Beckel had worked as a liaison between the White House and the Senate during the Panama debate and performed the same task during the SALT II debate, and George Moffett III, who directed the Committee of Americans for the Canal Treaties, joined the White House staff after the canal treaties were approved to work on the ratification of the SALT II Treaty.

There were several individuals who played particularly important roles in the SALT II debate. Paul Nitze was one of the most respected national security experts in Washington and had served in a variety of positions dating back to the Truman administration, most recently as a member of the SALT I delegation.[17] He was, according to Ralph Earle, "the first person I saw with a Carter bumper sticker."[18] Before the 1976 election, Nitze went to Plains, Georgia, to brief Carter about defense issues, and according to reports, Nitze gave a long, detailed presentation that bored Carter, who did not call on Nitze for advice following his election. Nitze was essentially cut out of defense policy discussions in the new administration and felt "abused and was mad" as a result.[19] Nitze became one of the cofounders of the Committee on

the Present Danger and wrote detailed analyses of the various Carter administration SALT proposals. These papers became some of the most widely read
and influential on Capitol Hill.

A second key participant in the SALT II debate was Paul Warnke, who
served as director of the Arms Control and Disarmament Agency (ACDA)
and chief SALT II negotiator from his appointment and contentious confirmation in March 1977 until his resignation in October 1978. Warnke had
proved to be a kind of lightning rod for conservatives to attack since they
believed that he was in favor of unilateral disarmament and was weak on
defense. President Carter indicates that Warnke resigned because he "had
already stayed away from his law firm longer than he or I had anticipated."[20]
In an interview with me, Warnke elaborated: "In 1978, I had three children
in college and my government salary simply could not meet the demands of
my family. . . . In addition, I had decided that the administration was not
making progress fast enough on arms control."[21] At the time, many observers
felt that Warnke had resigned in order to make the ratification of the SALT
II Treaty easier, but Warnke insists that his resignation was for personal
reasons and not dictated by the administration's ratification strategy.

President Carter appointed Gen. George Seignious to replace Warnke as
director of ACDA and Ralph Earle II as the chief SALT II negotiator.
General Seignious, who at the time of his selection was the president of The
Citadel, a military college in South Carolina, was chosen for two reasons: as a
retired military officer he would be a good symbolic supporter of the treaty,
and he was reportedly a good friend of Sen. Fritz Hollings, the conservative
Democrat from South Carolina who many thought would play an influential
role in the SALT II debate.

On the eve of Carter's departure for his meeting with Brezhnev in Vienna,
Lt. Gen. Edward L. Rowny announced that he was retiring from the army.[22]
At the time of his announcement, many assumed that Rowny was resigning
out of principle in order to campaign against the ratification of the SALT II
Treaty. Rowny had been a long-time protégé of Sen. Henry Jackson and had
officially served as the representative of the Joint Chiefs of Staff on the
delegation. Informally, Rowny was Senator Jackson's eyes and ears on the
delegation.

When the new administration assumed office, it had a perfect opportunity
to get rid of Rowny "because it was tradition that that position [JCS repre-
sentative] would change with a new administration."[23] However, in mid-
January 1977, just before the administration assumed office, the Department
of Defense transition team was considering the appointment of General
Rowny as the sole representative from DOD on the SALT delegation. An
adviser to the transition team exclaimed: "Are you out of your mind? You

don't invite a snake like that to come to a party that you're giving! Get serious; use your chance to dump him because this man is trouble!"[24] In the end, the transition team did not appoint Rowny as the sole DOD representative; however, he was reappointed as the JCS representative. Clearly, Carter's advisers had hoped to win points with Senator Jackson by reappointing Rowny, but in retrospect, critics of Rowny's reappointment called this decision a "foolish mistake" that was made as a result of "political ignorance."

Some Carter administration supporters were aware of and critical of General Rowny's activities. In December 1977, Rep. Bob Carr wrote to President Carter urging him to replace General Rowny as a member of the U.S. SALT delegation: "If Gen. Rowny disagrees with your arms control policies he is free to dissent within the Delegation, and has done so on many occasions. . . . Alternatively, he is free to resign and take his case to the public, as did Mr. Nitze. But he is not free to remain on the delegation while publicly issuing declarations which undercut United States national security posture, as he has done."[25] Members of the administration recognized the possibility that Rowny might resign in protest over the SALT II Treaty long before he actually did so; in November 1978, a deputy of Gerald Rafshoon, director of White House communications, warned Rafshoon of this possibility.[26] However, despite the recognition of the danger that Rowny posed to the administration, no one in a position to do so made a move to remove him from the U.S. SALT delegation. In retrospect, a number of administration officials and protreaty senators believed that President Carter and Secretary of Defense Brown made a serious error in failing to remove General Rowny from the SALT delegation at the beginning of the administration.[27]

In order to make his position on SALT clear, General Rowny sent a memorandum (classified "secret") to the chairman of the Joint Chiefs of Staff in January 1978.[28] In this memo, Rowny addressed four questions: "First, is a treaty along currently envisaged lines one which preserves deterrence? Second, would it represent essential equivalence and equality? Third, what other concerns do we have regarding the impending agreement? And finally, what should be done at this, *the eleventh hour?*"[29] In answering his four questions, Rowny painted a pessimistic picture of both Soviet intentions and the status of the U.S.-Soviet strategic nuclear balance and concluded: "I am deeply concerned that entry into the presently envisioned SAL [Strategic Arms Limitation] agreement would not enhance deterrence. In fact, the continuing trend of force imbalance favoring the Soviet Union may indeed erode deterrence."[30] Rowny updated the pessimistic assessment contained in this memo and subsequently resubmitted it to the Joint Chiefs of Staff in January 1979 and March 1979.[31]

General Rowny's resignation just prior to Carter's departure for the Vienna summit was represented in the press as a resignation of principle, or an act of protest and political courage. This view, however, distorts the facts. According to former high-level Department of Defense officials, Defense Secretary Harold Brown told General Rowny in early 1978 that President Carter had decided that the United States would not demand that the USSR eliminate its 308 heavy ICBMs and the Backfire bomber and that Rowny should resign from the delegation if he could not live with this decision. Rowny did not resign and "continued to be obdurate on the heavies and Backfire."[32] Because of his continued opposition to the administration's negotiating position, a number of former Carter administration officials now say that Rowny should have been fired. Rowny's reappointment to the SALT delegation and continued active service in the army had required a special waiver because by 1977 he had already served thirty-six years and was sixty years old. Army personnel regulations called for normal retirement after thirty-five years of service and age sixty. In fact, Rowny was scheduled to retire in the summer of 1979 and his retirement just prior to the Vienna summit in June was propitiously timed for the maximum political effect. According to a former Carter administration official, General Rowny's actions constituted "great selfishness for self-aggrandizement" rather than the altruistic picture that has previously been presented.[33]

THE TIMING OF THE RATIFICATION CAMPAIGN

Given their own experience and the priority that the president placed on the SALT II agreement, members of Carter's staff had devoted attention to the domestic politics of the agreement from the beginning of the administration. Landon Butler, Jordan's deputy, wrote a memo to Jordan concerning the "politics of SALT" in May 1977, just six weeks following the disastrous Vance trip to Moscow.[34] In the memo, Butler described a six-point strategy for broadening "the base of political support for SALT by reaching out to the public at large." The memo included the following suggestions:

1. The President should use a Town Hall Meeting or a telephone call-in show to discuss SALT.
2. The State Department should consider producing a film presenting the President's viewpoint on arms control.
3. We need carefully to broaden our base of support in the Senate.
4. The General Advisory Committee of ACDA can be broadened to play a very useful role.
5. We should develop a special program to relate to interested private groups.
6. We should develop a direct mail capability only as a last resort.

This is the earliest memo concerning a SALT ratification strategy that I was able to locate in the Carter Library, and it is significant for several reasons. First, from early in the administration, it appears that the Panama Canal treaties ratification strategy served as the template for the SALT II ratification strategy. An important implication of this is that Carter's advisers chose to influence the public, rather than approaching the Congress directly. Second, there are indications that Butler downplayed the idea of obtaining Senator Jackson's approval of SALT II. At one point in the memo, Butler wrote, "Everyone agrees that we should not allow Senator Jackson to monopolize Senate commentary on our SALT positions."[35] Third, the production of a pro-SALT film is mentioned in this memo (as well as in later memos), but the government never produced such a film. Given the impact that several anti-SALT films, particularly *The SALT Syndrome*, had on public opinion, this was, in retrospect, a serious mistake.

Others in the Carter administration were also thinking about the ratification of SALT II. In March 1978, the Office of the Historian in the Department of State issued a report focusing on previous administrations' efforts to gain the ratification of the Limited Test Ban Treaty, the Non-Proliferation Treaty, and the ABM Treaty.[36] This paper focused on the roles of the president, the Senate, public opinion, and public interest groups in the ratification of these three treaties. It provided a comparative view of arms control treaty ratification within the United States.

Members of the Carter administration were not the only ones thinking about a SALT II ratification strategy. According to William Kincade, then president of the nongovernmental Arms Control Association:

> As early as April 1977, a delegation of arms control supporters went to the White House saying that the administration should start the SALT II ratification effort. The arms control specialists within the administration said, 'That's a good idea, but the political people—Jordan, Powell and Rafshoon—need to be convinced.' When we talked with the politicos, they said, 'We need a treaty before we can start the ratification effort.' We [nongovernmental arms control supporters] thought that the ratification effort needed to be started long before the agreement was signed, and we went away from the meetings with heavy hearts.[37]

The fact that the Carter administration waited to campaign for the ratification of SALT II has caused some to conclude that SALT II failed due to the ineptitude of the administration.[38]

There were, however, good reasons why the Carter administration did not seriously begin the SALT II ratification effort until after the treaty was initialed by leaders of the United States and the USSR. The most obvious reason is that the provisions of the treaty were not formally settled until the agreement was signed by Carter and Brezhnev in Vienna on June 18, 1979, and the members of the administration felt they could not defend the specific terms of the treaty until they were finalized. As Hamilton Jordan noted, "We will not give the appearance of promoting a treaty which is still being negotiated."[39]

In addition, there were a number of issues competing for the attention of the president and his closest advisers, and their attention could only be devoted to SALT II once it moved to the top of the administration's agenda. Advisers were constantly guarding "their" issues against the incursion of other concerns. For example, Stuart Eizenstat, the president's chief domestic affairs adviser, wrote to Carter in October 1977: "Please permit me to urge you in the strongest possible way not to announce a SALT agreement until after the energy bill has passed both houses and Congress has adjourned. Such an announcement will simply draw attention away from the energy bill and throw yet another controversial issue into the melting pot."[40]

Finally, the president and his advisers did not decide that the SALT II agreement would be in the form of a treaty until just prior to the summit. There were a number of news reports that Carter was considering concluding SALT II as an executive agreement.[41] Such an agreement would have to be approved by a simple majority vote of both houses of Congress, a much simpler task than achieving the two-thirds approval of the Senate.

In a February 1979 *Atlantic Monthly* article based in part on an interview with President Carter, Professor James MacGregor Burns raised the executive agreement possibility: "While he plans to recognize the Senate's full role in treaty-making, if a SALT agreement is blocked or emasculated in the upper chamber, he will ask both House and Senate for a simple majority vote of approval . . ."[42] Burns had interviewed Carter in November 1978 as Carter was considering signing SALT II as an executive agreement. Following the publication of Burns's article, both supporters and opponents of SALT II in the Senate objected to concluding it as an executive agreement.[43] Sen. Frank Church, chairman of the Senate Foreign Relations Committee, wrote to Carter noting, "Some may see in the quoted characterization of your views a derogation of the Constitutional role of the Senate, as well as an attempt to threaten the Senate to either approve SALT or be removed from the decision-making process."[44]

In late February, Carter announced that he was no longer considering joint House-Senate approval as an option and that SALT II would be submitted to the Senate in the form of a treaty.[45] Apparently, Carter made the decision after consulting with key senators who strongly recommended that the agreement be concluded as a treaty and submitted to the Senate for "advice and consent."

Carter's decision to conclude a treaty rather than an executive agreement was made about the same time that the treaty was being wrapped up, and

once it was signed at the Vienna summit meeting, the White House inten-
sified ratification activities. Overall responsibility for the ratification effort
rested with the SALT Task Force, under the chairmanship of Hamilton
Jordan. Task force members from the White House staff included: Frank
Moore and Bob Beckel (Office of Congressional Relations), Jody Powell
(Press Office), Anne Wexler (Public Liaison Office), Gerald Rafshoon
(Communications Office), Phil Wise (Appointments), and Landon Butler
and George Moffett (Chief of Staff's Office). Other members drawn from
executive agencies and departments were: Warren Christopher and Matthew
Nimetz (State Department), David Aaron (NSC), Gen. George Seignious
(ACDA), Charles Duncan (DOD), Frank Carlucci (CIA), and Richard Moe
(Vice President's Office).[46]

Several White House groups were responsible for particular aspects of the
ratification campaign and were de facto subcommittees of the SALT Task
Force. The SALT Working Group under the chairmanship of NSC staff
member Roger Molander was responsible for answering technical questions
about the treaty both from members of the executive branch and from the
Senate. The administration's strategy for dealing with the media was developed by Gerald Rafshoon. Anne Wexler directed the public outreach effort
by the White House. In addition to these groups, the Department of State
and the Department of Defense each had separate SALT task forces; Matthew Nimetz headed State's and Walter Slocombe chaired DOD's.

Frank Moore and Bob Beckel in the White House Office of Congressional
Relations were responsible for directly interacting with senators on a day-to-
day basis. Moore had worked with Jimmy Carter since 1966 and had no
experience in dealing with the Congress prior to coming to Washington.
After he arrived, he did little to cultivate the support of important legislators.
One senior Senate staff member noted that when he saw Senator Stennis,
chairman of the Senate Armed Services Committee, at the White House in
January 1979, the senator told him that it was the first time that he had been
invited to the White House for a briefing on SALT.[47]

Moore, according to a respected Senate staff member, "was not up to the
job in a whole host of ways. He couldn't even do the technical job in the
most limited sense, much less lay out a strategic plan."[48] An NSC official
recalled that after the treaty was signed, an important White House meeting
was called to work out the administration's ratification strategy, and "Frank
Moore's only contribution in the entire four hour meeting was to get up and
periodically change the radio from one country music station to another
country station. That's when I knew we were in trouble!"[49] According to
almost all accounts, Moore was notoriously ineffective; Beckel received much
higher marks.

Initially, the director of White House communications, Gerald Rafshoon, was given the assignment to work out the administration's plan to ratify the SALT II Treaty. Rafshoon contacted the various groups within the administration working on SALT II and requested their recommendations. In the communications between Rafshoon and other officials, some interesting differences are evident. For example, Matthew Nimetz, who was counselor of the State Department and the chair of the department's SALT task force, wrote Rafshoon, "Members of Congress will, to a substantial degree, play a leading role in shaping public opinion towards the agreement."[50] This view differed in a fundamental way from the White House perspective (evident in Landon Butler's previously cited memo) that the key to ratification was to gain public support. Nimetz recommended that the White House "be involved in the ratification effort at an early date, and its direct participation would increase as the Congressional debate advances." Nimetz also noted that President Carter's personal contact with "key congressional leaders" and senior public figures would "be important to winning a broad consensus in support of SALT TWO."[51]

After receiving recommendations from a number of individuals and organizations, Rafshoon and his staff developed two plans: a communications plan for their office and an overall strategic plan for the administration. In the communications plan, Rafshoon described an ambitious list of tasks to be completed in support of SALT II, including establishing a speakers' bureau, writing speeches and briefing papers, producing a film, arranging for presidential addresses and press conferences, coordinating media appearances by senior members of the administration, arranging interviews of high-level members of the administration by prominent columnists, and distributing positive editorials to members of the Senate.[52]

In early December 1978, Rafshoon wrote an "eyes only" memo to President Carter outlining a strategic plan to develop public support for the SALT II Treaty.[53] Rafshoon began the memo by emphasizing the importance of the agreement: "Continuation of the SALT process will be one of the most significant achievements of your Presidency." Reflecting the age-old adage that in politics timing is everything, Rafshoon hoped that the negotiations would be concluded prior to the State of the Union address in January and that a summit meeting would then take place in late January or early February. Rafshoon believed that the administration needed to develop "*simple and easily understood*" themes that would "strike a *responsive chord*" and appeal to the public's "*common sense.*"[54] The goal of the ratification effort should not be "to educate the public either about the complexities of strategic planning or the details of the treaty." Rather, the administration's arguments "must make more sense—intuitively—than the opposition's. They must be supported by common sense . . ." As in both his earlier memo and Landon Butler's, Rafshoon recommended the production of a pro-SALT film "as quickly as possible." Rafshoon concluded the memo by noting that "high level coordination at the White House is critical to the success of this effort," and recommended that Jordan be given the responsibility to "effectively bring everyone together."

After considering Rafshoon's recommendations, President Carter gave Jordan the responsibility to develop the SALT II ratification strategy and to chair the SALT Task Force. By the end of January 1979, Jordan had prepared a "SALT II Ratification Work Plan" and sent it to Carter for his review.[55] The plan was broken down by time periods and functional tasks (congressional relations, public outreach, media, press, contacts with major public figures, and liaison with allied governments). This detailed document was the blueprint for the administration's ratification effort.

In the first months of 1979, members of the administration worked out detailed plans for the SALT ratification campaign. The White House chief of administration, Hugh Carter, developed a computerized master list of tasks to be completed and the person responsible for completing each of these tasks.[56] In early May, Rafshoon accurately predicted that "the debate over SALT II will be long, rancorous and confused" and urged the president to "take the time to show that you are the country's foremost SALT expert . . ."[57]

As the summit approached, the administration stepped up activities related to the upcoming ratification debate. The White House Office of Congressional Relations sent each senator lengthy briefing books on SALT on May 10, May 29, and June 14.[58] Two weeks before the summit, Rafshoon launched the press component of the ratification campaign by sending a letter and materials on SALT II to forty-seven prominent journalists, including Shana Alexander, David Broder, William Buckley, Rowland Evans, Joseph Harsh, and Tom Wicker.[59]

In his January memo, Jordan noted the importance of Carter's meeting with Brezhnev in Vienna: "The summit will provide our first opportunity to explain the full treaty to the American public. . . . Immediately after the summit, the Administration's activities should leave no doubt that we plan an all out fight for ratification."[60] According to plan, as soon as Carter returned from Vienna, the administration's all-out campaign to ratify the treaty began.

Anne Wexler was the liaison between the White House and special interest groups, and during the SALT debate she was responsible for public outreach. Her office worked with business, labor, religious, local, and state leaders in order to broaden the pro-SALT coalition and support for the treaty. Because federal statute prohibits federal funds from being "used directly or indirectly to pay for any personal service, advertisement, telegram, telephone, letter, printed or written matter, or other devices intended or designed to influence in any manner a Member of Congress, to favor or oppose, by vote or otherwise, any legislation . . .," Wexler's office worked through various nongovernmental pro-SALT groups such as Americans for SALT.[61]

In a year-end report on the activities of her office, Wexler wrote to President Carter, Hamilton Jordan, and Lloyd Cutler in December 1979: "We have been meeting every week or two with a coalition of unions, religious groups, and Americans for SALT. These meetings are expected to lead to important input regarding Senators."[62] Religious leaders were singled out for attention. Materials on SALT were sent to more than one thousand members of the clergy in the hope that they would preach sermons related to SALT. The administration actively sought the support of popular evangelist Billy Graham, and Wexler recommended that the president and vice president invite the Reverend Mr. Graham to the White House in order to discuss SALT.[63] In addition to these activities, Wexler's office was also responsible for acting as liaison between the White House and grassroots, pro-SALT organizations in many states and local communities.

Wexler's office was part of a much broader effort within the federal government to win public support for SALT II. This effort quickly became known as "the selling of SALT" among both proponents and opponents of the treaty. In May 1978, the Department of State created the SALT Working Group within the Bureau of European Affairs in order to respond to the anticipated increased public need for information about U.S.-Soviet relations as a result of the conclusion of the SALT II negotiations. Five foreign service officers and two secretaries were assigned to the group, which took the responsibility for arranging for State Department and ACDA officials to make speeches and to be interviewed by the news media, distributing informational materials, and organizing conferences on SALT. State Department officers who volunteered to speak to groups around the country (called "SALTies" by critics) went through a four-day training program, complete with a videotaped critique of their presentation at the end of the course.[64]

By the end of 1978, the group had furnished speakers for at least 138 engagements in forty-five states and 34 engagements in Washington, D.C.; distributed four hundred thousand copies of SALT-related documents available for public distribution; and organized nine major conferences throughout the United States.[65] The State Department, Arms Control and Disarmament Agency, and Defense Department estimated that their costs for SALT II public affairs expenditures during 1978 were, respectively, $347,000, $248,000, and $5,000, for a total of about $600,000. During the first six months of 1979,

State Department and ACDA officials participated in another 650 speaking engagements in forty-eight states and the District of Columbia and organized twenty-eight conferences at an estimated total cost of $624,000.[66] In addition to these expenditures, several White House offices also distributed SALT materials and arranged conferences on SALT at a total estimated cost of $19,000.

Many conservatives were infuriated by the activities of the "SALT sellers." Sen. Barry Goldwater requested that the U.S. General Accounting Office investigate these activities and issue a report on them.[67] *The National Security Record,* a publication of the conservative Heritage Foundation, published a detailed breakdown of the number of State Department briefings, speeches, town meetings, and media events related to SALT.[68] Kenneth Adelman referred to the administration's campaign as "Rafshooning the Armageddon,"[69] and the American Conservative Union became so alarmed that it filed suit seeking an injunction to halt the government's SALT-selling operations.[70] When Wexler was asked what she thought of the criticism that the White House was spending too much money to "drum up public support for the SALT treaty," she responded, "It's perfectly legitimate for the government to spend money to educate the public and respond to information requests on one of its policies—certainly a policy that is as important as SALT to the future of this country."[71]

ALTERNATIVE PRESENTATIONS OF THE CASE FOR SALT II

There were several ways in which the administration could present the SALT II Treaty to the public and the Senate. The first possibility was to present the treaty as a part of the broader fabric of Soviet-American relations, an approach observers called "warmed over Kissinger" or "rococo Kissinger."[72] This was the approach favored by Cyrus Vance and the State Department. According to this view, arms control was the most important aspect of détente, and the SALT II Treaty simply represented an improvement in the U.S.-Soviet relationship. The problem with this approach, of course, was that it did not appeal to many conservatives. In fact, it was President Ford's détente policy that almost led to his defeat at the 1976 Republican Convention. While détente was supported by moderates and liberals, it was anathema to conservatives.

Several senators and their staff members became concerned about how the administration was presenting the case for SALT II, and they organized a small group to develop an alternative way of presenting the treaty. This group included senators Dale Bumpers, Alan Cranston, John Culver, and Gary Hart and staff members Larry Smith (Armed Services Committee) and Charles Stevenson (Senator Culver's office). At the first meeting of this group, Smith told the members: "We have to do something to counter the effective attack of conservatives on the treaty. . . .We need to develop a 'pin-down' strategy, and any time one of the opponents criticizes the treaty, we need to respond."[73] Accepting Smith's advice, the group developed a highly organized, effective strategy for responding to attacks on the treaty. Senators who were treaty supporters signed up for "watches" on particular committees and would respond to attacks on the treaty that occurred whenever they were serving as "watch officer of the day." In addition, the group made sure that at least one protreaty senator always attended important committee meetings.

Perhaps an even more important contribution of this group than the pin-down strategy was the development of the "national security case" for SALT II. As its name implies, this approach emphasized the advantages for U.S. defense that resulted from SALT II, rather than simply portraying SALT II as an ingredient of détente. The national security case for SALT had a much broader appeal than the administration's initial approach because it appealed to a much wider segment in the Senate. After a number of discussions with pro-SALT senators, the Carter administration begrudgingly accepted the national security case for SALT, but there were lapses. One Senate staffer recalled:

> I took a group of politically influential Democrats to the White House, and they were important enough that Vice President Mondale agreed to meet with them. One of the visitors asked Mondale what he thought of SALT II, and he replied, 'I'm in favor of SALT II because it's in our national security interest.' So far, so good, but then he added, 'I've always been a believer in détente and that's another reason that I'm in favor of SALT II.' It was as if the tape was running the new message, but it ran out and Mondale went back to the 1975 rationale for SALT.[74]

Curiously, one case was not even presented during the SALT ratification campaign; it was, to borrow from Sherlock Holmes, "the dog that didn't bark"—until 1982. This was the "nuclear war" case for SALT. As public opinion polls reveal, the American people were not particularly concerned about the threat of nuclear war in 1979.[75] By the autumn of 1982, however, there was significant public concern about the danger of nuclear war, and this concern was evident in the popularity of the nuclear freeze movement. Roger Molander, a nuclear engineer who had served on the National Security Council under presidents Nixon, Ford, and Carter, said that no one ever proposed "anything even close to the nuclear war case for SALT." By 1982, millions of Americans feared a possible nuclear war, but in 1979 they did not. As one former SALT negotiator lamented in 1983, "I am delighted that the American people have now become aware of the dangers that nuclear weapons pose, but where were they in 1979 when we needed their help to get SALT II ratified?"[76]

CRITICISMS OF THE CARTER ADMINISTRATION'S RATIFICATION STRATEGY

A number of criticisms of the Carter administration's strategy for gaining the ratification of the SALT II Treaty have been voiced. Perhaps the most serious criticism was that "those in the administration who knew about the substance of SALT were either politically naïve or condescending toward politics, and those who were politically skilled, were almost totally ignorant of the substance. This is one of those issues where a deep fusion of the political and policy arts was required."[77] The administration eventually attempted to achieve this required fusion but not until the treaty was signed. According to someone who worked in the ratification effort, "We started two years too late; the opponents had been working against the treaty for two years before we even started."[78]

Once the administration began its effort, it used the Panama Canal treaties ratification plan as its model. In the case of the Panama Canal, the Senate was generally in favor of the treaties and the public was opposed. With SALT, the situation was exactly opposite; the Senate was generally opposed, and the public in favor. This should have elicited a different ratification strategy rather than simply relying on the earlier Panama strategy.

By almost all accounts, Frank Moore, the chief White House lobbyist on Capitol Hill, was inept. During the Panama Canal treaties ratification campaign, Bob Beckel performed well and was called on to repeat his performance for the SALT II Treaty. But overall, the poor performance of the White House Office of Congressional Relations hurt the ratification chances of the SALT II Treaty.

Early in the administration, a number of people suggested that President Carter appoint a senior adviser who was respected on Capitol Hill to oversee the SALT ratification effort. Robert Straus, a prominent adviser to Democratic presidents, was one of those recommended. Rather than accepting this recommendation, Carter relied on his own staff and then on several midlevel officials in the State Department and the Department of Defense to oversee the planning for and the initial implementation of the ratification strategy. But these officials did not have the respect or the visibility to command the Senate's attention.

It was not until August 1979 that Carter appointed several "non-Georgians with gray hair," including prominent Washington attorney Lloyd Cutler and former *Time* magazine editor Hedley Donovan.[79] Carter gave Cutler the responsibility for the SALT II ratification plan. Some in the administration who had been working on SALT for years were bitter when Cutler announced that he would not begin working on the SALT ratification campaign until after he had returned from a long-planned cruise on the canals of France. Carter's appointment of Cutler came too late to make a difference.

Like the captain of a ship in the navy in which he served, President Carter was ultimately responsible for the actions of his administration, including the SALT II Treaty ratification strategy. The president clearly wanted to conclude and ratify the SALT II Treaty. But he believed that if something was right (and Carter fervently believed that SALT II was right), the public and the Congress would support it. Although the president met with a number of influential citizens who came to the White House for briefing sessions, he did not place the highest priority on spending time with individual senators. This was an unfortunate mistake. With the Panama Canal treaties, public opinion needed to be reversed, and the administration's strategy was effective in achieving this. In the SALT II case, senators' opinions needed to be reversed, but the Carter administration's strategy was geared primarily to changing public opinion.

NOTES

1. "Letter from Jimmy Carter to Top Administration Officials," April 28, 1979, reprinted in *Newsweek*, May 21, 1979.

2. For a firsthand account of the negotiations, see William J. Jorden, *Panama Odyssey* (Austin: University of Texas Press, 1984). The following books describe the ratification process: George D. Moffett III, *The Limits of Victory: The Ratification of the Panama Canal Treaties* (Ithaca, N.Y.: Cornell University Press, 1985); William L. Furlong and Margaret E. Scranton, *The Dynamics of Foreign Policymaking: The President, the Congress and the Panama Canal Treaties* (Boulder, Colo.: Westview Press, 1984); and J. Michael Hogan, *The Panama Canal in American Politics: Domestic Advocacy and the Evolution of Policy* (Carbondale: Southern Illinois University Press, 1986).

3. Polling data cited in Moffett, *Limits of Victory*, 210.

4. Landon Butler, interview with author, Washington, DC, October 21, 1987.

5. Jimmy Carter, *Keeping Faith: Memoirs of a President* (New York: Bantam Books, 1982), 162.

6. Zbigniew Brzezinski, *Power and Principle: Memoirs of the National Security Adviser, 1977– 1981* (New York: Farrar, Straus and Giroux, 1983), 138–39.

7. Ibid., 136.

8. Carter, *Keeping Faith*, 165.

9. Cyrus Vance, *Hard Choices: Critical Years in America's Foreign Policy* (New York: Simon and Schuster, 1983), 151–52.

10. Letter from Jimmy Carter to Henry Kissinger, May 1, 1978, in "Kissinger," Name File, Jimmy Carter Library.

11. Carter, *Keeping Faith*, 88.

12. Ibid., 184.

13. Moffett, *The Limits of Victory*, 207.

14. *Time*, January 8, 1979, 21.

15. Carter, *Keeping Faith*, 262.

16. Quoted in Strobe Talbott, *Endgame: The Inside Story of SALT II* (New York: Harper and Row, 1979), 204.

17. Paul Nitze, with Ann M. Smith and Steven L. Rearden, *From Hiroshima to Glasnost: At the Center of Decision* (New York: Grove Weidenfeld, 1989).

18. Ralph Earle II, interview with author, Washington, DC, October 23, 1987.

19. Barry Blechman, interview with author, Washington, DC, October 23, 1987.

20. Carter, *Keeping Faith*, 233.

21. Paul Warnke, interview with author, Los Angeles, May 20, 1987.

22. Jack Nelson, "Troubled Carter to Leave Today for SALT Summit," *Los Angeles Times*, June 14, 1979.

23. Author's confidential interview.

24. Author's confidential interview.

25. Letter from Bob Carr to Jimmy Carter, December 9, 1977, WHCF–Subject File, FO 6–1, Jimmy Carter Library, 1.

26. Memorandum from Alan Raymond to Gerald Rafshoon and Greg Schneiders, November 20, 1978, Folder "SALT [3]," "Rail Strike through Soviet Postcards," Box 6, Gerald Rafshoon Files, Jimmy Carter Library, 3.

27. Author's interviews.

28. Memorandum from Edward Rowny to the Chairman, Joint Chiefs of Staff, January 6, 1978; declassified version obtained by the author from the Department of Defense under the Freedom of Information Act, request no. 87–FOI–1263, May 12, 1988.

29. Ibid., emphasis added, 1.

30. Ibid., 5.

31. "Statement of Lt. Gen. Edward L. Rowny," in U.S. Congress, Senate, Committee on Foreign Relations, *The SALT II Treaty*, hearings, 96th Cong., 1st sess., pt. 1:537.

32. Author's confidential interview.

33. Author's confidential interview.

34. Memorandum from Landon Butler to Hamilton Jordan, May 11, 1977, Folder "SALT [3]," "Rail Strike through Soviet Postcards," Box 6, Gerald Rafshoon Files, Jimmy Carter Library.

35. Ibid., 2.

36. U.S. Department of State, Office of the Historian, Bureau of Public Affairs, "Administration Strategy toward Congress on Three Nuclear Arms Issues (Limited Test Ban Treaty, Nonproliferation Treaty, SALT I Agreements)," Research Project No. 1189, March 1978 (originally classified secret; declassified as result of request by author under the Freedom of Information Act, March 23, 1988).

37. William Kincade, interview with author, Washington, DC, July 13, 1988.

38. Ibid. and Alan Platt, "The Politics of Arms Control and the Strategic Balance," in Barry Blechman, ed., *Rethinking the U.S. Strategic Posture* (Cambridge: Ballinger, 1982), 155–78.

39. Memorandum from Hamilton Jordan to Jimmy Carter, January 30, 1979, in Carter Presidential Papers, Staff Offices, Chief of Staff (Jordan), Subject File, "SALT Notebook [CF, O/A 648]," Box 53, Jimmy Carter Library.

40. Memo from Stuart Eizenstat to Jimmy Carter, October 22, 1977, "Arms Control [O/A 6245]," Box 147, Stuart Eizenstat Files, Jimmy Carter Library.

41. Norman Kempster, "Carter May Bypass Treaty Vote Process on Arms Pact," *Los Angeles Times*, October 7, 1978.

42. James MacGregor Burns, "Jimmy Carter's Strategy for 1980," *Atlantic Monthly*, March 1979, 41–46.

43. In December 1978, Gerald Rafshoon recommended that Carter not accept the "executive agreement option"; see Memorandum from Gerald Rafshoon to Jimmy Carter, December 6, 1978, in Carter Presidential Papers, Staff Offices, Assistant for Communications, Subject Files, SALT [5] folder, Jimmy Carter Library.

44. Letter from Frank Church to Jimmy Carter, February 28, 1979, in Box 70–41, WHCF–Subject File, Foreign Affairs, Executive, Folder FO 6–1 (2/11/79–3/31/79), Jimmy Carter Library, 2.

45. Press Release, Office of the White House Press Secretary, February 24, 1979, in Box 70–41, WHCF–Subject File, Foreign Affairs, Executive, Folder FO 6–1 (2/11/79–3/31/79), Jimmy Carter Library.

46. "SALT Task Force," undated list, Folder "[SALT–2]," "Rail Strike through Soviet Postcards," Box 6, Gerald Rafshoon Files, Jimmy Carter Library.

47. Author's confidential interview.

48. Author's confidential interview.

49. Author's confidential interview.

50. Memorandum from Matthew Nimetz to Gerald Rafshoon, October 6, 1978, "SALT II through Solar Initiatives," Box 60, Gerald Rafshoon Files, Jimmy Carter Library.

51. Ibid.

52. "SALT—Office of Communications Plan," written by Gerald Rafshoon, October 12, 1978, "Rail Strike through Soviet Postcards," Box 6, Gerald Rafshoon Files, Jimmy Carter Library.

53. Memorandum from Gerald Rafshoon to Jimmy Carter, December 6, 1978, in Carter Presidential Papers, Staff Offices, Assistant for Communications, Subject Files, SALT [5] folder, Jimmy Carter Library.

54. Ibid., 2 (emphases in the original).

55. Memorandum from Hamilton Jordan to Jimmy Carter, January 30, 1979, in Carter Presidential Papers, Staff Offices, Chief of Staff (Jordan), Subject File, "SALT Notebook [CF, O/A 648]," Box 53, Jimmy Carter Library.

56. "SALT II Ratification: Master Work Plan," April 11, 1979, WHCF, Hugh Carter Files, Box 77, Jimmy Carter Library.

57. Memorandum from Gerald Rafshoon to Jimmy Carter, May 8, 1979, "FO 6–1, 5/9/79–5/15/79," Box 70–41, WHCF–Subject Files, Foreign Affairs, Executive, Jimmy Carter Library, 1–2.

58. "Reference Guide to SALT," in Henry M. Jackson Papers, Accession no. 3560–6, Box 50, Folder 9, University of Washington Libraries.

59. Letter from Gerald Rafshoon to Shana Alexander and other journalists, June 4, 1979, "FO 6–1, 6/1/79–6/11/79," Box 70–41, WHCF–Subject Files, Foreign Affairs, Executive, Jimmy Carter Library.

60. Memorandum from Hamilton Jordan to Jimmy Carter (note 55), 8–9.

61. 18 USC 1913.

62. Memorandum from Anne Wexler to Jimmy Carter, Hamilton Jordan, and Lloyd Cutler, December 4, 1979, "Executive, FO–61 (11/1/79–12/30/79)," Box FO–42, WHCF–Subject File, Foreign Affairs, Jimmy Carter Library.

63. Memorandum from Anne Wexler to Phil Wise, March 30, 1979; letter from William Dyess to Anne Wexler, March 29, 1979, Folder FO–61 (2/11/79–3/31/79), Box 70–41, WHCF–Subject File, Foreign Affairs, Executive, Jimmy Carter Library.

64. "Selling SALT: President Pulls Out the Stops," *U.S. News and World Reports*, April 2, 1979, 35.

65. Letter from J. K. Fasick to Barry Goldwater, March 16, 1979, report no. ID–79–24 (Washington: U.S. General Accounting Office, 1979).

66. Letter from J. K. Fasick to Barry Goldwater, August 27, 1979, report no. ID–79–50 (Washington: U.S. General Accounting Office, 1979).

67. Ibid.

68. *National Security Record,* May 1979.

69. Kenneth L. Adelman, "Rafshooning the Armageddon: The Selling of SALT," *Policy Review* 9 (Summer 1979): 85–102.

70. *American Conservative Union v. Jimmy Carter* (Civil Action no. 79–2495).

71. "Interview with Anne Wexler: White House and Congress: Why the Troubles," *U.S. News and World Report,* June 18, 1979, 54.

72. Author's interviews.

73. Larry Smith, interview with author, Washington, DC, October 20, 1987.

74. Ibid.

75. See polling data in chapter 4.

76. Speech by Ralph Earle II.

77. Larry Smith, interview with author.

78. Author's confidential interview.

79. The quoted phrase is Donovan's; see Hedley Donovan, *Roosevelt to Reagan: A Reporter's Encounters with Nine Presidents* (New York: Harper and Row, 1985), 212.

CHAPTER FOUR

Public Opinion
and SALT II

Given the democratic nature of American government, public opinion clearly plays an important role in American politics. Politicians pay close attention to public opinion polls, particularly at election time. At other times, they look to polls to inform them how the public feels about certain issues. Public opinion has a significant influence on the making of domestic and foreign policies. In this chapter, I will (1) describe Americans' attitudes toward foreign policy in general, (2) present the results of polls on SALT II, (3) review the factors that influenced public opinion on SALT II, and (4) assess the role that public opinion played in the SALT II debate.

AMERICAN ATTITUDES CONCERNING FOREIGN POLICY

One of the findings of political science that has been shown in study after study during the past several decades is that most Americans do not care about foreign policy issues most of the time. In fact, Americans only become concerned about foreign policy issues when they perceive their interests as threatened. Prominent instances in which this occurred include the Vietnam War from 1968 on, and during the mid–1970s following the Arab oil-export embargo and the ensuing increased price of gasoline. Because Americans do not perceive foreign policy issues as affecting their interests most of the time, their attitudes on these issues are generally, as Charles Kegley and Eugene Wittkopf have pointed out, "uninformed, uninterested, unstable, acquiescent and manipulable."[1]

In his classic study, *The American People and Foreign Policy*, Gabriel Almond found that only about 15 to 20 percent of Americans were knowledgeable about foreign policy and followed issues related to it on a regular basis. Almond called this group the "attentive public."[2] More recent studies of public opinion have challenged Almond's characterization of this group; for example, W. Russell Neuman found that only about 5 percent of the American population was politically knowledgeable and active, while 75 percent move in and out of politics and the remaining 20 percent are apolitical.[3] The size of this group of politically knowledgeable and active Americans is not particularly relevant to this study; however, the level of the public's knowl-edge about SALT is important.

Since the beginning of the nuclear age, a number of public opinion ana-lysts have focused on Americans' attitudes toward nuclear weapons and nu-clear war. In the days immediately following the bombing of Hiroshima, the Gallup Organization asked, "Do you approve or disapprove of using the new atomic bomb on Japanese cities?" About 89 percent of those Americans questioned approved and only 11 percent disapproved.[4] Over time, Ameri-cans were less certain that the decision to drop atomic bombs on Japanese cities was correct; in 1971, 64 percent approved of this decision and in 1982, 63 percent approved.[5] In 1945 and 1946, a number of polling organizations asked whether those questioned had "read or heard about" or "know of" the atomic bomb.[6] Between 96 and 100 percent responded affirmatively to this question, a percentage that has not been equalled by any other question related to the public's knowledge of the nuclear weapons issue during the past forty years. So it is clear that Americans know that the atomic bomb exists, but what else do they know and believe about nuclear weapons?

The United States was the only state that possessed nuclear weapons until 1949 when the Soviet Union exploded its first nuclear device. During the 1950s, the United States and the Soviet Union developed and deployed hydrogen bombs that were one hundred times as powerful as atomic bombs and intercontinental ballistic missiles that could travel from the United States to the USSR (or vice versa) in approximately thirty minutes. In addition, Great Britain and France developed and deployed their own nu-clear weapons. As nuclear-weapons technology proliferated, Americans be-came more concerned about these new weapons and less sure that they would be able to survive in a world in which they were used. In 1956, the Gallup Organization asked, "Do you think you and your family would be likely to live through an atomic war?" While 29 percent thought that they would be likely to live through such a war, 38 percent thought that they would not and 33 percent were unsure.[7] In subsequent years, Gallup asked a similar question, "If we should happen to get into an all-out nuclear war, what do you think your own chances would be of living through it—very good, poor, or just 50–50?" In 1961, 47 percent thought that their chances of surviving were poor; this figure grew to 55 percent by 1963 and to 60 percent by 1981.[8]

A number of social and political factors contributed to the public's increas-ing concern over nuclear weapons during the 1950s and early 1960s. The first U.S. hydrogen bomb test, conducted in 1952, produced unexpectedly high levels of radioactivity, and a 1954 test in the South Pacific spread radioactive fallout over thousands of square miles and resulted in the death of a Japanese fisherman on a boat eighty-five miles from the test.

By 1959, a radioactive isotope, strontium 90, began to appear in signifi-cant amounts in wheat and milk. Atmospheric nuclear tests released radioac-tive isotopes into the atmosphere, which would return to earth in rain and snow. These isotopes then entered the human food chain via cows' or moth-ers' milk. Scientists and parents became concerned that this isotope would cause leukemia among children drinking milk; a two-part article in the *Satur-day Evening Post* in 1959, entitled "Fallout: The Silent Killer," illustrated public concern.[9] Books, articles, and movies reflected and fanned increased public concern over nuclear weapons. Best-selling books such as *Fail-Safe,* *Cat's Cradle,* and *On the Beach* were examples of this literature, and Stanley Kubrick's classic film *Dr. Strangelove* satirized the thinking of the new nuclear strategists. The government itself contributed to an increasing public con-cern over nuclear weapons by emphasizing the dangers of nuclear war and calling for preparations for civil defense. More than thirty-five million copies of one civil defense booklet were distributed throughout the country. By the early 1960s, a full-blown public scare over fallout, the Soviet threat, and civil defense swept the nation.

The high point of the cold war occurred in October 1962 when the Soviet Union secretly attempted to install missiles in Cuba, and the United States responded with a quarantine of Cuba and demanded that the missiles be removed. During the crisis, according to former Secretary of State Dean Rusk: "For the first time nuclear powers had to look at nuclear exchange as an operational matter. Men had a chance to peer into the pit of the inferno."[10] In the wake of the crisis, President Kennedy and Premier Khrushchev moved quickly to conclude several agreements to lessen the danger of nuclear war and the costs of preparing for such a war.

The Hot Line Agreement and the Limited Nuclear Test Ban Treaty, both signed in 1963, were first steps toward reducing the danger of nuclear war, and the public viewed these agreements in positive terms. In 1959, 64 per-cent of those questioned had listed "war (especially nuclear war)" as the country's most urgent problem. Just six years later, this figure had fallen to 16 percent, and within several more years, this issue had dropped from the list entirely.

Several factors contributed to the demise of the nuclear issue in the public mind. Historian Paul Boyer has described five factors that contributed to the public's decreased concern about nuclear weapons and the dangers that they posed.[11] First, there was a public perception of diminished threat. Arms control successes bred a decreased sense of public concern about nuclear weapons. Ten American-Soviet bilateral and nine multilateral arms control agreements were signed in the period from 1963 to 1979. Norman Cousins, editor of *Saturday Review,* complained: "Hardly anyone talks anymore about nuclear stockpiles as the world's No. 1 problem. . . . The anti-testing clamour of the Sixties now seems far off and almost unreal."[12] A second reason for decreased public concern was the loss of immediacy. As the years passed, "memories of Hiroshima and Nagasaki began to dim . . ."[13] and it appeared that the world and its leaders had learned how to "live with the bomb."

Boyer points to a third factor: the neutralizing effect of the "peaceful nuclear atom." The Eisenhower administration had launched the Atoms for Peace program in 1953, promising that if the United States helped non-nuclear-weapons states develop peaceful nuclear power, they would be less inclined to develop nuclear weapons. Consequently, the U.S. government and American companies actively marketed nuclear power all over the world. Subsequent administrations continued to push nuclear power; in 1967, President Lyndon Johnson gave a speech entitled "Nuclear Power: Key to a Golden Age of Mankind."[14]

A fourth element that contributed to the public apathy about nuclear weapons was related to the complexity and reassurance of nuclear strategy. In the 1950s, nuclear deterrence was based on a simple threat as old as humanity: if another country attacked the United States, the United States would counterattack. By the 1960s, deterrence had grown far more complex; for example, strategists wrote about a number of different types of deterrence including minimum deterrence, extended deterrence, massive retaliation, and flexible response. The strategists developed their own vocabulary which was liberally strewn with acronyms such as ICBM, SLBM, MAD, BMEWS, and NORAD. Only the most interested member of the public had even a vague idea of what these terms and acronyms represented, much less what they actually meant.

A final reason that the public's attention was diverted from the nuclear weapons issue was the Vietnam War. As the war drew out and escalated, Americans became more and more interested in it. In 1969, when Gallup asked respondents to list the "two or three most important problems facing the nation," 63 percent mentioned Vietnam and only 2 percent identified the danger of nuclear war.[15] Coincidentally, this was almost the identical number (64 percent) who had identified "war (especially nuclear war)" as the nation's most urgent problem ten years before.

Soon after the Paris peace accords ending U.S. involvement in the Vietnam War were signed, the American public identified a new concern as the country's most important: economic problems. In fact, "since the end of the Vietnam War, economic concerns have ranked far above foreign policy matters as the nation's 'most important problem,' usually by margins of five or six to one."[16] From 1973 to 1978, respondents consistently named economic concerns as the most important.[17] In mid-December 1978, an NBC/Associated Press survey asked people to name the single issue on which Congress should act, and the responses were as follows:[18]

Inflation	32%
Cuts in federal spending	16
Crime	11
Energy	10
National health insurance	10
Tax cuts	7
U.S. military strength	5
Treaty with Russia to limit nuclear weapons	4

Thus, of the eight issues cited by those questioned, the six most frequently cited concerned economic (inflation, cuts in federal spending, and tax cuts) and social issues (crime, energy, and national health insurance); foreign policy and defense issues were the least frequently mentioned. A Gallup poll of November 1979 found these results: 63 percent felt that the "high cost of living/inflation" was the most important problem facing the nation in 1979, and only 6 percent felt that foreign policy was the most important.[19]

When Americans were asked about foreign policy issues specifically, from 1964 to 1974, their overriding concern was peace, and from 1974 to 1981, military strength became most important.[20] In fact, as William Schneider has pointed out, "Virtually every month from 1974 to 1981 saw greater support for increasing the size of the defense budget."[21] Figure 4–1 shows the growing public support for increasing the defense budget during this period. As the graph shows, in 1977 for the first time since the early 1960s, more Americans believed that "too little" rather than "too much" was being spent on defense. Two Harris polls showed that support for increased defense spending went from 28 percent in December 1976 to 52 percent in November 1978, a situation that Louis Harris called a "remarkable turn-around."[22] Louis Kreiberg and Ross Klein identified three related changes between 1973 and 1978 that appear to have produced the clear trend toward greater public support for increased defense spending: "(1) the decline in the impact of the Vietnam war, (2) a rise in particular elements of conservative ideology, and (3) an increase in anti-Soviet and anti-communist sentiment."[23]

These changes had a significant impact on the groups within the public that took an interest in foreign policy. Based on different sets of data, political scientists have identified three dominant foreign-policy opinion groups. Based on their analysis of public opinion polls sponsored by the Chicago Council on Foreign Relations in 1974 and 1978, William Schneider and Michael Mandelbaum identified "liberal internationalists" (who were pro-détente and antimilitary), "conservative internationalists" (who were anti-détente and promilitary), and "noninternationalists" (who were opposed to

Figure 4-1: Support for Defense Spending, 1973–1982

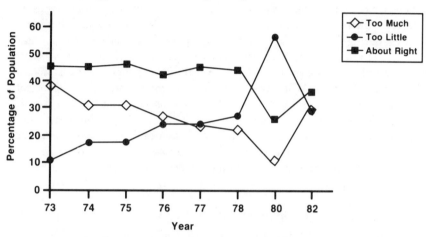

Source: National Opinion Research Center

greater United States involvement in international affairs).[24] Based on a survey of elites, Ole Holsti and James Rosenau identified three foreign-policy opinion groups; interestingly, they are very similar to those identified by Schneider and Mandelbaum: "cold war internationalists," "post–cold war internationalists," and "semi-isolationists."[25]

In sum, the Vietnam War both destroyed the foreign policy consensus that had existed from the late 1940s to the late 1960s and shifted public concern away from foreign policy issues to domestic economic and social issues. By the late 1970s, rather than one relatively united body of foreign policy opinion, there were three. There were signs of growing conservatism, such as increasing support for greater defense spending, and of increasing support for an isolationist foreign policy. In fact, the proportion of the American public that identified itself as isolationist increased from 8 percent in 1964 to 23 percent in 1974.[26]

Before turning to American opinion on SALT II, several observations concerning general public opinion on arms control and dealing with the Soviet Union need to be made. In poll after poll conducted since the beginning of the nuclear age, two attitudes were clear: (1) Americans, by about 75 percent, supported efforts to control nuclear weapons, and (2) about two-thirds of the American public did not trust the Soviet Union to abide by its international agreements.[27] Based on an extensive review of questions on nuclear weapons, Everett Carll Ladd concluded that "American opinion on nuclear weapons and war has changed scarcely at all over nearly four decades."[28]

Public opinion analysts have shown that Americans are not interested in foreign policy and defense issues unless they perceive their interests as affected. Americans were alarmed by the danger of nuclear war and the Soviet threat during the 1950s; however, during the 1960s, public perception of the danger of nuclear war receded due to several factors, including the Vietnam War which shattered the post–World War II foreign policy consensus. By the end of the Vietnam War, Americans were most concerned about economic and social issues. Despite their variable attention and concern over foreign policy and defense issues, Americans have maintained some consistent views about nuclear weapons, arms control, and the degree to which the Soviet Union can be trusted. These general orientations to foreign policy and defense issues constitute the foundation on which public opinion about SALT II was based.

PUBLIC OPINION ON SALT II

During a visit to his home state of North Carolina in August 1979, Sen. Jesse Helms wanted to air his opposition to the SALT II Treaty, which had been signed just two months before. He reported: "No one wants to talk about SALT II and nuclear weapons. They want to discuss inflation, energy, tax cuts, recession and business regulations. You go out on the street and ask the average fellow about MIRVs, and he says, 'Oh yeah, the TV show host.'"[29]

Senator Helms's experience was far from unique during the period in which the Senate debated the SALT II Treaty, for most Americans knew very little, if anything, about the agreement. And most people were willing to admit their ignorance. A CBS/*New York Times* poll taken in June 1979 (the same month that the SALT II Treaty was signed) asked: "The Senate will debate the US treaty with the Soviet Union which limits strategic nuclear weapons—called SALT. From what you know about this SALT treaty, do you think that the Senate should vote for or against it, or don't you know enough about it to have an opinion?" Some 27 percent were in favor of the agreement, 9 percent opposed, 10 percent did not have an opinion, and 54 percent said they did not know enough about the treaty.[30] In February 1978, the Opinion Research Corporation asked respondents how much they had heard or read about the SALT negotiations. The majority, 61 percent, reported that they had heard or read very little or nothing at all, 29 percent a fair amount, and only 8 percent a great deal.[31] In a December 1978 survey, only 34 percent of those questioned could correctly identify the two countries involved in the SALT negotiations.[32] Another poll taken in 1979 found that even fewer people—23 percent—knew which two nations were involved in the talks.[33]

The public neither knew very much about SALT II, as the above poll findings demonstrate, nor did the public consider it particularly important. In May 1979, one month before the SALT II Treaty was signed, Louis Harris asked: "I'd like to ask you about some issues and problems that some people would like to see Congress do something about. If you had to choose, which one do you feel is most important for Congress to do something about?" The results:[34]

Keeping inflation under control	31%
Passing an energy bill to make the United States more energy self-sufficient	20
Helping the elderly and the poor get a better break	10
Keeping the military strength of the United States at least as strong as that of the Russians	9
Giving relief to taxpayers	9
Cutting federal spending	7
Supporting stronger measures to control crime	3
Backing a SALT agreement with Russia to control nuclear weapons	2
Achieve peace in the Middle East	2
Passing a comprehensive health insurance bill	2
Not sure	5

As is obvious from these results, the public did not consider a SALT agreement to be particularly important; indeed, the public ranked a SALT agreement at the bottom of the list of its concerns.

The public opinion polls on SALT II are confusing; they indicate that the number of those supporting SALT ranged from a high of 81 percent (NBC poll of January 1979) to a low of 20 percent (Committee on the Present Danger poll of March 1979). Figure 4–2 indicates the wide variation in a number of the polls conducted on SALT II. In its summary of SALT polls, the editors of *Public Opinion* commented, "SALT polls are poles apart."[35] One can see the reason for this comment in Figure 4–2.

There are several possible reasons why the results of these polls are so different. First, public opinion expert Daniel Yankelovich has pointed out: "Conventional survey techniques are most accurate when reflecting the public's state of mind on well-thought-through issues. They are not as sensitive in judging how the public might react after it has the opportunity to learn the facts, to listen to competing views, to think through the questions, and to see how well any particular policy accords with their deeper values, attitudes, and beliefs."[36] Clearly, the public had not "thought through" the issues related to SALT II, and the wide divergence in the SALT polls reflects this.

Second, research on public opinion indicates that there is a tendency for

Figure 4-2: Public Opinion Polls on SALT II

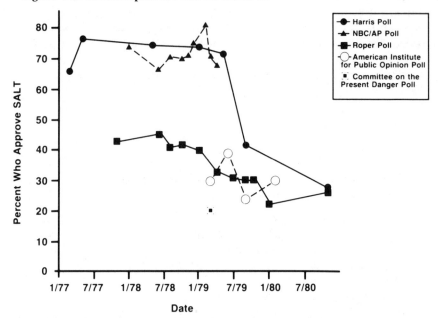

Source: Data taken from Thomas W. Graham, "The Politics of Failure: Strategic Nuclear Arms Control, Public Opinion and Domestic Politics in the United States, 1945–1985" (Ph.D. diss., Massachusetts Institute of Technology, 1989). I would like to thank Dr. Graham for providing me with this data.

people to give positive responses when asked about unfamiliar issues, and this tendency is indicated in the SALT polls.

Third, many criticized the wording of a number of the polls on SALT; for example, the Committee on the Present Danger noted, "Highly generalized, hypothetical and simplistic questions with no effort to measure gradations of response provide data which furnish little insight into relevant public attitudes and are apt to be completely misleading."[37] Many of the questions supposedly concerning SALT really asked people what they thought about arms control in general, rather than SALT II in particular. For example, an NBC/Associated Press poll asked, "Do you favor or oppose a new agreement between the United States and Russia which would limit nuclear weapons?" And 81 percent answered that they favored a new agreement. But it was not clear what people had in their minds when they indicated an affirmative response to this question. Did they have in mind a comprehensive test ban, the Non-Proliferation Treaty, SALT II, or some other agreement? Pollster Burns Roper was also critical of the NBC poll: "The NBC question comes very close to asking whether people would like to have peace. In fact by saying 'a new agreement' instead of 'the new agreement,' it could almost be interpreted as asking whether people would like to see the present draft renegotiated."[38]

It is no wonder that President Carter and his advisers were confused by the public opinion polls on SALT II. Given the conflicting results of the polls, where did they turn to assess what the public really believed? Within the State Department, the Bureau of Public Affairs tracked public opinion on SALT II on a regular basis, and the assistant secretary of state for public affairs summarized polls and forwarded these summaries to the secretary of state, the director of the Arms Control and Disarmament Agency, and the counselor of the State Department. President Carter and the White House staff relied primarily on the polls conducted by Carter's own in-house poll-ster, Patrick Caddell. In his memoirs, Carter noted, "Caddell's polls, I knew from experience, were remarkably accurate."[39] A comparison of the polls summarized by the State Department and Caddell's provides insight into the way that the executive branch viewed public opinion on SALT II.

Within the State Department, Bernard Roshco was responsible for sum-marizing publicly available polls for Hodding Carter, the assistant secretary of state for public affairs. Roshco developed several important themes in the memos that he drafted for the assistant secretary. In September 1978, Roshco analyzed the reasons for divergent poll results and noted, "We know that the public has expressed a desire to be 'tougher,' in some undefined way, toward the Soviet Union . . .," which could explain the 56 percent opposition to SALT indicated in a poll at that time. In addition, Roshco perceptively noted that polls such as an August 1978 NBC poll ("Do you favor or oppose a new agreement between the United States and Russia which would limit nuclear weapons?") "should not be taken as an assurance the public would accept the [SALT II] agreement actually negotiated."[40]

In a December 1978 memo, Hodding Carter warned: "The public's desire to limit Soviet deployment of nuclear weapons does *not* mean it will give careful, extended consideration to detailed expositions about SALT. It does mean *the public will be highly susceptible to attention-arresting, seemingly plausible criticisms of SALT.*"[41] During the ensuing months, Hodding Carter's warning proved to be prescient; opponents of SALT II produced a number of hard-hitting, thirty-second television commercials and simplistic brochures that proved to be very influential. In the same memo, the reasons and implica-tions of the wide divergence in two polls—one by NBC and one by Roper—were analyzed. According to the memo, the Roper poll, which indicated much lower support for SALT II than the NBC poll, "adds credence to our previously stated concern that support for an actual SALT *treaty* would be sizably lower than support [for] the *idea* of reaching an agreement with the Soviet Union to control strategic nuclear arms."[42]

Figure 4-3: Roper Polls on SALT II

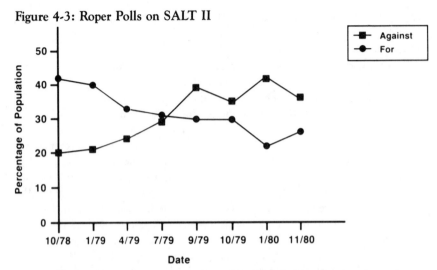

Source: Thomas W. Graham, "The Politics of Failure: Stategic Nuclear Arms Control, Public Opinion and Domestic Politics in the United States, 1945–1985" (Ph.D. diss., Massachusetts Institute of Technology, 1989).

State Department analysts believed that Roper "posed the most appropriately worded question" and they therefore gave "more credence to Roper's data than to the data produced by any of the other polls."[43] Roper himself thought that "most of the polls are conveying misleadingly high levels of approval," and his polls indicated support levels from a low of 20 percent to a high of 42 percent. Figure 4–3 shows the results of Roper's polls over a two-year period.

While the State Department relied primarily on Roper's polls, President Carter and the White House staff depended upon Caddell's polls. In a dramatic memo that Caddell sent to President Carter and Hamilton Jordan in May 1978, Caddell reported the results of his most recent poll: "Since foreign policy/defense concerns have been secondary matters in recent years, nothing in our structured quantitative research prepared us for the below surface anxiety and concern over these issues that the open end interviews revealed."[44] Caddell warned that *"For the first time since the Vietnam War, defense/foreign affairs is emerging,"* and that the public was moving in a more conservative direction. Concerning SALT, Caddell predicted: *"SALT itself seems destined to be caught in the vertex [sic] of these larger concerns over our defense and foreign policy posture. I fear that a SALT agreement will not be judged on its own merits but rather become a vehicle for these concerns. Given the attitudes we see emerging, SALT could become a firestorm."*[45] Caddell urged that the issue of "peace as well as defense are [sic] considered."

Table 4–1: Caddell Polls on SALT II

	Yes, favorable	Yes, unfavorable	Yes, don't know	No, have not heard	Not sure
1975	37%	13%	15%	22%	13%
1976	33	18	15	21	12
1977	39	15	24	22	--
1978	37	19	17	21	6

Source: Data derived from Cambridge Reports, Inc., "An Analysis of Current Public Opinion on SALT," February 15, 1979, folder "SALT II–Information [CF 1986]," box 60, "SALT Speech through Solar Initiatives," Gerald Rafshoon's Files, Jimmy Carter Library, 2.

What is striking about Caddell's memo is that he was surprised by the results of his poll. As noted in the first part of this chapter, public support for increasing the defense budget grew almost monthly from 1974 to 1981, and while peace was the dominant concern of most Americans from 1964 to 1974, military strength became paramount from 1974 to 1981.[46] Caddell urged the president to emphasize the issue of "peace" just as the public was moving in the opposite direction. The evidence of this movement was clear in public opinion polls of the time, except Caddell's.

In February 1979, Caddell prepared a report summarizing his previous poll results on SALT. The following question was asked: "Have you heard of the Strategic Arms Limitation Talks—or SALT talks—with the Russians? (If yes) Do you have a generally favorable or unfavorable opinion of such talks?"[47] Table 4–1 summarizes the responses.

Caddell's results were much closer to Roper's than to those polls (such as the NBC polls) that showed much greater public support for SALT II. In addition, Caddell and the State Department's public opinion analysts agreed that about 20 percent of the public was opposed to SALT II.[48] However, Caddell's and the State Department's conclusions differed in a very important respect. Whereas the State Department argued that public support for "generic" arms control should not be confused with specific support for SALT II, Caddell concluded "that Americans support both arms limitation in general and SALT in particular."[49] In retrospect, it appears that the information provided by the State Department was more accurate than that provided by Caddell, but Jimmy Carter, to his detriment, believed Caddell's polls.

Two weeks prior to the signing of the SALT II Treaty, the State Department summarized public opinion concerning the agreement at that time:

1. *Support outweighs opposition* among those who have *firm* views on this issue, but the polling questions have been so differently worded that the results

have produced no consensus regarding the actual levels of support and opposition.

2. *Much of the expressed opinion is "soft"*; moreover, an exceptionally large proportion of the rest describe themselves as undecided or unsufficiently [sic] informed to express an opinion.[50]

In short, the polls were inconclusive about SALT II, a conclusion that was clearly noted in a November 1979 memo: "the finding to which all the current SALT polls seem to point is that public opinion on SALT is now so closely divided that *one cannot weigh with confidence whether the predominant attitude is to favor SALT or oppose it.*"[51]

FACTORS THAT INFLUENCED PUBLIC OPINION ON SALT II

Just as President Carter was about to present the SALT II Treaty to the Senate for ratification, a member of his administration commented: "If Eisenhower was [sic] President, all he'd have to do is say: 'I've read the treaty, and I think it's good,' and he'd get a tremendous number of people to follow him."[52] This was not to happen with Jimmy Carter.

The data presented above indicate the wide divergence in the polls taken on SALT II. What factors influenced public opinion on this issue? During the time that the Senate was debating the SALT II Treaty, political scientist David Moore examined several variables that he expected to correlate with support for SALT. These variables included "public confidence in U.S. negotiators, attitudes toward the Panama Canal treaties, perceptions of the relative strength of the U.S. and USSR, support for internationalism, ideological orientation, party identification, education, and level of interest in U.S.-Soviet arms negotiations."[53] Moore found that one variable acted as a strong predictor of support for SALT: the degree of confidence people expressed in the American officials negotiating with the Soviets. Those who had confidence in U.S. negotiators supported the treaty, while those who did not have such confidence were critical of it. "Regardless of one's political ideology, the more confidence one has in U.S. negotiators, the more supportive he will be of a new SALT treaty."[54]

Moore's findings underscore the importance of President Carter's popularity ratings as a factor in determining the level of support for SALT II. Table 4–2 summarizes public approval ratings and the major foreign policy events of the Carter administration. In scoring public opinion before and after these events, I have summed the changes in approval and disapproval to reach a total *net change* of public approval. As one can see from the table, the most dramatic changes in net public approval occurred following the signing of the Egyptian-Israeli Peace Treaty by President Sadat and Prime Minister Begin in March 1979 (a net rise of 17 percent) and the takeover of the U.S. embassy in Tehran in November 1979 (a net increase of 12 percent). Iron-

Table 4-2: Carter Approval Ratings and Major Foreign Policy Events, 1977–1980 *

Date and Event	Approval	Disapproval	No Opinion	Net Change **
August (early) 1977	60%	23%	17%	
U.S. and Panama agree to transfer canal.				
August (middle) 1977	66	26	8	
	+6	−3		+3
April 1978	40	44	16	
Second Panama Canal Treaty ratified.				
April/May 1978	41	42	17	
	+1	+2		+3
September (middle) 1978	45	40	15	
Camp David agreements concluded.				
September (late) 1978	48	34	18	
	+3	+6		+9
December (middle) 1978	51	34	15	
U.S. recognizes the People's Republic of China.				
January (early) 1979	50	36	14	
	−1	−2		−3
March (early) 1979	39	48	13	
Sadat and Begin sign peace treaty.				
March (middle) 1979	47	39	14	
	+8	+9		+17
June (early) 1979	29	56	15	
SALT II Treaty signed.				
June (late) 1979	29	57	14	
	0	−1		−1
November (early) 1978	32	55	13	
American embassy in Tehran seized.				
November (middle) 1978	38	49	13	
	+6	+6		+12
December (middle) 1978	54	35	11	
USSR invades Afghanistan.				
January (early) 1980	56	33	11	
	+2	+2		+4
April 1980	39	50	11	
Hostage rescue attempt fails.				
May (early) 1980	43	47	10	
	+4	+3		+7

* Source: *The Gallup Opinion Index,* Report No. 182 (October–November 1980), 13–14.
** Net change was calculated by subtracting the earlier approval rating from the later approval rating plus/minus subtracting the later disapproval rating from the earlier disapproval rating.

ically, the first event was one of the greatest successes of the Carter administration and the latter, one of the greatest failures.

Although paradoxical, these results are consistent with earlier public opinion findings concerning presidential leadership during crises. President Kennedy, for example, achieved his highest public approval ratings in the days following the disastrous Bay of Pigs invasion. Table 4–2 also shows that the least popular foreign policy event of the Carter administration was the recognition of the People's Republic of China (a net loss of 3 percent). Closely following this was the signing of the SALT II Treaty which resulted in a decrease of 1 percent, barely a ripple in the ocean of public opinion. Thus, rather than building his public support, SALT II barely affected the public's opinion of President Carter.

While Table 4–2 indicates the changes in President Carter's popularity, Figure 4–4 shows Carter's popularity from February 1977 through February 1980. The high point in his popularity occurred very early in his administration, in March 1977. There was a gradual downward trend during the ensuing two years, and the low point (until that time) occurred in July 1979, one month after the SALT II Treaty was signed. Figure 4–4 also shows the level of public support for the SALT II Treaty as revealed by the Roper polls. It is clear that Carter's popularity and public support for SALT II were closely related.

President Carter's popularity ratings were among the lowest recorded; as Gallup pointed out, "President Carter . . . holds the unfortunate distinction of having received the lowest popularity rating given any President in the last four decades—21 percent, in July 1980—and won only a 34 percent approval rating in the public's final assessment of his performance in office."[55] Of the seven presidents who served after World War II, Carter's 47 percent rating was the third lowest average rating behind Truman (41 percent) and Ford (46 percent).

The SALT II Treaty was signed at a time when several trends in public opinion were developing, all of which worked to the disadvantage of SALT II ratification. Public support for increased defense spending was increasing, public approval of President Carter was decreasing, and the public's opinion of the Soviet Union was growing increasingly critical, as Figure 4–5 shows.

Political scientist Bruce Russett has noted that "Arms control treaties . . . may not be well received in times of economic adversity."[56] Judged in light of this proposition, the SALT II Treaty was forwarded to the Senate at a bad time, for the United States was in the throes of a recession in 1979. As Russett points out, "Future leaders contemplating such agreements [as SALT II] may wish to take into account the state of the domestic economy as they ponder the degree of popular support and try to adjust their timing accordingly."[57]

Figure 4-4: President Carter's Popularity

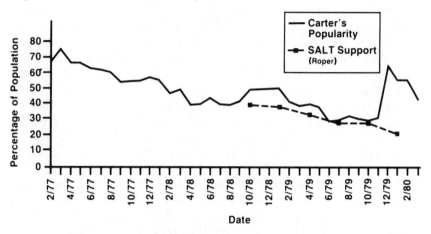

Source: *The Gallup Opinion Index*, no. 182 (October–November 1980).

Figure 4-5: U.S. Public Opinion of the Soviet Union

Question: How do you feel about the Soviet Union?

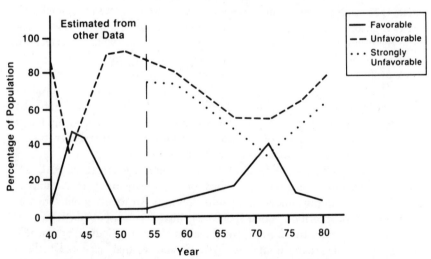

Source: Joseph S. Nye, Jr., "Can America Manage Its Soviet Policy?" In Joseph S. Nye, Jr., ed., *The Making of America's Soviet Policy* (New Haven: Yale University Press, 1984), 329; used by permission.

CONCLUSIONS

Many studies have shown that most Americans do not care about foreign policy issues most of the time. In addition and perhaps as a result of this indifference, they are not knowledgeable about these issues. At the time that the SALT II Treaty was debated, most Americans did not perceive the issue of arms control as affecting their interests and, consequently, they did not follow the debate over SALT II very closely.

President Jimmy Carter and his advisers recognized that public acceptance of the SALT II Treaty was important in helping to achieve ratification by the Senate, and they sought to gain public approval of the agreement in a number of ways. Central to the administration's ratification strategy, as described in chapter 3, was the White House effort to win the approval of influential citizens from states with undecided senators. The White House sponsored a number of briefings for such citizens in Washington, D.C. Typically, Cyrus Vance, Harold Brown, and/or Zbigniew Brzezinski would describe the elements of the treaty and then respond to questions from the audience. President Carter made an attempt to drop by these meetings in order to add to the aura. The administration hoped that these citizens would be so convinced of the need for the treaty that they would go home and urge their senators to vote in favor of the agreement.

But the Carter administration's ratification strategy overlooked a fact of contemporary political life: about two-thirds of the American public relies on television as its primary source of news and information.[58] On the one hand, television has created an audience for news about foreign policy, since it is the television producers and not the public who decide what is covered on television programs. Of course, even news programs must have a public following, or they will lose their commercial sponsors. And if most Americans don't care about foreign policy issues most of the time, the prudent producer will not emphasize foreign policy–related stories. In addition, the entire text of the average thirty-minute nightly news program on the major networks can be contained on one side of a single page of a newspaper. So the amount of information that is covered is not great.

Either consciously or fortuitously, the conservative critics of SALT II based their strategy of defeating ratification on a recognition of the importance of television in influencing public opinion. Antitreaty groups such as the American Security Council sponsored thirty-second spots on television opposing the treaty. In addition, the American Security Council produced a thirty-minute antitreaty film, *The SALT Syndrome*, that appeared to be a factual documentary complete with a number of former government officials noting the weaknesses of the SALT II Treaty. According to one study of the role of interest groups in the SALT II debate, "No other interest group activity seemed to influence public opinion so much as this movie."[59]

President Carter and his advisers sought to create a public constituency for the SALT II Treaty, and they failed in this effort. The public was not interested in SALT either at the beginning of the ratification debate or at the end of it. In fact, public opinion polls conducted in late 1979 indicated that the public had learned little or nothing during the course of the debate. The administration was not able to convince members of the public that arms control was a subject that affected them; that task was, ironically, accomplished by Ronald Reagan following his landslide election in 1980. The careless rhetoric of President Reagan and members of his administration convinced large numbers of Americans that something had to be done about nuclear weapons, a feeling that led to widespread public support for a freeze on the production and stockpiling of nuclear weapons.[60]

By mid–1979, when the SALT II Treaty was signed, President Carter's approval rating was down, the country was in an economic recession, support for increased defense spending was up, public opinion was increasingly critical of the Soviet Union, and public support for the SALT II Treaty was down. This was the domestic atmosphere in which the Carter administration sought to win the ratification of the SALT II Treaty.

NOTES

1. Charles W. Kegley, Jr., and Eugene R. Wittkopf, *American Foreign Policy: Pattern and Process*, 3d ed. (New York: St. Martin's Press, 1987), 305.

2. Gabriel A. Almond, *The American People and Foreign Policy* (New York: Praeger, 1960).

3. W. Russell Neuman, *The Paradox of Mass Politics: Knowledge and Opinion in the American Electorate* (Cambridge: Harvard University Press, 1986).

4. Survey by the Gallup Organization, August 10–15, 1945, cited in "Opinion Roundup: Americans Assess the Nuclear Option," *Public Opinion* (August–September 1982): 33.

5. Ibid.

6. Polls conducted by the Social Science Research Council, the American Institute of Public Opinion, and others, cited in Thomas W. Graham, "The Politics of Failure: Strategic Nuclear Arms Control, Public Opinion and Domestic Politics in the United States, 1945–1985" (Ph.D. diss., Massachusetts Institute of Technology, 1989). I would like to thank Dr. Graham for sharing his data with me.

7. Survey by the Gallup Organization, June 15–20, 1956, cited in "Opinion Roundup," 35.

8. Ibid.

9. Robert A. Divine, *Blowing on the Wind: The Nuclear Test Ban Debate, 1954–1960* (New York: Oxford University Press, 1978).

10. "Testimony of Secretary of State Dean Rusk," U.S. Congress, Senate, Committee on Foreign Relations, *Nuclear Test Ban Treaty*, hearings, 98th Cong., 1st sess., August 1963, 33.

11. Paul Boyer, "From Activism to Apathy: The American People and Nuclear Weapons, 1963–1980," *The Journal of American History* 70, no. 4 (March 1984): 821–44.

12. Norman Cousins, "The Nightmare That Won't Go Away," *Saturday Review*, April 17, 1976, 14.

13. Boyer, "From Activism to Apathy," 830.

14. Lyndon B. Johnson, "Nuclear Power: Key to a Golden Age of Mankind," *Department of State Bulletin*, December 25, 1967, 862–64.

15. Cited by Boyer, "From Activism to Apathy," 836.

16. William Schambra, "More Bucks for the Bang: New Public Attitudes toward Foreign Policy," *Public Opinion* (January–February 1979): 47.

17. Eugene R. Wittkopf, "Elites and Masses: Another Look at Attitudes toward America's World Role," *International Studies Quarterly* 31, no. 2 (June 1987): 132.

18. Cited by Schambra, "More Bucks for the Bang," 47.

19. *Gallup Opinion Index*, Report no. 172 (November 1979), 17.

20. William Schneider, "Conservatism, Not Interventionism: Trends in Foreign Policy Opinion, 1974–1982," in Kenneth A. Oye, Robert J. Lieber, and Donald Rothchild, eds., *Eagle Defiant: United States Foreign Policy in the 1980s* (Boston: Little, Brown, 1983), 60.

21. Ibid., 43.

22. Quoted by Schambra, "More Bucks for the Bang," 48.

23. Louis Kreiberg and Ross Klein, "Changes in Public Support for U.S. Military Spending," *Journal of Conflict Resolution* 24 (March 1980): 79–110.

24. William Schneider and Michael Mandelbaum, "The New Internationalism: Public Opinion and American Foreign Policy," in Kenneth Oye, Donald Rothchild, and Robert Lieber, eds., *Eagle Entangled: U.S. Foreign Policy in a Complex World* (New York: Longman, 1979).

25. Ole R. Holsti and James Rosenau, *American Leadership in World Affairs: Vietnam and the Breakdown of Consensus* (Boston: Allen and Unwin, 1984).

26. Samuel P. Huntington, "Renewed Hostility," in Joseph S. Nye, Jr., ed., *The Making of America's Soviet Policy* (New Haven: Yale University Press, 1984), 272.

27. Daniel Yankelovich, Robert Kingston, and Gerald Garvey, eds., *Voter Options on Nuclear Arms Policy: A Briefing Book for the 1984 Elections* (New York: Public Agenda Foundation and the Center for Foreign Policy Development, 1984). In a June 1978 CBS/*New York Times* survey, 64 percent of the respondents said that the USSR would not live up to its share of an agreement if the United States and USSR were to sign one limiting weapons. An October 1978 NBC News/Associated Press poll also indicated that 64 percent of those surveyed did not trust the Soviets to live up to agreements to "relax tensions between them"; see "Opinion Roundup: The Realities of U.S./U.S.S.R. Intentions and Position," *Public Opinion* (August–September 1982): 36.

28. Everett Carll Ladd, "The Freeze Framework," *Public Opinion* (August–September 1982): 20 (emphasis in original).

29. Associated Press, August 25, 1979 (referring to television personality Merv Griffin).

30. CBS/*New York Times* poll, June 1979, cited in Graham, "The Politics of Failure."

31. David W. Moore, "The Public Is Uncertain," *Foreign Policy* 35 (Summer 1979): 70.

32. Ibid., 70–71.

33. Robert Erikson, Norman Luttbeg, and Kent L. Tedin, *American Public Opinion*, 2d ed. (New York: Wiley, 1980), 19.

34. Louis Harris poll, May 1979, cited in Graham, "The Politics of Failure."

35. *Public Opinion* (March–April 1979): 27.

36. Daniel Yankelovich, "Cautious Internationalism: A Changing Mood toward U.S. Foreign Policy," *Public Opinion* 1, no. 1 (March–April 1978): 16.

37. Committee on the Present Danger, "Public Attitudes on SALT II: The Results of a Nationwide Scientific Poll of American Opinion," March 1979, 4.

38. Letter from Burns W. Roper to Sen. Frank Church, March 2, 1979, attached to a memo from William J. Dyess to George Seignious and Matthew Nimetz, April 4, 1979, in "SALT II through Solar Initiative," Box 60, Gerald Rafshoon Files, Jimmy Carter Library.

39. Jimmy Carter, *Keeping Faith: The Memoirs of a President* (New York: Bantam Books, 1982), 114.

40. Memo from Hodding Carter III to Paul Warnke, Matthew Nimetz, and Marshall Shulman, September 19, 1978, Department of State, Bureau of Public Affairs, 1–2. I am indebted to Thomas W. Graham for providing me with a copy of this memo.

41. Memo from Hodding Carter III to George Seignious and Matthew Nimetz, December 19, 1978, Department of State, Bureau of Public Affairs, 4 (emphasis in original).

42. Ibid., 1 (emphasis in original).

43. Memo from William J. Dyess to George Seignious and Matthew Nimetz, April 4, 1979, in "SALT II through Solar Initiative," Box 60, Gerald Rafshoon Files, Jimmy Carter Library, 1.

44. Memo from Patrick H. Caddell to Jimmy Carter and Hamilton Jordan, May 10, 1978, in Folder "SALT [5], Rail Strike through Soviet Postcards," Box 60, Gerald Rafshoon Files, Jimmy Carter Library, 1 (emphasis in original).

45. Ibid., 3 (emphasis in original).

46. Schneider, "Conservatism, Not Interventionism," 43, 60.

47. Cambridge Reports, Inc., "An Analysis of Current Public Opinion on SALT," February 15, 1979, Folder "SALT II—Information [CF 186]," Box 60, Gerald Rafshoon Files, Jimmy Carter Library, 2.

48. See ibid. and memo from Hodding Carter III to Paul Warnke, Matthew Nimetz, and Marshall Shulman, 3.

49. Cambridge Reports, Inc., "An Analysis of Current Public Opinion on SALT," 10.

50. Memo from Hodding Carter III to George Seignious, Matthew Nimetz, and J. Brian Atwood, November 23, 1979, Department of State, Bureau of Public Affairs, 3 (emphasis in original).

51. Ibid.

52. Quoted by Steven V. Roberts, "Arms Pact Friends and Foes Rally for Senate Battle," *New York Times*, April 13, 1979.

53. David W. Moore, "SALT: A Question of Trust," *Public Opinion* (January–February 1979): 50; also see Moore, "The Public Is Uncertain," 68–73.

54. Ibid.

55. *Gallup Opinion Index*, no. 182 (October–November 1980), 3.

56. Bruce Russett, "Democracy, Public Opinion, and Nuclear Weapons," in Philip E. Tetlock, Jo L. Husbands, Robert Jervis, Paul C. Stern, and Charles Tilly, eds., *Behavior, Society, and Nuclear War*, vol. 1 (New York: Oxford University Press, 1989), 191.

57. Ibid.

58. Schneider, "Conservatism, Not Interventionism," 61.

59. David Carl Kurkowski, "The Role of Interest Groups in the Domestic Debate on SALT II," Ph.D. diss., Temple University (Ann Arbor: University Microfilms, 1982), 240.

60. Robert Scheer, *With Enough Shovels: Reagan, Bush and Nuclear War* (New York: Random House, 1984).

CHAPTER FIVE

The Battle of the Interest Groups

Public opinion, the Congress, and interest groups have had an increasing role in the making of American foreign policy since the beginning of the twentieth century. This trend was evident after World War I when the U.S. Senate blocked America's entry into the League of Nations. In recent decades, the Congress has played a more active and important role in fulfilling its appropriations, confirmation, and oversight functions in foreign policy. Congressional actions during the Vietnam War illustrated the new activism of the Congress. Public opinion has also had a significant effect on the making of U.S. foreign policy, as the influence of the nuclear weapons–freeze campaign on U.S. governmental policies demonstrated in the early 1980s.

In his classic study, *The American People and Foreign Policy*, originally published in 1950, Gabriel Almond referred to interest groups infrequently and sporadically.[1] More recent books contain some material on interest groups and American foreign policy, but their authors devote not more than a chapter and often just several pages to this subject.[2]

Because the debate over the SALT II Treaty was significant and involved a large number of interest groups, it provides a good case study of the important, but somewhat neglected, subject of the role of interest groups in the making of American foreign and defense policy.

INTEREST GROUPS AND AMERICAN POLITICS

In the tenth Federalist Paper, James Madison noted that the tendency to form factions was "sewn in the nature of man" and that "among the numerous advantages promised by a well-constructed Union, none deserves to be more accurately developed than its tendency to break and control the violence of faction."[3] Madison was particularly concerned about the potential of such factions for sowing dissension in the newly created United States, and he sought to establish a form of government that would check these tendencies. The result was a republican form of government with shared, not separated, powers. Madison was not the only early observer of American politics to note its fractious nature. Alexis de Tocqueville noted the prevalence of "associations" in his classic study, *Democracy in America*.

Political scientists were somewhat slow to recognize the importance of groups in American politics; it was not until David B. Truman published *The Governmental Process* in 1951 that political scientists began to pay systematic attention to the role of groups.[4] Truman pointed out that groups naturally made demands on government and that it was the decentralized, diffuse nature of American government that gave groups their leverage.

David Truman established the importance of groups in American domestic politics; however, the degree to which groups influenced the conduct of U.S. foreign policy was questionable. For most of its history, debates over American foreign policy "stopped at the water's edge," meaning that there was bipartisan support for most U.S. foreign policy initiatives. However, at the end of World War I, the Senate debated whether or not the United States should join the League of Nations. President Woodrow Wilson argued passionately that the United States should enter the new international organization, and Sen. Henry Cabot Lodge led the opposition. In the end, the opponents won, the United States did not enter the league, and it was moribund within several years. A number of prominent Americans were disappointed and concerned by this turn of events and believed that the United States should take an active role in international relations in order to create a more peaceful world. To this end, the Foreign Policy Association was established in 1918, and the Council on Foreign Relations was created in 1921. These were two of the earliest interest groups oriented exclusively to foreign policy issues, and they remain two of the most important of this type of group.

While political scientists have devoted considerable attention to the role of groups in American politics, they have not devoted much attention to the role of interest groups in foreign policy—making. Perhaps the major reason for this lack of attention is that interest groups have not had significant effects on the outcomes of previous foreign policy decisions. In his study of the peace settlement with Japan at the end of World War II, Bernard Cohen found that interest groups had little impact on the policy outcomes except in those cases where economic interests were involved.[5]

In the mid–1960s, several political scientists focused on the role of interest groups in American politics. Lester Milbrath interviewed lobbyists and persons in Congress in order to discover who communicated with whom and with what results. Milbrath concluded that lobbyists were much weaker than was generally assumed, and that they had little power over legislators.[6] Confirming this finding, Harmon Ziegler concluded, "The influence of interest groups in the legislative process depends more on the harmony of values between the group and the legislators than it does on the ability of the group to wield its 'power' either through skillful techniques or presumed electoral influence."[7] Thus, these important studies concluded that the influence of interest groups was not as great as had been assumed.

Several trends increased the influence of interest groups in the making and implementation of American foreign policy.[8] First, from the late 1960s, Congress played a more active and important role in foreign and defense policy debates; many date this greater activism and involvement to the debate that took place in 1969 over the deployment of the anti-ballistic missile (ABM) system.[9] This debate resulted in the mobilization of many citizens and interest groups, and in responding to these constituent concerns over ABM, members of Congress and their staffs became better informed about ABM in particular and defense issues more broadly. Not only did the quality of information on Capitol Hill increase after the ABM debate, but the number of staff members, committees, subcommittees, and other organizations, such as the Office of Technology Assessment, mushroomed beginning in the late 1960s.

A second development that has increased the role that interest groups play in foreign policy has resulted from technological developments. Radio, television, and computerized mailings enable contemporary interest groups, with a relatively small investment, to communicate with millions of people. Third, political parties in the United States are weak and have declined in importance over time.[10] American political parties have few resources to distribute to politicians, and there is almost no way that parties can effectively discipline their members who are legislators. At the same time, representatives of literally thousands of interest groups besiege legislators, and it is not surprising that these groups play a more important role in some congressional elections than the major political parties.

Recent studies of interest groups have described and analyzed their purpose, structure, organization, and strategy. A number of analysts have noted that interest groups serve as intermediaries between citizens and the government. The primary task of an interest group is to convert the desires of its members into particular objectives and policies. In this way, interest groups serve as conduits linking public opinion and public policies.[11]

In *Lobbying for the People*, Jeffrey Berry analyzes a particular type of group: the "public interest group," which Berry defines as "one that seeks a collective good, the achievement of which will not selectively and materially benefit the membership or activists of the organization."[12] In his study, Berry found that public interest groups were pivotal in defeating various proposals to build the B–1 bomber.

A number of public interest groups were active in the SALT II ratification debate. Despite the number of groups involved in the debate, they can be distinguished from one another in several different ways. First, groups may be differentiated according to whether contributions to them are tax-deductible. Some groups are classified by the Internal Revenue Service in Section 501(c)(3) of the IRS code as nonprofit groups whose principal purpose is educational. Any contribution to a 501(c)(3) group is tax-deductible, and by law this type of group is not allowed to spend more than 20 percent of its funds for lobbying activities.

A second distinction concerns the target audience of groups. Broadly speaking, groups can target the "attentive public" (the most knowledgeable citizens) or the "mass public." The choice of these target audiences will affect the tactics and strategy that a group adopts. In the SALT II debate, the Carter administration focused its attention primarily on the attentive public, while the public interest group Americans for SALT focused its attention on the mass public. Of those groups that opposed the treaty, the Committee on the Present Danger focused on the attentive public, and the American Security Council and the Coalition for Peace through Strength concentrated on the mass public.

Third, interest groups can be independent of one another, or umbrella organizations can be created in order to present the views of a number of like-minded groups. Because interest groups are commonly oriented to a single issue and therefore have limited membership, they often cannot achieve their legislative goals without the assistance of other groups. Faced with the necessity of coalition building, groups will find others with similar orientations and form umbrella groups. One political scientist referred to such groups as "catalytic groups" since they are formed for a specific period of time in response to a single issue.[13] The Coalition for Peace through Strength, Americans for SALT, and the Religious Committee on SALT were examples of umbrella groups whose founding was catalyzed by the SALT II debate.

Fourth, groups may be distinguished from one another according to the tactics that they adopt in advancing their case. Broadly considered, three types of lobbying are conducted by interest groups: direct, indirect, and lobbying through constituents.[14] Direct lobbying tactics include personal presentations to those the group is attempting to influence, testifying at congressional hearings, and legal action. Political contributions, evaluating and publishing voting records, and releasing research results are examples of indirect lobbying. Members of groups and constituents of the interest group's target can be used to lobby on the group's behalf when the group sponsors political protests, encourages its influential members to contact policymakers, and sponsors letter-writing campaigns. All of these tactics were used by various groups during the SALT II debate.

Finally, interest groups may be differentiated by the resources that are at their disposal. Ornstein and Elder have identified five types of interest group resources: physical, organizational, political, motivational, and intangible.[15] Interest groups vary widely in their physical resources, with budgets ranging from thousands to millions of dollars. If an issue, such as SALT II, is perceived as important, groups tend to coalesce in order to pool their resources. Despite such pooling, interest groups are commonly short of money, information, personnel, and time. Perhaps because of these shortages, groups almost always perceive the other side to be stronger and better endowed with resources. As Raymond Bauer and his collaborators found, "Each side sees itself as David against Goliath."[16]

THE OPPOSITION GROUPS

The formation of interest groups in favor of and opposed to SALT II in many ways reflected the disintegration of bipartisanship in foreign policy that resulted from the contentious debate over the Vietnam War in the late 1960s and early 1970s. To those who had supported the U.S. war effort, the withdrawal of the United States from the war and the ensuing defeat of South Vietnam in April 1975 marked a humiliating and unnecessary defeat for the United States, the first in its history. To those who opposed American involvement in the war, the United States had been involved in Vietnam too long and had committed far too many resources to fighting the war, the most precious of which were the fifty-eight thousand Americans who died in Vietnam.

Many supporters of American involvement in the Vietnam War believed that liberals and the U.S. Congress had defeated the United States and South Vietnam, and they pledged that such a defeat should never occur again. Consequently, a number of influential citizens who favored a strong, assertive defense policy for the United States began meeting informally in several different groups. The Committee for a Democratic Majority was a group of conservative Democrats from the "Henry Jackson wing" of the party. In the summer of 1974, Eugene Rostow delivered a broadside attack on the Nixon-Kissinger policy of détente with the Soviet Union. In June 1974, the widely respected former Democratic government official and defense intellectual, Paul Nitze, resigned from the American SALT delegation with what Henry Kissinger has called "a blistering public attack on Nixon."[17] Referring to Nixon's Watergate problems, Nitze commented, "It would be illusory to attempt to ignore or wish away the depressing reality of the traumatic events now unfolding in our nation's capital . . ."[18] In December 1975, Rostow, Nitze, and a small number of other like-minded, influential, former government officials began meeting to discuss U.S. defense policy and what could be done to strengthen it.[19]

Despite the fact that a Republican had been president since January 1969, conservative Republicans were also concerned about the Nixon-Ford-Kissinger foreign and defense policies. President Ford was widely criticized within his own party and responded in March 1976 by ordering his staff not to use the word "détente." This semantic change did not satisfy conservatives within the Republican party, and in June 1976 CIA Director George Bush appointed a group of known hard-liners to evaluate the estimates and evaluations that the Central Intelligence Agency had completed of Soviet military objectives and capabilities. "Team B," as it was known, was chaired by Harvard history professor Richard Pipes and its members included, among others, Paul Nitze, Foy Kohler, William Van Cleave, Lt. Gen. Daniel Graham, Thomas Wolfe, Maj. Gen. George Keegan, Brig. Gen. Jasper Welch, Paul Wolfowitz, and Seymour Weiss. (Pipes, as well as Nitze, Kohler, and Van Cleave, subsequently became founding board members of the Committee on the Present Danger.) The Team B report was highly critical of the CIA's estimates and resulted in calls for much higher defense spending.

In November 1976, the candidate who had been "Jimmy Who" just a year and a half earlier was elected president. Hard-liners were not sure exactly where Carter stood on defense. He had graduated from the Naval Academy and had served eleven years in the navy. Carter had given the speech nominating Henry Jackson for president at the 1972 Democratic convention. And during the 1976 campaign, Carter had met with Senator Jackson, Nitze, and other hard-liners for advice on defense policy. These credentials and actions were reassuring to those who favored increased defense spending.

During the campaign, however, Carter's beliefs became clearer, and these beliefs were not reassuring to hard-liners. On November 11, 1976, just three days after Carter's electoral victory, the Committee on the Present Danger was formally founded. The 141 board members of the new organization read like a "Who's Who" of American politics and included: C. Douglas Dillon and Henry Fowler, both former secretaries of the treasury; Gen. Andrew Goodpaster, former NATO Supreme Allied Commander; Lane Kirkland, then secretary-treasurer of the AFL-CIO; Gen. Lyman Lemnitzer, former chairman of the Joint Chiefs of Staff; David Packard, former deputy secretary of defense; Norman Podhoretz, editor of *Commentary*; Dean Rusk, former secretary of state; and Adm. Elmo Zumwalt, Jr., former chief of naval operations.[20] Of its members, 60 percent were Democrats and 40 percent were Republicans.[21] Fowler, Kirkland, and Packard were the cochairmen of the committee; Paul Nitze was the chairman of policy studies, and Eugene Rostow was the chairman of the executive committee. Charles Walker was the treasurer and Max Kampelman was counsel.

Charles Tyroler II served as the director of the committee; a former member of the committee's staff described him as "the force behind the committee's day-to-day operations, including fund raising."[22] The staff consisted of three professional staff members—Tyroler, Paul Green, and Charles Kupperman—plus four secretaries. The committee was incorporated as a nonprofit research and educational organization and received 501(c)(3) status from the Internal Revenue Service, making it a tax-exempt charity. Therefore, any contributions to the committee were tax-deductible for the giver. The committee was financed by voluntary contributions from individuals and, according to the committee's publications, would "under no circumstances solicit or accept contributions from companies or persons who derive a substantial portion of their income from the defense industry."[23] The budget of the committee was relatively small by Washington standards: $90,000 in 1977, $200,000 in 1978, and $300,000 in 1979.[24] Despite the committee's public pledge to limit annual contributions from any single source, conservative philanthropist Richard Mellon Scaife donated approximately $260,000 to the committee.[25]

Following the founding of the Committee on the Present Danger, its leaders had to decide on the tactics the organization would adopt to get its message across. According to Rostow: "When we commenced operations in 1976, a considerable number of our founding members urged that we purchase media advertising including TV and radio time, employ direct mail, create regional and local chapters and the like to reach John Q. Citizen. Seeing our special function in quite another light, we firmly rejected that advice."[26] Instead, the committee focused its efforts on influencing the attentive public. According to former staff member Charles Kupperman: "The committee . . . is not a grassroots organization. To the contrary, the Committee on the Present Danger deliberately focused on the upper echelon of American opinion leaders."[27] At its height, the committee's mailing list consisted of about thirteen thousand names, hardly a large list by Washington interest group standards.[28]

Shortly after the disastrous trip by Secretary of State Cyrus Vance to Moscow in March 1977, the committee published its first pamphlet, "What Is the Soviet Union Up To?"[29] The committee distributed more than fourteen hundred copies of the report to influential citizens, newspaper reporters, and editorial writers. Drafted by Richard Pipes, the report ominously warned, "The ultimate Soviet objective—a Communist world order—requires the reduction of the power, influence, and prestige of the United States," and "Soviet nuclear offensive and defensive forces are designed to enable the USSR to fight, survive and win an all-out nuclear war should it occur."[30] The only reference to SALT in this first report was a brief note that SALT I had had "no visible effect on the Soviet [military] build-up." The report ended by warning, "if past trends continue, the USSR will within several years achieve strategic superiority over the United States."[31]

The committee fired its "first salvo in the SALT II debate" in July 1977 when it published a pamphlet entitled "Where We Stand on SALT."[32] The

committee argued that under American SALT proposals then being considered, "the Soviets would destroy more strategic targets and damage more
people [sic] and industry in a nuclear war," and the committee therefore
opposed the U.S. government's SALT proposals including both the comprehensive proposal that Secretary Vance had presented to the Soviets in
March 1977 and his subsequent proposal in May. The committee's position
went beyond that of many conservatives, such as Senator Jackson, who had
supported the March comprehensive proposal.

As correspondence in the Carter Library indicates, Eugene Rostow regularly sent Zbigniew Brzezinski copies of the committee's reports and pamphlets and expressed increasing alarm at the Carter administration's personnel appointments, policies, and actions.[33] In August 1977, following release
of the committee's report on SALT, a meeting was arranged between President Carter and the Committee on the Present Danger's executive committee. According to one press account, the meeting was requested and arranged
by Hamilton Jordan and was erroneously announced by the White House as a
meeting with "a group of leaders from private industry."[34]

The meeting did not go well. Carter told the group that he believed his
proposals at the SALT II negotiations had been fair and that they protected
U.S. national security interests. He also indicated that he had read the
committee's July report and that he did not like it. As Carter spoke, Nitze
reportedly quietly murmured, "No, no, no . . ." and the president responded
by saying, "Paul, would you please let me finish?"[35] The relationship between
Carter and Nitze thus further deteriorated.

By the summer of 1977, the "facsimile ratification debate" had begun, a
full two years before the treaty was signed.[36] The Committee on the Present
Danger was widely acknowledged as "the brains behind the opposition,"[37]
and the press conferences that it held were characterized as "more like academic seminars given by Nitze to a small, select group of Washington-based
journalists covering the national security beat for their papers, journals, and
wire services."[38] The ripple effect from these meetings was significant since
journalists would distill Nitze's detailed, esoteric analyses of the SALT II
negotiations for their readers. Nitze's "white paper" on SALT II was updated,
revised, and published by the committee on eleven different occasions.[39]

From the time of its founding in 1976 through the end of December 1979,
members of the executive committee and board of the Committee on the
Present Danger participated in 479 TV and radio programs, press conferences, debates, public forums, and speaking engagements. The committee
distributed more than two hundred thousand copies of its pamphlets and
reports. During the Senate's hearings on the SALT II Treaty, executive
committee and board members testified on seventeen different occasions
before the Armed Services and Foreign Relations committees.[40]

By all accounts, the Committee on the Present Danger was the single most effective organization opposing the treaty; however, there were a large number of other groups allied with the committee including, most prominently, the American Security Council, the American Conservative Union, and the Coalition for Peace through Strength. Whereas the Committee on the Present Danger focused on elite decision makers, these other groups focused on the mass public. According to Kupperman, when the committee received a request for information from the general public, it passed this to the American Security Council for a response.[41] Thus, there was a clear division of labor among interest groups opposing the treaty.

Several of the opposition interest groups had substantial resources. For example, the American Conservative Union had 325,000 members and had spent an estimated $1 million opposing the ratification of the Panama Canal treaties.[42] During the SALT II debate, this group produced a thirty-minute anti-SALT film that was shown on more than two hundred television stations across the nation. The most important single mass-membership organization in the SALT II debate was the American Security Council, which had a membership of 200,000. Annual dues for members were $20 per person and the budget of the organization in 1979 was $4 million. Unlike the Committee on the Present Danger, the American Security Council, founded in 1955, was a lobbying organization and not a tax-exempt, nonprofit organization. The council was led by John M. Fisher as president and retired army Lt. Gen. Daniel O. Graham as executive director.

In keeping with its focus on the mass public, the council produced a series of short, hard-hitting films designed to underscore dramatically the alleged military weaknesses of the United States. The first of these films, *Only the Strong*, was followed in 1978 by *The Price of Peace and Freedom* and in the summer of 1979 by *The SALT Syndrome*. Conservative organizations would purchase copies of these films and make them available to educational institutions, churches, civic groups, unions, and professional associations at nominal or no charge. *Only the Strong* was shown on television more than eight hundred times, and *The SALT Syndrome* was shown more than six hundred times in 1979 alone.[43] One scholar who studied the role of interest groups in the SALT II debate found that *The SALT Syndrome* had a greater impact on public opinion than any other single activity.[44] The Carter administration took *The SALT Syndrome* so seriously that it published and distributed a sentence-by-sentence rebuttal of the film.[45]

Conservatives had learned from two important previous skirmishes during the Carter administration: the confirmation battle over Paul Warnke's appointment and the Panama Canal treaties debate. They had learned that they could achieve greater influence by forming an ad hoc umbrella organization to oversee and coordinate the activities of like-minded conservative groups. Consequently, the Coalition for Peace through Strength was founded in August 1978 to unite the efforts of organizations and individuals who were concerned about the direction of U.S. defense policy in general and SALT II in particular. The coalition included 204 members of Congress, 106 national organizations, and 2,500 retired generals and admirals.[46] In practice, it was often hard to tell the difference between the American Security Council and the Coalition for Peace through Strength, for the two organizations worked hand in hand. The two organizations, for example, jointly produced and distributed *The SALT Syndrome.* [47]

In addition to the organizations that opposed SALT II, a number of prominent individuals opposed the agreement. Former Texas governor and secretary of the treasury John Connolly stated that the SALT II Treaty would do nothing "but legitimize and condone the Soviets' overtaking the United States in strategic arms between now and 1985."[48] Moral Majority leader Jerry Falwell noted, "It's my conviction every Christian should work as aggressively as possible between now and when the United States Senate should be called on to ratify or refuse to ratify SALT II to stop its ratification."[49]

In opposing the treaty, the anti-SALT groups had several advantages. First, they were united in their opposition to SALT II; the same kind of unity did not characterize the protreaty groups. Second, the antitreaty groups had superior resources and were more effective in organizing public opinion. Third, as Ornstein and Elder have noted, "in a political system geared toward slow change with numerous decision points and checks and balances, a group's likelihood of success is enhanced if it focuses on blocking rather than initiating action."[50] The opponents of SALT II therefore had the advantageous position. Fourth, scholars have found that conservatives tend to write their legislators more than liberals and those who are opposed to a policy tend to write more often than those who favor a policy.[51] SALT II was a case in which conservatives were opposed to ratification of the treaty and, not surprisingly, mail to senators ran strongly against ratification.

THE PROTREATY GROUPS

As would be expected on an issue as important as the SALT II Treaty, a large number of interest groups became involved in the ratification debate. These included church groups, unions, professional associations, veterans' organizations, and ad hoc interest groups. Given the ways in which the Carter administration tried to influence the Senate, the administration itself resembled an interest group.[52] Administration officials met extensively with senators to try to win their votes; they traveled throughout the country giving speeches, press conferences, and radio and television interviews; and they met with leaders of protreaty interest groups. The administration structured its efforts according to the specialized offices in the White House. Frank Moore and the Office of Congressional Relations arranged meetings between the administration and senators. Anne Wexler and her office worked with interest groups, unions, professional associations, and grassroots protreaty groups. On the whole the administration's efforts were focused primarily on the mass and attentive publics.

The activities of the European allies of the United States also closely resembled those of an interest group, and the Carter administration treated the allies accordingly. For example, the administration literally lobbied the Western European defense ministers and was able to obtain formal endorsements of the SALT II Treaty from West Germany, France, Great Britain, Italy, Canada, Norway, and NATO. Norway's Prime Minister Odvar Nordl noted: "I am aware that the SALT II agreement does not solve all outstanding problems with respect to strategic stability. But we cannot let the best be the enemy of the good."[53] West German Chancellor Helmut Schmidt forcefully argued:

> This treaty has been negotiated by three American presidents, Nixon, Ford and Carter, by three American secretaries of state, Rogers, Kissinger and nowadays, Vance. . . . If, after such a long period of negotiations and agreement, in the end parliaments refused to ratify that sort of treaty, the world becomes incalculable. How could you in the future depend on a policy carried out by an American president? It would be a disastrous blow to the nuclear leadership of the United States as regards the west as a whole.[54]

Within the United States, a number of groups reflected the diversity of interests that supported the ratification of the SALT II Treaty, including: the AFL-CIO, the American Committee for East-West Accord, Americans for Democratic Action, the Arms Control Association, the Center for Defense Information, the Coalition for a New Foreign and Military Policy, Common Cause, the Communication Workers of America, the Council for a Livable World, the Federation of American Scientists, the Friends Committee on National Legislation, the International Association of Machinists, the National Council of Churches, the Union of Concerned Scientists, the U.S. Catholic Conference, the United Auto Workers, the United Steelworkers, and the Committee for a Sane Nuclear Policy (SANE).

Despite the number and diverse character of protreaty interest groups, there was no nongovernmental, protreaty analogue to the Committee on the Present Danger. The Carter administration itself came closest to performing the tasks in support of SALT II that the Committee on the Present Danger did in opposing the treaty.

There were, however, several umbrella organizations formed in order to support ratification of SALT II. The Religious Committee on SALT consisted of twenty-seven religious organizations, and the membership of the denominations represented by the committee included more than fifty million people. In September 1979, 175 religious leaders representing many of the member groups of this committee met with President Carter and other cabinet members at the White House. Following this meeting, they went to Capitol Hill in order to meet with senators to urge them to vote in favor of SALT II. Commenting on this meeting, the Reverend William Howard, president of the National Council of Churches, noted, "Never before has the leadership of so great a diversity of American religious organizations come together to say with one voice that arms limitation—through SALT II and SALT III—must be a priority for this nation."[55] Other prominent religious leaders also endorsed SALT II, including conservative evangelist Billy Graham.[56] Perhaps influenced by the Reverend Mr. Graham's support and President Carter's own evangelical religious beliefs, some groups that had not previously supported arms control efforts, such as the Southern Baptist Convention, came out in favor of the ratification. Like many interest groups, the Religious Committee on SALT was handicapped by limited financial resources; the budget for a two-year period was less than $20,000.[57] Despite this limitation (and disproportionate to it), the committee had an impact on the SALT II debate due to the extensive network of the religious organizations that were associated with the committee.

Just as anti-SALT groups had learned certain lessons from the past, the pro-SALT interest groups had also learned that coalition building was an important key to success. Prodisarmament groups had been ineffective in the past, and it was only during the ABM debate that these groups came close to stopping a major weapons program. A group of organizations banned together in the mid–1970s in order to stop the production and deployment of the B–1 bomber. By pooling their resources and talents, these groups were able to effectively pressure the Carter administration and the Congress not to build and deploy the B–1.[58] This effort laid the foundation for later pro–arms control efforts.

During the summer of 1978, Americans for SALT was founded in order to generate "a national campaign for ratification of the SALT II Treaty." The sole goal of the organization was to lobby in favor of the treaty by organizing programs to increase the visibility of growing public support for SALT II, to coordinate local pro-SALT activities in communities and states with the efforts of national organizations, and to conduct extensive educational programs.[59] Thus, the avowed focus of Americans for SALT was on the grassroots level, rather than on the attentive (or elite) public.

Americans for SALT was founded with the support of a number of organizations including the American Committee on East-West Accord, the Arms

Control Association, the Council for a Livable World, the National Council of Churches, several labor unions, and New Directions (a public interest group designed to be the "Common Cause of foreign policy"). The cochairpersons of the organization were all distinguished in their respective fields and included former presidential adviser and secretary of defense Clark Clifford, University of Notre Dame president Father Theodore Hesburgh, former Defense Department official Townsend Hoopes, and former ambassadors Henry Cabot Lodge and Charles Yost. Americans for SALT organized a speakers bureau and offered speakers to organizations planning programs concerning SALT II. The group published thirteen issues of an "action newsletter," *SALT Talk,* which carried news of its activities, descriptions of the treaty, and suggestions for "what you can do." The committee also distributed special reports from time to time including a rebuttal to a report published by the Coalition for Peace through Strength. Another special report consisted of a set of guidelines for organizing state and local groups, planning a speaking event, writing letters to the editor, holding news conferences, and writing press releases.[60]

Three weeks after the SALT II Treaty was signed, Americans for SALT sponsored full-page advertisements in the *New York Times* and the *Washington Post* in which a number of prominent Americans announced their support for the treaty.[61] Ten days later, Americans for SALT convened a "field organizing conference" for more than one hundred treaty supporters from twenty-four states in order to develop strategies to promote Senate ratification of the treaty. Following briefings by government experts, President Carter spoke to the group and stressed the need for ongoing citizen involvement in the ratification effort.[62]

Americans for SALT, however, was hampered by several factors. First, the organization was created only one year before the SALT II Treaty was signed; many of the antitreaty organizations had been founded much earlier. The Committee on the Present Danger, for example, was founded in November 1976 and began actively lobbying against the treaty in the summer of 1977. Second, an umbrella interest group requires effective leadership in order to function. Americans for SALT had major personnel problems during its first year of existence. During that time, two executive directors and an assistant executive director were fired. When Nancy Ramsey was appointed executive director in July 1979, the organization had neither an operations plan nor a budget, shortcomings that reflected its organizational problems. A third problem was funding. Ramsey was able to pull the organization together, but spent one-third to one-half of her time raising the $34,000 per month necessary to keep Americans for SALT operating.[63] Eventually, approximately $300,000 was raised to support activities and programs. A fourth problem concerned the nature of the pro-SALT coalition. As the former president of the nongovernmental interest group, the Arms Control Association, William Kincade, has pointed out: "The protreaty groups were not effective because they were not unified. Nobody on the left is satisfied with half a loaf, and consequently, they usually get nothing. That's what happened with SALT II."[64]

The disunity of the left was evident when Jeremy Stone, executive director of the Federation of American Scientists, a public interest lobby of scientists, published an article in the *New York Times* in March 1979 that criticized the emerging SALT agreement for failing to place meaningful limits on Soviet and American strategic nuclear arsenals.[65] After the SALT II Treaty was signed, Stone refused to endorse it, despite the fact that the Federation of American Scientists did so. Others followed Stone's lead. In May, Robert Johansen, president of the Institute for World Order, published an article in *Harper's* magazine in which he argued that "the achievement of both SALT I and SALT II is to curtail relatively insignificant parts of a quantitative arms race so that more money and brainpower can be devoted to a significantly more dangerous qualitative arms race."[66] In March 1979 senators Hatfield, McGovern, and Proxmire published a critical assessment of the agreement, and in August, *Progressive* magazine called for the outright rejection of the treaty on the grounds that it did not do enough to achieve "genuine" arms control.

THE ARGUMENTS: PRO AND CON

During the course of the debate over the SALT II Treaty, literally hundreds of arguments in favor of and opposed to the treaty were advanced by individual senators, members of the Carter administration, scholars, journalists, interest groups, and involved citizens. Broadly considered, these arguments concerned four questions: (1) were the terms of the treaty in the national security interests of the United States? (2) was the treaty verifiable? (3) was the Carter administration's defense program sufficient to assure the national security of the United States? and (4) what effect would the treaty have on broader issues of Soviet-American relations?

The Terms of the Treaty

Those who supported the ratification of the SALT II Treaty argued that the terms of the treaty were advantageous to the national security of the United States for seven principal reasons. First, the treaty established equal numerical limits on the total number of "strategic nuclear launch vehicles" (i.e., intercontinental ballistic missiles plus submarine-launched ballistic missiles plus long-range bombers) for the United States and the Soviet

Union. Second, the treaty placed qualitative limits on "multiple, independently targetable reentry vehicles" (MIRVs) deployed on ICBMs and SLBMs, weapons that many considered to be the most destabilizing in the Soviet and American arsenals. Both sides were limited to deploying no more than fourteen warheads per SLBM and no more than ten warheads per ICBM. Many, including Secretary of State Cyrus Vance, considered these limits on "missile fractionation" to be among the most significant in the treaty.[67]

Third, each side was limited to developing and deploying one "new type" ICBM. Thus, the United States would be free to develop and deploy a new large ICBM to counter the Soviet large SS–18 ICBM. Fourth, the treaty called for a reduction of the total number of Soviet strategic nuclear launch vehicles from 2,500 to 2,250 within two years of the signing of the treaty. SALT II, therefore, was actually the first arms treaty that called for reductions in the number of nuclear weapons.

Fifth, the treaty would save the United States money. Secretary of Defense Harold Brown estimated that it would enable the United States to save approximately $30 billion over the ten-year life of the treaty. Sixth, treaty supporters argued that the SALT II Treaty would "pave the way" for other arms control agreements, possibly including a ban on antisatellite weapons and a comprehensive test ban treaty. Last, some observers noted that the greatest nuclear danger was that more and more states would develop, test, and deploy nuclear weapons. The Non-Proliferation Treaty, signed in 1968. placed restrictions on the development of nuclear weapons by non-nuclear-weapons states. However, the nuclear-weapons states, including the United States and the USSR, pledged in Article VI of the treaty to work toward nuclear disarmament. The SALT II Treaty would be a step in that direction.

Treaty supporters noted a number of areas in which the Soviets had made concessions to the United States, including the Soviet decision to omit from the SALT II negotiations American forward-based systems (U.S. nuclear weapons based in Europe that could reach the Soviet Union), the banning of the Soviet SS–16 mobile ICBM, the decision to publish a database of Soviet and American strategic forces, and the counting rule for cruise missiles deployed on bombers.[68]

The opponents of the treaty argued that the terms were detrimental to the national security interests of the United States. First, the treaty allowed the Soviet Union to keep 308 modern, large (or heavy) SS–18 intercontinental ballistic missiles, which, opponents argued, meant that the treaty favored the USSR. Second, opponents argued that the SALT II Treaty granted the Soviet Union strategic superiority over the United States and that this was very important. Paul Nitze claimed that it was principally American strategic superiority that had caused the Soviet Union to back down in the Berlin crisis of 1961 and the Cuban missile crisis of 1962.

Third, opponents contended that SALT II weakened the United States' commitment to defend its European allies. Fourth, a protocol to the treaty called for a three-year ban on the deployment of cruise missiles and mobile ICBMs. Opponents argued that this protocol would create an impetus not to deploy these weapons. Fifth, opponents were quite concerned that the Soviet Backfire bomber was not included in the treaty because it was not classified as a long-range bomber by the Carter administration. Sixth, opponents argued that the SALT II Treaty would not save the United States any money.

The Verification Issue

Verification has been one of the central issues in arms control and disarmament negotiations since the end of World War II; some would argue that this has been *the central* issue. Obviously, arms control agreements cannot simply be based on trust since two (or more) potential adversaries are the negotiating parties. Just as a good attorney insists that his or her client's interests be protected with a well-drafted contract, the U.S. Senate has insisted in almost all cases that other nations' compliance with international agreements be monitored. An exception to this general rule was the 1972 Biological Weapons Convention which contained no provisions for verification.

Members of the Carter administration recognized the central importance of the verification issue. The president pledged, "I would not sign or present to the Congress or to the American people any treaty which in my opinion could not be adequately verified from the first day it's effective."[69] Secretary of State Vance noted: "No arms control treaty is worthwhile if it cannot be policed. But in SALT II that ability is based on our own proven and extensive technical means of monitoring Soviet strategic forces."[70] And Secretary of Defense Brown said that the verification issue was "in a class by itself."[71]

In his testimony to the Senate Armed Services Committee, Secretary Brown noted that "verification refers to the continuing process of assessing compliance with the provisions of arms control agreements."[72] Brown also noted that "no arms limitation can ever be absolutely verifiable," and because of this, each U.S. administration must make a judgment on whether particular arms control agreements can be "adequately verifiable." This test, according to Brown, is "the practical standard of whether we can determine compliance adequately to safeguard our security—that is, whether we can identify attempted evasion if it occurs on a large enough scale to pose a significant risk, and whether we can do so in time to mount a sufficient response."[73]

The SALT I agreements—the Anti-Ballistic Missile Treaty and the Interim Agreement on Offensive Forces—contained several provisions concerning verification. Significantly, both the SALT I agreements and the SALT II

Treaty called for verification by "national technical means," which was a bureaucratic euphemism for satellite photography and the monitoring of electronic signals. Because of the sensitivity of this subject, no government official, including the president of the United States, had ever publicly referred to U.S. spy satellites; however, in October 1978, President Carter noted that the United States had the capability of taking high-resolution photographs of the Soviet Union from satellites.[74] In the SALT I agreements, the United States and the USSR pledged not to interfere with the "national technical means" of the other country. In essence, this meant that the "eyes and ears" of the two countries were protected by the SALT agreements. Advisers had encouraged the president and the secretary of state to declassify and publish satellite photographs of well-known American sights such as the Washington Monument, so the public could see the impressive capabilities of U.S. spy satellites. But the intelligence community would not authorize such disclosure, fearing that the publication of actual photos would compromise the American satellite reconnaissance program.[75]

The SALT I agreements called for the establishment of an organization, the Standing Consultative Commission, to oversee the implementation of the terms of the agreements and to consider any questions concerning compliance with the agreements. The commission was formally established and began meeting in 1973. From its establishment until the end of the Carter administration, most observers believed that the commission had a very good record of resolving compliance-related questions concerning the SALT I agreements.[76]

Despite the relatively good performance of the Standing Consultative Commission, verification remained a controversial issue. In response to a request from the Senate Foreign Relations Committee and in an attempt to allay fears that the SALT II Treaty could not be verified, the Carter administration published several special reports concerning Soviet compliance with the SALT I agreements and verification aspects of the SALT II Treaty.[77] These reports described some of the issues with which the Standing Consultative Commission had successfully dealt. In sum, supporters believed that the verification procedures called for in SALT II amounted to one of the major advantages of the treaty.

In contrast to this view, many opponents of the SALT II Treaty believed that it was not verifiable. Some of the opponents' skepticism was fueled by leaks of highly classified information from inside the intelligence community to senators and their aides. One CIA analyst, David Sullivan, became concerned that his superiors were unjustifiably modifying his conclusions to fit the Carter administration's predispositions. Consequently, Sullivan gave a copy of his report to retired admiral Elmo Zumwalt who suggested that it be given to Richard Perle, Senator Jackson's aide. Soon after giving his report to Perle, Sullivan came up for a random polygraph test and failed the test. As a result, Adm. Stansfield Turner, director of the CIA, fired Sullivan and demanded that Jackson reprimand Perle.[78] Sullivan went from the CIA to work on Capitol Hill where he wrote a number of articles that fueled skepticism about the verifiability of the SALT II Treaty.[79]

Treaty opponents were specifically concerned about several verification issues related to the treaty. First, they noted that the treaty called for ceilings on the numbers of launchers and not on the actual numbers of missiles. Therefore, the Soviets could legally increase the number of missiles in their stockpile and since several of the Soviet systems were "reloadable," the Soviets could achieve superiority over the United States, the opponents argued. Second, given the closed, secretive nature of Soviet society and the vastness of the USSR, opponents were concerned that the Soviets would be in a much better position to cheat on the agreement than the United States. Third, treaty opponents did not have a high opinion of the performance of the Standing Consultative Commission; according to Weinberger, the commission was "a diplomatic carpet under which Soviet violations have been continuously swept, an Orwellian memory hole into which our concerns have been dumped like yesterday's trash."[80]

The Carter Defense Program

Critics of the Carter administration contended that the president had ordered a number of actions that resulted in the weakening of U.S. national security. As evidence of their concern, they pointed in particular to the president's cancellation of the B–1 bomber, the slowdown of the construction of the Trident submarine and missile, the cancellation of the deployment of the enhanced radiation weapon (neutron bomb), and the closing of the country's only ICBM production line.

SALT II Treaty supporters pointed to strategic improvements that had taken place since the signing and approval of the SALT I agreements. The Minuteman III ICBM had been hardened and modernized with a new warhead, the Mark 12–A, and a new guidance system. These improvements doubled warhead yield and accuracy. The United States had developed and deployed a new submarine-launched ballistic missile, the C–4 (also called the Trident I), and deployed it in Poseidon submarines. The United States had improved the survivability and penetrability of B–52 bombers and equipped them with short-range air-to-ground missiles. In addition, the Stealth bomber program was begun. The total number of strategic nuclear warheads deployed by the United States increased from fifty-seven hundred in 1972 to ninety-two hundred in 1980, giving the United States an advantage in this important criterion of strategic power. And the United States moved ahead with the development of cruise missiles and the D–5 (or Trident II) SLBM.[81]

The major question mark in the Carter administration's defense program was a new ICBM labeled the MX, which stood for "missile experimental." Treaty critics were particularly concerned about the 308 large intercontinental SS–18 ballistic missiles that the treaty allowed the Soviet Union to retain; they strongly advocated the development and deployment of a similar weapon by the United States. The critics contended, and administration officials conceded, that in the future the SS–18 could carry from twenty to thirty warheads.[82] In the months prior to the signing of the SALT II Treaty, "MX and SALT became as intertwined as the fibers of a rope," according to one Senate staffer.[83]

There were several questions concerning the MX. The first concerned whether the missile should be built at all. The answer to this question quickly became as much a domestic political issue within the United States as an issue of military policy. Vance pointed out, "I had long felt, since the 1977 cancellation of the B–1 bomber, that ratification of the SALT II Treaty would be unlikely without a firm administration commitment to the MX program."[84] The second debate took place within the Carter administration and concerned the type of missile that should be built. Zbigniew Brzezinski, the national security adviser, favored building 100 large missiles that would carry ten warheads each, while William Perry, the deputy secretary of defense, favored building 330 smaller missiles that would carry three warheads each.[85] Each plan called for the deployment of approximately one thousand warheads.

Although President Carter had stated publicly that efforts to build support in the Senate for the treaty would not result in new weapons programs, he came to the conclusion that he would not be able to get the treaty ratified if he did not go ahead with the MX. Consequently, on June 7, 1979, just eleven days before he signed the SALT II Treaty, Carter announced plans to develop and deploy two hundred MX missiles that would be shuttled among eight thousand to nine thousand hardened shelters so that they would not be vulnerable to a first-strike attack.[86] The president hoped that his choice of the Brzezinski option, the large MX, would increase the chances of Paul Nitze, Henry Jackson, and other conservatives supporting the treaty, but those hopes soon proved unrealistic when Jackson and Nitze continued to criticize the treaty even after Carter had announced his support for the development and deployment of the MX.

The Debate over U.S. Policy toward the Soviet Union

When asked in retrospect why he thought the SALT II Treaty was not ratified, Matthew Nimetz, former State Department counselor and the person in charge of gaining public support for the treaty, said: "I thought that the debate on the SALT agreement would really be a major debate on our relations with the Soviet Union. . . . Every decade or so we have a major debate on our Soviet relations, and we hadn't had a debate like this in the country since the whole debate on détente and the end of the Vietnam War."[87] From this perspective, the debate over SALT II was a symptom of the deeper debate over the direction and objectives of post-Vietnam American foreign policy in general and U.S.-Soviet relations in particular.

At the end of World War II, the United States had no coherent policy toward the Soviet Union. Following the fall of the Eastern European countries to communist governments and reported communist insurgencies in Greece and Turkey, the Truman administration developed the doctrine of containment, which was designed to stop the expansion of communism. Despite varying emphases, containment was the common thread of post–1947 American foreign policy. The first policy to challenge the basic assumptions of containment since 1947 was the Nixon-Kissinger détente policy of the early 1970s.[88] This policy was developed and implemented at the same time that the United States was fighting the most divisive foreign war in its history.

Views concerning the proper U.S. policy toward the Soviet Union ran a full spectrum: on the left, some believed that the United States was to blame for the onset of the cold war and that the USSR simply responded to the American threat. Adherents of this view preferred a policy of concessions toward the USSR. At the other end of the spectrum, foreign policy conservatives compared the Soviet Union to Nazi Germany, and drew direct, pejorative parallels between the Nixon-Ford-Kissinger policy of détente and Neville Chamberlain's pre–World War II policy of appeasement.[89] These critics advocated a policy of competitive confrontation with the Soviet Union. Those in the middle of the political spectrum viewed U.S.-Soviet relations as characterized by both cooperation and competition and advocated a mixture of positive incentives and negative sanctions in dealing with the Soviet Union.[90]

By 1979, conservatives had lost a number of significant battles. First, and of great significance, the United States had lost the Vietnam War. Second, conservatives had lost the White House to someone they perceived as "soft on communism" and weak on supporting American defense efforts. Third, conservatives were unsuccessful in blocking Carter's appointment of Paul Warnke to direct the Arms Control and Disarmament Agency and serve as the chief American delegate at the SALT II negotiations. Fourth, conservatives had lost the battle to defeat the Panama Canal treaties. By the time the SALT II Treaty was signed and presented to the Senate, these losses were of great concern to conservatives, who became determined to win the battle to defeat SALT II.

Treaty opponents were concerned that, if the treaty were ratified, Americans would be lulled into complacency and that they would not sense any threat to the United States or its interests. Professor William Van Cleave argued that the "on-going SALT negotiations have a dampening effect on American options and programs far beyond the direct limitations themselves," and Richard Perle contended that "in the nine years since SALT got underway, there have been repeated efforts, by individuals in and out of the U.S. government, to halt or delay the procurement of weapons systems in the United States in the belief that the prospects for U.S.-Soviet arms control would be thereby brightened."[91] Even supporters of the treaty expressed a concern that SALT II could lull the American people into a false sense of security. Gen. David Jones, chairman of the Joint Chiefs of Staff during the Carter administration and a supporter of the SALT II Treaty, noted that the most serious concern of the JCS was that "SALT II could be allowed to become a tranquilizer to the American people . . ."[92] However, in a study of the lulling effects of the treaty, political scientist Sean Lynn-Jones concluded that "the negotiating and signing of the treaty . . . do not appear to have induced a sense of complacency about U.S. security."[93]

A central issue related to SALT II and American-Soviet relations was linkage. Critics of SALT argued that the United States should not conclude an arms control agreement with the Soviet Union as long as it pursued interventionist policies around the world that were antithetical to the interests of the United States and its allies. Within the Carter administration, Zbigniew Brzezinski was the most prominent proponent of this view. Outside the administration, conservative critics of the SALT II Treaty widely held this view. Supporters of SALT II, such as Cyrus Vance, believed that the issue of nuclear arms control was so important that it should be delinked from other issues of U.S.-Soviet relations.

CONCLUSION

Interest groups clearly played an active role in the SALT II debate, but how important were they? The answer to this question depends on the intended target of interest-group activity. The Carter administration's ratification activities, which resembled those of a nongovernmental interest group in a number of ways, sought to influence the elite public and sponsored a number of briefings at the White House for prominent citizens from states with senators whose votes were either uncertain or particularly important. Despite the effort that went into the organizing of these briefings, according to one scholar, they "failed to activate public opinion for the treaty."[94]

Nongovernmental interest groups did not have much of an impact on media coverage of SALT II. Out of 326 stories concerning SALT II listed in the Vanderbilt Television News Archive for 1979, only 19 stories (6 percent) mentioned interest groups by name. Nationally based interest groups were mentioned in the *New York Times Index* by name only ten times in 1979.[95] Thus, it appears that it was very difficult for SALT II–related interest groups to obtain media coverage, which is one of the most effective means that interest groups use to try to get their message across to the public.

Interest groups used a number of methods to attempt to influence senators concerning SALT II. In his research on the influence of interest groups on the SALT II ratification debate, David Kurkowski asked sixty-eight Senate staff members to evaluate the effectiveness of fourteen interest-group activities utilized during the debate. He found that staff members believed that a personal presentation to a senator or an aide was the most effective single interest-group activity. Following, in order of importance were: having an expert contact the senator; holding a briefing where an expert makes a presentation; having an influential constituent contact the senator; building a grassroots organization in the state; testifying at a hearing; publishing fact sheets and other materials; producing and showing films; encouraging letter-writing campaigns; giving speeches and sponsoring conferences; working for or against the senator's reelection campaign; publicizing voting records on foreign policy issues; holding press conferences; and sponsoring advertisements in newspapers.[96]

In his study of public interest groups, Jeffrey Berry found, "Of all the techniques open to pubic interest representatives, the personal presentation of arguments to government officials was thought to be the most effective."[97] This view confirmed earlier findings by Milbrath and by Ziegler and Baer.[98] Kurkowski's study of interest groups' influence on SALT II also confirmed this view.

It is possible that the Carter administration would have been more effective in dealing with the Senate if it had concentrated its efforts on influencing individual senators rather than attempting to bolster grassroots support for SALT II through the White House briefings and SALT public-information programs. Hamilton Jordan was immediately responsible for developing the SALT II ratification plan and is, therefore, responsible for this shortcoming. But ultimately, the "buck stops" on the president's desk, and President Carter was therefore responsible for the mistaken approach.

NOTES

1. Gabriel Almond, *The American People and Foreign Policy* (New York: Praeger, 1960), 139, 143, 150, and 236.

2. Barry Hughes, *Domestic Context of American Foreign Policy* (San Francisco: W. H. Freeman, 1978), 153–96; Bernard C. Cohen, *The Public's Impact on Foreign Policy* (Boston: Little, Brown, 1973), 96–106; Charles W. Kegley, Jr., and Eugene Wittkopf, *American Foreign Policy: Pattern and Process,* 3d ed. (New York: St. Martin's Press, 1987), 276–83; and Charles W. Kegley, Jr., and Eugene Wittkopf, eds., *Domestic Politics and American Foreign Policy* (New York: St. Martin's Press, 1988), 55–69.

3. Alexander Hamilton, James Madison, and John Jay, *The Federalist Papers,* no. 10 (New York: New American Library, 1961), 77–84.

4. David B. Truman, *The Governmental Process: Political Interests and Public Opinion,* 2d ed. (New York: Knopf, 1971).

5. Bernard Cohen, *The Political Process and Foreign Policy: The Making of the Japanese Peace Settlement* (Princeton: Princeton University Press, 1957).

6. Lester W. Milbrath, *The Washington Lobbyists* (Chicago: Rand McNally, 1963).

7. Harmon Ziegler, *Interest Groups in American Society* (Englewood Cliffs, N.J.: Prentice-Hall, 1964), 274.

8. David Carl Kurkowski, "The Role of Interest Groups in the Domestic Debate on SALT II," Ph.D. diss., Temple University (Ann Arbor, Mich.: University Microfilms, 1982), 173.

9. Edward J. Laurance, "The Changing Role of Congress in Defense Policy-Making," *Journal of Conflict Resolution* 20, no. 4 (June 1976): 213–53; Duncan L. Clarke, *Politics of Arms Control: The Role and Effectiveness of the U.S. Arms Control and Disarmament Agency* (New York: The Free Press, 1979), 160–64.

10. E. E. Schattschneider, *Party Government* (New York: Rinehart and Company, 1942) and James MacGregor Burns, *The Deadlock of Democracy* (Englewood Cliffs, N.J.: Prentice-Hall, 1963).

11. Truman, *The Governmental Process.*

12. Jeffrey M. Berry, *Lobbying for the People: The Political Behavior of Public Interest Groups* (Princeton: Princeton University Press, 1977), 7.

13. Fred W. Riggs, *Pressures on Congress: A Study in the Repeal of Chinese Exclusion* (New York: King's Crown Press, 1959), 22.

14. Berry, *Lobbying for the People,* 212–52.

15. Norman J. Ornstein and Shirley Elder, *Interest Groups, Lobbying and Policy-Making* (Washington: Congressional Quarterly Press, 1978), 66.

16. Raymond A. Bauer, Ithiel de Sola Pool, and Lewis Anthony Dexter, *American Business and Public Policy: The Politics of Foreign Trade* (Chicago: Aldine, 1972), 342.

17. Henry Kissinger, *Years of Upheaval* (Boston: Little, Brown, 1982), 1152.

18. Quoted in Kissinger, ibid.

19. Jerry W. Sanders, *Peddlers of Crisis: The Committee on the Present Danger and the Politics of Containment* (Boston: South End Press, 1983), 183.

20. Committee on the Present Danger, "Common Sense and the Common Danger," (Washington: Committee on the Present Danger, 1976), 7–12.

21. Paul H. Nitze with Ann M. Smith and Steven L. Rearden, *From Hiroshima to Glasnost: At the Center of Decision* (New York: Grove Weidenfeld, 1989), 354.

22. Charles Martin Kupperman, "The SALT II Debate" (Ph.D. diss., University of Southern California, September 1980). Dr. Kupperman served on the staff of the Committee on the Present Danger and presents a highly complimentary view of the committee and its activities in contrast to the critical perspective of Jerry Sanders, *Peddlers of Crisis*.

23. Committee on the Present Danger, "How the Committe on the Present Danger Will Operate—What It Will Do and What It Will Not Do," (Washington: Committee on the Present Danger, November 10, 1976), 1–2.

24. Charles Tyroler II, interview with Charles Martin Kupperman, March 1, 1980, cited in Kupperman, "The SALT II Debate," 192.

25. Karen Rothmyer, "Citizen Scaife," *Columbia Journalism Review* (July–August 1981): 41.

26. Memorandum from Eugene V. Rostow to the Members of the Committee on the Present Danger, October 13, 1987, 2.

27. Kupperman, "The SALT II Debate," 192.

28. Sanders, *Peddlers of Crisis*, 23, n. 44.

29. Committee on the Present Danger, "What Is the Soviet Union Up To?" (Washington: Committee on the Present Danger, April 1977).

30. Ibid., 6, 8–9.

31. Ibid., 12.

32. Committee on the Present Danger, "Where We Stand on SALT," (Washington: Committee on the Present Danger, July 1977).

33. Letter from Eugene V. Rostow to Zbigniew Brzezinski, February 21, 1977, in "FG 6–1–1/Brzezinski, Zbigniew 2/16/77," Box FG–25, WHCF–Subject File, Federal Government–Organizations, Jimmy Carter Library.

34. Rowland Evans and Robert Novak, "A Touchy Carter: Shades of Former Presidents?," *Washington Post*, August 13, 1977.

35. Ibid.

36. John Newhouse, "Reflections: The SALT Debate," *New Yorker*, December 17, 1979.

37. *Congressional Quarterly*, June 23, 1979, 1217.

38. Kupperman, "The SALT II Debate," 203.

39. Paul N. Nitze, "Current SALT II Negotiating Posture," unpublished paper (Washington: Committee on the Present Danger, November 1, 1977).

40. "Memorandum from Eugene V. Rostow, Chairman, Executive Committee, to Friends and Supporters of the Committee," December 5, 1979.

41. Charles Kupperman, interview with author, Washington, DC, June 5, 1987.

42. *Time*, January 8, 1979, 21.

43. Kurkowski, "The Role of Interest Groups," 137–39.

44. Ibid.

45. *"The SALT Syndrome:* Charges and Facts: Analysis of an Anti-SALT 'Documentary,'" *Congressional Record–Senate,* July 30, 1980, S 10366–71.

46. Ibid., 134.

47. Coalition for Peace through Strength, *The SALT Syndrome,* unpublished script (Boston, Va.: American Security Council Education Foundation, n.d.).

48. *Time,* March 5, 1979, 11.

49. *Washington Post Magazine,* August 19, 1979, 4.

50. Ornstein and Elder, *Interest Groups,* 58.

51. Lewis A. Dexter, "What Do Congressmen Hear: The Mail," *Public Opinion Quarterly* 20 (Spring 1956): 17–27.

52. Kurkowski, "The Role of Interest Groups," 310.

53. Associated Press, June 12, 1979.

54. *Economist,* October 6, 1979.

55. "Church Leaders to Ask Senate to Support SALT II Accords," *Los Angeles Times,* September 8, 1979.

56. "Billy Graham Supports SALT as Step toward Disarmament," *Los Angeles Times,* August 4, 1979.

57. Kurkowski, "The Role of Interest Groups," 121.

58. Berry, *Lobbying for the People.*

59. Americans for SALT brochure.

60. "Comment on the Report of the Coalition for Peace through Strength," unpublished paper (Americans for SALT, April 19, 1979); "SALT II Campaign," unpublished guidelines (Americans for SALT, n.d.).

61. "7 out of 10 Americans Approve of the SALT II Treaty," *Washington Post,* July 9, 1979.

62. "Americans for SALT Conference," *SALT Talk* 1, no. 7 (August 7, 1979): 6.

63. Nancy Ramsey, interview with author, Washington, DC, June 5, 1987.

64. William Kincade, interview with author, Washington, DC, July 13, 1988.

65. Jeremy Stone, "SALT, in Perspective," *New York Times,* March 11, 1979.

66. Robert C. Johansen, "Arms Bazaar," *Harper's,* May 1979, 21.

67. Cyrus Vance, interview with author, New York City, July 14, 1988.

68. Testimony of Ralph Earle II, U.S. Congress, Senate, Committee on Foreign Relations, *The SALT II Treaty,* Hearings, 96th Cong., 1st sess., pt. 1:248–49.

69. "Transcript of the President's News Conference on Foreign and Domestic Matters," *New York Times,* May 1, 1979.

70. Cyrus Vance, "Limiting the Strategic Arms Race" (Speech to the Institute of World Affairs of the University of Wisconsin-Milwaukee, Current Policy no. 73, U.S. Department of State, Washington, DC, July 24, 1979), 3.

71. Harold Brown, "SALT II and the National Defense" (Speech to the Council on Foreign Relations and the Foreign Policy Association, New York, Current Policy no. 62, U.S. Department of State, Washington, DC, April 1979), 7.

72. "Statement of Hon. Harold Brown," U.S. Congress, Senate, Committee on Armed Services, *Military Implications of the Treaty on the Limitation of Strategic Offensive Arms and Protocol Thereto (SALT II Treaty)*, Hearings, 96th Cong., 1st sess., 1979, pt. 1:15.

73. Ibid.

74. Don Irwin, "Satellite Spying on Soviets, Carter Says," *Los Angeles Times*, October 2, 1978.

75. Matthew Nimetz, interview with author, New York City, July 15, 1988.

76. Robert W. Buchheim and Dan Caldwell, "The Standing Consultative Commission: Description and Appraisal," in Paul Viotti, ed., *Conflict and Arms Control* (Boulder, Colo.: Westview Press, 1984); Dan Caldwell, "The Standing Consultative Commission: Past Performance and Future Possibilities," in William C. Potter, ed., *Verification and Arms Control* (Lexington, Ma.: Lexington Books, 1985); and Sidney Graybeal and Michael Krepon, "Making Better Use of the SCC," *International Security* 10, no. 2 (Fall 1985).

77. "SALT One: Compliance, SALT Two: Verification," Selected Documents no. 7 (U.S. Department of State, Washington, DC, February 1978); see also "Compliance with SALT I Agreements," Special Report no. 55 (U.S. Department of State, Washington, DC, July 1979).

78. Stansfield Turner, *Secrecy and Democracy: The CIA in Transition* (New York: Harper and Row, 1985), 122–23.

79. See the following publications by David S. Sullivan: "The Legacy of SALT I: Soviet Deception and U.S. Retreat," *Strategic Review* 7 (Winter 1979): 26–41; "Lessons Learned from SALT I and SALT II: New Objectives for SALT III," *International Security Review* 6 (Fall 1981): 355–86; *The Bitter Fruit of SALT: A Record of Soviet Duplicity* (Houston: Texas Policy Institute, 1982).

80. "Responding to Soviet Violations Policy," Memorandum from Secretary of Defense Caspar Weinberger to President Ronald Reagan, December 9, 1985, 9.

81. "Statement of Prof. Robert Legvold," Senate Committee on Foreign Relations, *The SALT II Treaty*, pt. 3:74–75; Stephen J. Flanagan, "SALT II," in Albert Carnesale and Richard N. Haass, eds., *Superpower Arms Control: Setting the Record Straight* (Cambridge: Ballinger, 1987), 121.

82. See the testimony of Cyrus Vance and Harold Brown to the Senate Committee on Foreign Relations, *The SALT II Treaty*, pt. 1:91, 104.

83. Larry Smith, interview with author, Washington, DC, October 20, 1987.

84. Cyrus Vance, *Hard Choices: Critical Years in America's Foreign Policy* (New York: Simon and Schuster, 1983), 365.

85. William Perry, interview with author, Menlo Park, Calif., January 15, 1988.

86. "Carter Reportedly OKs Mobile Missile," *Los Angeles Times*, June 8, 1979.

87. Matthew Nimetz, interview with author.

88. Dan Caldwell, *American-Soviet Relations: From 1947 to the Nixon-Kissinger Grand Design and Grand Strategy* (Westport, Conn.: Greenwood Press, 1981).

89. Richard Perle, "Echoes of the 1930s," *Strategic Review* 7 (Winter 1979).

90. Marshall Shulman, *Beyond the Cold War* (New Haven: Yale University Press, 1966).

91. William R. Van Cleave, "U.S. Strategic Forces in the 1980s," in Gordon Humphrey, et al., *SALT II and American Security* (Cambridge: Institute for Foreign Policy Analysis, 1980), 20;

Richard Perle, "Echoes of the 1930s," 13; these examples are quoted in Sean M. Lynn-Jones, "Lulling and Stimulating Effects of Arms Control," in Carnesale and Haass, eds., *Superpower Arms Control,* 223–74.

92. Testimony of Gen. David C. Jones, U.S. Congress, Senate Committee on Foreign Relations, *The SALT II Treaty,* pt. 1:373.

93. Lynn-Jones, "Lulling and Stimulating Effects of Arms Control," 258.

94. Kurkowski, "The Role of Interest Groups," 400.

95. Ibid., 265.

96. Ibid., 177–78.

97. Berry, *Lobbying for the People,* 214.

98. Milbrath, *The Washington Lobbyists;* L. Harmon Ziegler and Michael Baer, *Lobbying* (Belmont, Calif.: Wadsworth, 1969).

CHAPTER SIX

The Debate in the Senate

The greatest consultative privilege of the
Senate—the greatest in dignity—is its right
to a ruling voice in the ratification of treaties
with foreign powers.
Woodrow Wilson, 1885

When President Carter signed the SALT II Treaty and submitted it to the Senate for advice and consent, a new set of negotiations concerning SALT II began, negotiations between the executive branch and the Senate. Carter recognized this fact: "My restraints were just as much with the Senate as they were at the bargaining table with the Soviets."[1] Members of the Senate believed that the task before them was very significant. Minority Leader Howard Baker called SALT II "the most important treaty this country has undertaken since World War I."[2] Democrat John Glenn agreed: "Not since Woodrow Wilson's time and the League of Nations debate has a treaty been so important, yet so contentious, as the SALT II Treaty."[3] In this chapter, I will describe: (1) the political environment in the Senate in 1979; (2) the prominent senators, committees, and staff members who played important roles in the SALT II debate; and (3) the Senate's action on the treaty.

THE POLITICAL ENVIRONMENT IN THE SENATE IN 1979

Many observers have noted that for years the United States Senate resembled a gentleman's club rather than a serious legislative body. In the "old Senate," influence and power were centralized and determined by seniority; deference was paid to certain older, "bellweather" members; only rarely would younger members challenge senior, established members; and senators often deferred to the White House. Vietnam and Watergate destroyed this atmosphere, for both of these episodes demonstrated the disastrous consequences of inadequately checked executive power. The "new Senate" was decentralized, democratized, and junior member–oriented.[4] As I. M. Destler has noted, "In the cold war period, three things combined to make Congress a tolerable policy partner: deference to the president on the big things;

centralization of power; and, if not consensus, a functioning internationalist coalition. By the 1970s all had disappeared."[5]

A number of those elected to the Senate in 1974 had been caught up in the anti–Vietnam War movement; these new senators included Gary Hart (who had been George McGovern's campaign manager in the 1972 presidential race), John Culver, and Dale Bumpers. Each of these three freshman senators requested and received a place on the Senate Armed Services Committee where they were able to exert their influence on defense issues. The presence of these three outspoken, liberal senators on the Armed Services Committee in itself was a departure from past practice; previously, members of the committee had rarely challenged the positions or budgets of the Department of Defense.

As the 1970s wore on, public opinion about Soviet-American relations and presidential power took a more conservative turn, and this change was reflected in the composition of the Senate. In the 1978 election, twenty new senators were elected—eleven Republicans and nine Democrats. This was the biggest single turnover in the Senate since 1946. Included in this group were a number of conservatives including Gordon Humphrey and Alan Simpson. In many respects the "gadfly role" that liberal senators such as Proxmire, McGovern, Hatfield, and Church had played in the early 1970s was played in the late 1970s by conservatives Garn, Wallop, Humphrey, and Helms.[6]

Thus, the Senate that Jimmy Carter faced in the debate over the SALT II Treaty in 1979 was composed of a diverse group of politicians including some elected in the early 1970s who reflected the antiwar sentiments of that period and others of a conservative orientation who reflected the more assertive attitude of the 1980s. As a political body, however, the Senate went from being the "most dovish body in the U.S. government" to being the most hawkish by the end of the 1970s, and this orientation had a dramatic impact on the SALT II debate.[7]

JIMMY CARTER AND THE CONGRESS

Jimmy Carter was the first elected president following Watergate, and the residual tension from both Vietnam and Watergate added significantly to the normal amount of conflict that exists between the executive and congressional branches even in the best of times. Added to this, Carter had campaigned as a Washington outsider, trying to make a virtue out of his lack of Washington experience. Once elected, Carter and his advisers did little to dispel the wariness that many members of Congress felt toward the new president.

Things did not begin well. When Speaker of the House Tip O'Neill requested tickets for his family to attend a gala at the Kennedy Center the night before Carter was inaugurated, he was given seats in the last row of the second balcony. The Speaker blamed Carter's chief of staff, Hamilton Jordan, for slighting his family, and although Jordan apologized, O'Neill believed that the slight had been intentional. Subsequently, after Jordan failed to return several of the Speaker's phone calls, O'Neill thereafter referred to Jordan as "Hannibal Jerken."[8] O'Neill concluded that "during the Carter years, congressional Democrats often had the feeling that the White House was actually working against us."[9] There were other petty slights that alienated some members of Congress; for example, the White House sent bills to House and Senate leaders for meals that they ate at the White House.

Carter had an obvious disdain for legislators. During the presidential campaign, Carter was asked whether some cattle on a South Dakota farm reminded him of Georgia's legislators, and he replied sarcastically, "No, they're more intelligent."[10] Carter later recognized his problems with the legislative branch; he entitled one chapter of his memoirs "My One-Week Honeymoon with Congress."[11]

Neither Carter nor his senior staff members and cabinet members enjoyed spending time with members of Congress. Carter and his principal cabinet members with foreign policy responsibilities, Cyrus Vance and Harold Brown, enjoyed mastering the technicalities of complex issues and simply did not like interacting with members of Congress. According to political scientist Charles O. Jones, "Separation was preferred to intimacy in presidential-congressional relations."[12]

Carter's problems with Congress were not simply due to personality conflicts. During the ninety-fifth Congress (1977–78), Carter sought to deal with a number of complex and controversial issues including windfall profits, comprehensive energy legislation, Taiwan, the Panama Canal treaties, defense spending, and Iran. Interestingly, despite his problems in dealing with Congress, Carter was able to accomplish a great deal. The Panama Canal treaties were ratified; sales of aircraft to Saudi Arabia and Egypt were approved; an arms embargo against Turkey was lifted; the sanctions against trading with Rhodesia were retained; the Taiwan Relations Act was passed; and the largest development assistance bill in history was passed.[13] These victories were achieved at some cost, as President Carter later recognized: "The battles with Congress over the Panama Canal treaties and energy legislation had been long, drawn-out, and debilitating to the members [of Congress] and to me."[14]

Carter's problems with Congress were exacerbated by another factor: the White House Office of Congressional Relations was not effective. Jimmy Carter had brought the director of the office, Frank Moore, with him from Georgia, and Moore had no previous experience in Washington. In the interviews conducted for this book, both senators and Senate staff members were very critical of Moore. Several went as far as to say that Moore was the worst White House congressional liaison with whom they had dealt.[15]

Early in the administration, senators Gary Hart and Alan Cranston went to the president and suggested that he appoint a senior official to act as a liaison between the White House and the Senate. They suggested that the president appoint Robert Straus who, as the special trade representative, had served as the administration's chief lobbyist for the legislation on the multi-lateral trade negotiations.[16] Sen. William Proxmire believed that the president should have appointed the respected former Senate majority leader Mike Mansfield to such a position rather than naming him as ambassador to Japan.[17] Instead, the president relied on Frank Moore until it became obvious that he needed help. Bob Beckel, who had assisted with the ratification of the Panama Canal treaties, was brought in and did a creditable job according to almost all accounts.

In early 1978, the White House decided that an overall coordinator for the SALT II ratification effort was needed and Matthew Nimetz, the number three person at the Department of State, was appointed. Although the members of both the executive branch and the Senate interviewed for this book believed that Nimetz did a good job, they also felt that he was not at a high enough level within the bureaucracy. Finally, in August 1979 the president brought the respected Washington attorney, Lloyd Cutler, into the White House to act as the "SALT II czar," but his appointment came late in the process. Cutler had had little experience in national security matters and needed time that was not available to learn the issues.

Despite the problems in dealing with the Congress, the executive branch devoted substantial resources to working with the Congress. Although the White House Office of Congressional Relations had a small staff of 7 professionals, there were at least 675 staff members from executive branch departments and agencies who were directly involved in congressional liaison work, more than one congressional liaison staff person for each member of Congress.[18] The Department of Defense alone had a congressional liaison staff of 227.[19]

In sum, according to Department of Defense official William Perry, "The Carter administration did not have a good working relationship with the Congress, partly because the president didn't recognize the importance of that and didn't work at it hard enough and partly for reasons out of his control."[20]

THE SENATE'S INVOLVEMENT IN SALT

During the negotiations that led to the first strategic arms limitation agreements, the Senate was not actively involved in the oversight of the negotiations conducted by the Nixon administration.[21] Following the conclusion of the SALT I negotiations, the Anti-Ballistic Missile Treaty was submitted to the Senate for its advice and consent, and the Interim Agreement on Offensive Forces was submitted to both houses of Congress. Sen. Henry Jackson was concerned about the greater number of missiles that the agreement allowed for the USSR, and he sponsored an amendment calling for equal levels in all future agreements. The Jackson amendment marked the first significant congressional involvement in the SALT process.

Vietnam and Watergate had stimulated the involvement of the Congress in foreign policy, and the Carter administration recognized that increased congressional involvement was a fact of life. In May 1977, Paul Warnke, the director of the Arms Control and Disarmament Agency, wrote to Vice President Walter Mondale and requested that he designate several senators to serve as advisers to the SALT delegation "in order to facilitate Congressional knowledge and involvement and to increase public understanding of the objectives of these negotiations."[22] Subsequent to this, Secretary of State Vance wrote to the entire membership of the Senate and extended an invitation to visit Geneva to observe the SALT II negotiations firsthand. By the time the treaty was signed by the leaders of the two superpowers, thirty-six senators had visited.[23] In addition, in mid–1977 the administration named twenty-five senators and fourteen representatives as official advisers to the American SALT II delegation. Although this action was clearly designed to assure the members of Congress that their views were being taken into account in the negotiations, not all members of Congress were convinced that their views were seriously considered.

Tension, struggle, and competition have characterized executive-congressional relations throughout most of American history. But during the Carter years, the Congress was more activist than during previous periods. Congress had not only the will to challenge the executive branch; it also had expanded legal, structural, institutional, and political capabilities to do so.[24]

By the late 1970s, the Congress had significantly increased its staff support over previous decades. In the mid–1960s, the total staff for House and Senate committees equaled approximately 1,100. By the late 1970s, there were more than 3,000 staff members. The personal staffs of individual members of Congress also increased dramatically from fewer than 6,000 in the mid–1960s to more than 10,000 in the late 1970s.[25] In percentage terms, the growth in the personal staffs of senators from 1947 to 1979 was 512 percent, and the growth of the Senate's committee staff was 373 percent.[26] In addition to the increase in the number of staff members, there was also a difference in quality. In the early 1960s, it was unusual for a senator to have an aide whose specific responsibility was foreign policy; however, by the late 1970s, this was the rule rather than the exception.

In addition to increasing the number of staff members during the 1970s, Congress also increased the number and the analytical capabilities of congressional support agencies. The Office of Technology Assessment was established in 1972, and by 1979 it had a staff of 145. The Legislative Reference Service was reorganized into the Congressional Research Service (CRS) and was given greater responsibilities, more staff, and a larger budget, which enabled CRS staff members to focus on a wide variety of topics including SALT II.[27] Between 1965 and 1979 the CRS staff grew from 231 to 847, an increase of 367 percent. The Congress directed the General Accounting Office to increase its staff and to expand its scope to evaluate the implementation of programs. Its staff went from 4,278 in 1965 to 5,303 in 1979, an increase of 125 percent. The Congressional Budget Office (CBO), founded in 1974, was designed to provide the Congress with an in-house capability to analyze budgets and programs presented by the executive branch. During the SALT II debate, for example, CBO staff members prepared analyses concerning the costs of strategic weapons programs with and without SALT II.[28] By 1979, CBO had a staff of 207.[29]

Members of the Congress also had added to their power by increasing the number of committees and subcommittees. By the ninety-sixth Congress (1979–80), all but two Democratic senators chaired either a committee or a subcommittee, and nearly half of the Democratic members of the House of Representatives also chaired either a committee or a subcommittee.

The interaction of the White House and the Senate during the debate over the Panama Canal treaties sensitized senators to both their responsibilities and their power in the treaty-ratification process. According to William Bader, the staff director of the Senate Foreign Relations Committee at the time that SALT II was debated: "It was during the Panama Canal treaties' deliberations that the Senate re-wrote the 'marriage manual' on ratification procedures. The Senate developed a taste and a technique for modifying and not simply reviewing submitted treaties."[30]

Given the power and the inclination of Congress to use that power, President Carter, Hamilton Jordan, and Frank Moore considered the possibility of concluding SALT II as an executive agreement rather than a treaty. One of the SALT I agreements—the Interim Agreement on Offensive Weapons— was an agreement rather than a treaty, so there was a relatively recent precedent. Vice President Mondale was also concerned about sending the treaty to the Senate where it might become the hostage of a few conservative senators.[31] In addition, many members of the House of Representatives— including Robert Carr, Thomas Downey, and Clement Zablocki—had suggested that the administration submit the final agreement to both houses of Congress. In an interview, President Carter indicated that he might submit

SALT II to the Congress as an agreement, rather than a treaty.[32] After a strongly negative reaction to this trial balloon, the president backed away from this alternative.[33] Once this decision was made and SALT II was signed as a treaty, it was submitted to the Senate for its advice and consent.

SENATORS' POSITIONS ON SALT II

Once the treaty was submitted to the Senate, four groups of senators emerged. First, there was a group of senators who were irreconcilably opposed to the ratification of SALT II in the form that it was submitted to the Senate. This group included, among others, Henry Jackson, John Tower, Jake Garn, and Jesse Helms. A second group consisted of those senators who were strong supporters of the treaty and included Alan Cranston, John Culver, Gary Hart, and Joseph Biden. A third group that emerged during the debate on the treaty consisted of the liberal critics of SALT II who believed that the treaty did not do enough to control the arms race. This group was led by Mark Hatfield, George McGovern, and William Proxmire. The fourth group consisted of the "undecideds," those who had not made up their minds about how to vote for the treaty. The senators in this group were clearly the most significant, for their votes would determine whether the treaty was ratified or rejected. The most important members of this group were Majority Leader Robert Byrd, Minority Leader Howard Baker, and Armed Services Committee members John Stennis (the chairman of the committee) and Sam Nunn.

Senators influenced the debate on SALT II in a number of different ways: some were experts in their own right and issued press releases concerning the treaty; others worked through their committees. In the following, I will first review the positions of a number of prominent individual senators and their staff members, and I will then review the debate within the three Senate committees that held hearings on SALT II.

The Irreconcilable Opponents

A number of senators were irreconcilably opposed to the SALT II Treaty. According to one Senate staff member, speaking only partly facetiously, "There are 20 members [of the Senate] who would vote against ratification if the treaty provided for unilateral Russian disarmament."[34]

Henry M. Jackson was the most prominent of the irreconcilable opponents of the treaty. Jackson first came to Washington, D.C., in January 1941 as a young, twenty-eight-year-old member of the House of Representatives from the state of Washington. He was elected to the Senate in 1952 and served there until his death in 1983 at age seventy-three. During his forty-one years of service in the Congress, Jackson devoted his attention to two principal issues: energy and national security. He closely reviewed any matters concerning arms control, and often influenced the way in which the Senate dealt with these matters. Paradoxically, during his service in the Senate, Jackson voted in favor of every arms control agreement that was reported to the Senate for a final vote, including the Antarctic Treaty, the establishment of the Arms Control and Disarmament Agency, the Limited Test Ban Treaty, the Outer Space Treaty, the Non-Proliferation Treaty, the Seabed Treaty, the Anti-Ballistic Missile Treaty, the Interim Agreement on Offensive Forces, the Biological Weapons Convention, and the Environmental Modification Treaty.[35]

Despite this apparent support for arms control, Jackson had demanded a price from the executive branch for his support on a number of these agreements. When the Limited Test Ban Treaty was considered by the Senate, Jackson demanded and received a promise from the Kennedy administration to continue nuclear tests permitted by the treaty, at the same level as or higher than before the treaty was put into force. Jackson authored the amendment to the 1972 Interim Agreement demanding that future agreements contain "equal aggregates" of weapons for the United States and the USSR. After the SALT I agreements were concluded, Jackson demanded that the Nixon administration replace almost all of the high-level officials of the Arms Control and Disarmament Agency. It was during this "purge" of ACDA that Gen. Edward Rowny replaced Gen. Royal B. Allison as the representative of the Joint Chiefs of Staff on the U.S. SALT delegation. Subsequently, General Rowny provided a constant flow of information to Senator Jackson's office concerning the course of the negotiations.[36] Given the central role that Jackson had played in the Senate on national security affairs, it was clear that he would continue this role when SALT II was submitted to the Senate.

Columnist Rowland Evans has noted: "Of all the sources of power in Washington today, the most nearly invisible—yet in some ways the most influential—is the congressional staff. . . . A staff of professionals is no less essential to the care, feeding and orderly operation of Congress than Merlin was to King Arthur or Cardinal Richelieu to Louis XIII."[37] With allowances for journalistic license, the point that Evans makes is a good one: the staffs of members of Congress perform vital roles. Henry Jackson's staff advisers remained with him for a much longer period than the staff members of most other senators. Jackson's professional assistant and adviser on foreign and defense policy, Dorothy Fosdick, worked for him for twenty-eight years from 1955 until the senator's death in 1983.[38]

Of all of Jackson's advisers, Richard Perle was the most influential and effective. Perle served Jackson in various professional and staff positions from 1969 to 1979, and he attracted the attention of officials at the highest level of the executive branch throughout that period. Henry Kissinger noted: "I actually considered Jackson a good friend, and I agreed with many of his analyses of Soviet intentions. The difference between Jackson and me was that he wanted all-out confrontation, under the influence of one of his associates, Richard Perle. He wanted all-out confrontation with the Soviets, and he liked a policy of constantly 'needling' of the Soviet Union."[39] Looking back on his presidency, Jimmy Carter commented, "I never did have much hope that I could convince Richard Perle that we needed the SALT II Treaty or [that we] ought to negotiate any treaty with the Soviet Union."[40]

One reason Perle was so effective is that he had very good ties with Washington journalists. A correspondent for a national magazine recalled that Perle would frequently call him with various news items on early Saturday mornings several hours before his weekly deadline. Often, the correspondent would incorporate these tidbits in his stories even though he did not have time to check them.[41] According to a former Senate aide, "Richard Perle understood how to get his point of view across in a timely, appropriate and convincing way to the national media, and that created a symbiotic relationship with the media and Perle."[42]

Richard Perle was an effective opponent of the SALT II Treaty. Part of Perle's opposition to SALT II may have been personally motivated. He was a Democrat and Zbigniew Brzezinski had considered him for a position on the National Security Council; however, he was not offered anything in the Carter administration.[43] Nancy Ramsey, the executive director of Americans for SALT, the principal interest group working for the ratification of the treaty, when asked who the most effective opponent of the treaty was, replied, "Richard Perle, because everywhere we moved on the Hill, Perle had already been there, or he was right behind us."[44]

Perle was hardly alone; there were a number of conservative staff allies working for other senators. Sven Kramer had worked for Henry Kissinger before Senator Tower hired him to work for the Republican Policy Committee. Ty McCoy had worked in the CIA and the Department of Defense before going to work for Senator Garn. David Sullivan had also worked for the CIA before joining the staff of Sen. Gordon Humphrey in 1979. James Lucier and John Carbaugh were Senator Helms's foreign policy aides.[45] Other aides listed as "available to work on SALT" in Henry Jackson's files included "John Lehman, Sy Weiss, Fred Iklé, Burt Marshall, Charlie Kupperman (Committee on the Present Danger), Bill Schneider (Jack Kemp and Hudson Institute), Colin Gray (Hudson Institute), Bill Van Cleve [sic] (University of Southern California), Dick Pipes (Harvard), Ron Lehman (Senator Tower), Chris Lehman, Mark Schneider (Senator Garn) and Mark Edelman (Senator Danforth)."[46] A number of these aides began meeting regularly at the Madison Hotel for meals, and this group hence became known as the "Madison group."[47] The members of this group had very good ties to the Department of Defense from which they obtained sensitive information. They sought to draft amendments that would result in the renegotiation of the treaty, so-called "killer amendments."

Senator Jackson and the other irreconcilable opponents worked against the SALT II Treaty even before it was concluded; five weeks before the treaty was signed Jackson issued a press release that stated: "From what I know of the SALT II treaty it is substantially unequal and unverifiable. It favors the Soviet Union. In its present form it is not in the security interest of the United States."[48] Despite Jackson's opposition, President Carter tried to win his support for the treaty, but by the time the Senate was considering the treaty, Jackson's opposition was firm.

Senator Jackson was the most prominent of the opponents of the SALT II Treaty, although a number of other senators would have voted against SALT II irrespective of the changes that could have been made in the treaty.

The Treaty Supporters

Larry Smith, a former Senate Armed Services Committee staff member, recalled, "A number of the SALT II supporters were intimidated by the presumed expertise of Senator Jackson and his staff on SALT II."[49] In order to defend against Jackson's and other critics' attacks on the treaty, senators Cranston, Culver, and Hart developed a substantive case for the treaty and a strategy for dealing with the critics' attacks.[50] Their case was based on the premise that the SALT II Treaty would increase the national security of the United States, rather than on the idea that arms control was inherently good or that the treaty would contribute to détente. The "national security case for SALT" claimed that the treaty would cap the Soviet threat to the United States; that it would help the United States to assess the threat from the USSR; and that the treaty would help the United States to better evaluate Soviet capabilities.

Supporters of the treaty invited twenty senators to form a group, according to the organizer of the group, Senator Cranston, "to consider the strengths and weaknesses of the treaty and to develop supporters within the Senate so that we would be ready to deal with counterarguments."[51] The "Cranston group" met regularly with officials from the administration to discuss treaty issues. In my interviews, former Senate staff members gave the Cranston group high marks for stimulating support for the treaty in the Senate. William Bader commented: "The Cranston group was doing what the Foreign Relations Committee should have been doing: holding seminars, inviting people in, and building an internal constituency. The committee was not prepared to do that."[52] Senators Robert Dole and William Roth, Jr., organized their own SALT study groups, but these were not as active or as effective as the Cranston group.[53]

Just as the Senate staff members who opposed the treaty formed the Madison group, the staff members who supported the treaty formed several groups of their own. Larry Smith and Charles Stevenson were instrumental in developing the national security case for SALT while working for the Senate Armed Services Committee. Sen. Edward Kennedy's foreign policy adviser, Jan Kalicki, assembled a group of staff members to meet periodically to discuss various aspects of the treaty. In a memo to Deputy National Security Affairs Adviser David Aaron, the administration's SALT ratification coordinator, Matthew Nimetz, identified a "core of friendly Senate staffers meeting weekly for strategy meeting [sic], including (with the senator or committee for who [sic] or which they worked indicated in parentheses): Jan Kalicki (Kennedy), Tom Dine (Budget), Charlie Stevenson (Culver), Lynn Parkinson (Bumpers), Peter Gold (Hart), Larry Smith (Armed Services), Cas Yost (Mathias), John Haynes (Anderson), Bruce Van Voorst (Clark), Bill Miller (Intelligence) and Bill Ashworth (Foreign Relations)."[54]

The Liberal Critics

On March 2, 1979, senators Hatfield, McGovern, and Proxmire wrote to President Carter indicating, "After considerable thought we have concluded that the proposed SALT II treaty is very difficult, if not impossible, for us to support."[55] The "gang of three" was particularly concerned that "the price of SALT II" would be too high, and that to gain the support of conservative senators, the administration would agree to develop and deploy new weapons systems such as the MX missile.[56]

In an interview with the author, Senator Hatfield indicated that he and his two colleagues thought the Carter administration was trying to buy the support of conservatives: "We viewed our strategy as a way to slow down and perhaps stop the constant yielding and placating of the promilitary senators. . . .The more [the Carter administration] placated, then the more they demanded."[57] In fact, the Carter administration was not completely hostile to the criticism of the three senators. After they announced their position, several members of the White House Office of Congressional Relations met with the senators and their staffs on Capitol Hill. The administration members indicated that the "White House would support strong language in the Treaty, if the Senate were to put it in, suggesting that the next round [of the SALT negotiations] have very deep reductions." According to one of Proxmire's staff members who was present at this meeting, "We felt that this was a tactical victory of sorts, that we got their attention."[58]

Some in the White House believed that Hatfield, McGovern, and Proxmire were posturing and that they would vote in favor of the treaty if their votes were needed for ratification.[59] Looking back on the debate, Senator Proxmire believes that he probably would have voted for the treaty if the Senate had voted on it. In an interview, Senator Hatfield noted, "If I had been the deciding vote, I probably would have voted to approve the treaty."[60]

The Undecideds

There were approximately thirty senators who had not decided whether they would vote for or against SALT II by the time it was signed.[61] This clearly was the most important group since these senators would determine the fate of the treaty.

The two most important formal leaders of the Senate are the majority and the minority leaders. At the time that SALT II was signed, these two positions were held, respectively, by Robert Byrd and Howard Baker. Their support had been crucial during the Panama Canal treaties ratification effort, and the Carter administration wanted their support for the SALT II Treaty.

Majority Leader Byrd did not come out in favor of SALT II at the time that it was signed. Instead, the Democratic leader studied in great detail the hearings before the Foreign Relations, Armed Services, and Intelligence committees. Byrd carefully read not only the treaty, but also the transcripts of the testimony of various witnesses. William Perry said: "My single most impressive meeting with any senator was with Senator Byrd. We spent five or six hours one-on-one discussing the treaty, and I found Senator Byrd exceedingly well informed."[62] Byrd may have adopted his noncommittal approach in order to win over undecided senators. In early July, Byrd led a delegation of senators to Moscow where they were received by both Foreign Minister Gromyko and General Secretary Brezhnev. According to reports, Byrd was pleased with his trip to the USSR and the answers to his questions that he received there. Despite this, Byrd waited until late October to announce his formal support for the treaty.

The Senate minority leader has played an important role in the ratification of past treaties. During the debate on the Limited Nuclear Test Ban Treaty in 1963, President Kennedy was able to obtain the support of the minority leader, Everett Dirksen, in order to counter Henry Jackson's criticism of the treaty. Sixteen years later, another Democratic president, Jimmy Carter, sought to convince Senator Dirksen's son-in-law and Senate minority leader, Howard Baker, to support his arms control treaty, SALT II.

Senator Baker had supported several previous arms control agreements including the SALT I agreements and the Vladivostok Accord. In addition, he had supported President Carter on several important foreign policy issues, including the ratification of the Panama Canal treaties and the lifting of the embargo on arms shipments to Turkey. Perhaps because of this past support, Baker felt vulnerable to conservative attack within the Republican party. This was an important consideration at any time, but was even more signifi-cant in 1980 since Baker was seeking his party's nomination for president.

At the beginning of 1979, Baker indicated that he was undecided on SALT II and that his vote would depend upon how the Soviets conducted themselves in the world.[63] He also somewhat ominously implied that the era of bipartisanship in foreign policy was over, by referring to the formerly isolationist Republican senator who had supported President Truman's for-eign policy initiatives after World War II: "Vandenberg was right in his time, and I think I am right in my time."[64] Within several months, Baker said that he was "leaning against" the treaty because of his concerns about the restric-tions placed on U.S. strategic programs, the Soviet Backfire bomber, and verification.[65] As late as June 6, Baker was still publicly undecided. He told the National Press Club: "I would like to support SALT II, but my friends the issue is not whether I support SALT, the question is whether I support this treaty. And I simply cannot give you the answer to that question at this time."[66] The answer came on June 27 when Senator Baker announced his formal opposition to the treaty, saying, "If the Administration does not signal a willingness to consider amendments, and if the Soviet Government does not desist in trying to threaten the Senate, then I will work diligently and, I trust, effectively to defeat this treaty."[67]

Senator Baker was one of the first members of the Senate Foreign Relations Committee to question the Carter administration's first witness, Secretary of Defense Harold Brown. According to Paul Warnke, "On the first day of the hearings, Baker came armed for bear, and Brown, who had great experience in the [arms control] field, peeled Baker like an onion, and he [Baker] did not come back to the hearings."[68] On November 2, Baker formally announced his candidacy for the Republican nomination for president, and one week later in the Foreign Relations Committee, he voted against reporting the treaty favorably to the Senate. Baker had gone from the undecided to the opposed column of the vote count. According to Baker: "Salt II is a disaster for the deterrent effect of our weapons system. It gives us nothing of value in return, it validates Soviet strategic arms superiority, and it thus endangers national security."[69]

Both critics and supporters of SALT II viewed Sam Nunn's role in the debate over the treaty as crucial, because of his recognized expertise on defense matters. Just three weeks after his inauguration, President Carter sent Nunn, the Democratic senator from Carter's home state of Georgia, a handwritten, "personal and confidential" note in which he assured the senator, "As you know, I will be the monitor and actual negotiator in arms limitation talks, &

will stay close to you & others."[70] Eugene Rostow believed that the treaty was doomed when three senators—Nunn, Baker, and Jackson—requested research help from the Committee on the Present Danger.[71] One White House official commented: "I can envision winning SALT without Jackson and possibly even without Baker. . . . But without Nunn, we're dead."[72]

In January 1979, Frank Moore and Zbigniew Brzezinski wrote a memo to President Carter concerning the administration's ratification strategy in the Senate: "Nunn is, perhaps, the most crucial Senator in the SALT ratification battle. . . . He may be one of the only Senators who can effectively counter Jackson."[73] During the height of the debate over SALT II in the summer of 1979, Madeleine Albright, Brzezinski's assistant for congressional relations, wrote a memo to him, saying: "Sam Nunn is going to be crucial to the passage of SALT. Within 24 hours, he managed to switch the debate from one which was focused on verification, Protocol, and heavy missiles to one about overall defense posture."[74]

Prior to his election to the Senate, Sam Nunn had served as a state senator in Georgia and before that as president of the Perry, Georgia, chamber of commerce, his first elected office. Because Senator Nunn and President Carter came from the same state, they knew and dealt with one another before either man came to Washington. When he was a state legislator, Nunn supported Carter in both of his gubernatorial drives. In 1972, Nunn defeated the candidate for the U.S. Senate whom Carter had appointed to fill the vacancy created by the death of Richard Russell. During the early part of the 1976 Democratic presidential primaries, Nunn remained neutral, but strongly supported Carter in the general election. Following his election to the Senate in 1972 with a respectable 54 percent of the vote, Nunn went to Washington with his great-uncle, Congressman Carl Vinson, who served as chairman of the House Armed Services Committee. The two men called on senators John Stennis, Henry Jackson, Robert Byrd, and Mike Mansfield to request that Nunn be appointed to the Senate Armed Services Committee. The Senate leaders were impressed with Nunn and appointed him to the committee, and within several years of his arrival in the Senate, Sam Nunn was a respected expert concerning military affairs.

During the Carter administration, Nunn criticized the president for unilaterally canceling the B–1 bomber program, and he was influential in convincing the Senate not to cancel the enhanced radiation weapon (the neutron bomb). One senator told a reporter: "Nunn has more credibility on SALT than just about anybody in the Senate. When I first came to the Senate, we just naturally looked to Scoop (Henry) Jackson for leadership on arms control, but Jackson has used up a lot of his credibility in recent years."[75] Sen. Lawton Chiles noted: "SALT is incredibly complicated. It hurts your head. Most senators are involved in so many things they don't have time to be an expert on everything, so you look around for somebody you can trust. Sam is not an ideologue. He is not going to influence the kneejerks on the right or left, but his credibility will sway some votes among the uncommitted."[76]

Nunn was concerned about a number of aspects of the SALT II Treaty, including the vulnerability of U.S. land-based missiles, the Soviet Backfire bomber, the verification of the agreement, and the effect of the protocol to the agreement.[77] When asked about the strategic impact of the treaty, Nunn replied:

> One of the principal questions is whether we are tranquilized into thinking we really do have overall parity and that this treaty will allow us to continue our spending levels with the Soviets continuing theirs, as they are now. If that happens, they will achieve superiority. If the whole debate stimulates the United States to adopt strategic programs and overall military posture is substantially enhanced, then it will have served a good purpose, whether the treaty is ratified or rejected.[78]

To Nunn, the most important question was not the effect of the treaty on arms control, but rather the effect of the treaty on U.S. defense programs.

Following the signing of the treaty, Nunn led the effort to pressure the Carter administration to increase the defense budget in exchange for supporting the SALT II Treaty. The administration was committed to a 3 percent increase, but Nunn wanted an increase of 5 percent. In early September, Nunn criticized the administration's approach: "Voltaire once said of the Holy Roman Empire that it was neither holy, Roman, nor an empire. As of July 1979, the administration's 3 percent real growth was neither 3 percent, nor real, nor growth."[79]

President Carter recognized the key role that Nunn played in the SALT II debate:

> Sam was one of the senators who took the position that a SALT II Treaty was beneficial to our country, that it was a balanced treaty, and I was able to confide in Sam about the ultra-secret verification capabilities we had in nations around the Soviet Union. These couldn't be revealed to the public and couldn't be revealed to other senators. But Sam used the SALT II Treaty in a legitimate fashion to extract from me promises for a higher level of defense expenditures, and I didn't particularly object to that . . .[80]

THE COMMITTEE HEARINGS

Following President Carter's submission of the SALT II Treaty to the Senate, the treaty was referred to the Senate Foreign Relations Committee which, since its creation in 1816, has had exclusive jurisdiction over treaties. Since the 1960s, a rivalry has existed between the members of the Foreign Relations Committee and the Senate Armed Services Committee. In 1963 the Armed Services Committee held hearings on the Limited Test Ban Treaty. In 1968, Sen. J. William Fulbright, chairman of the Foreign Relations Committee, decided to hold hearings on the anti-ballistic missile system, and this decision antagonized members of the Armed Services Committee who felt that their committee should have exclusive jurisdiction over military weapons systems. Subsequently, the Armed Services Committee held hearings on the Non-Proliferation Treaty in 1969, the SALT I agreements in 1972, and the Panama Canal treaties in 1978. When the SALT II Treaty was submitted to the Senate, the conservative members of the committee, led by Senator Jackson, pressured Chairman Stennis to hold hearings on the treaty.

Founded in 1976 and specifically charged with the responsibility for overseeing intelligence activities of the executive branch, the Senate Intelligence Committee was given the task of assessing the verification procedures of the treaty. In this section the actions of the Senate Foreign Relations, Senate Armed Services, and Senate Intelligence committees will be reviewed.

The Senate Foreign Relations Committee

Because of the responsibility and the prestige of the Senate Foreign Relations Committee, membership on it has been avidly sought. Not only have senators sought positions on the committee, the chairmanship of the committee has traditionally been one of the most important positions in the Senate. The character and the effectiveness of congressional committees is heavily influenced by the person who chairs the committee, and previous chairmen of the Foreign Relations Committee have included some of the most influential members of the Senate, such as Henry Cabot Lodge, William Borah, and J. William Fulbright, who served for fifteen years as chairman. Following Fulbright's defeat in 1974, John Sparkman served as chairman from 1974 to 1978, and most observers considered his leadership of the committee to have been lackluster at best.

Soon after his election to the Senate in 1956, then Senate Majority Leader Lyndon Johnson appointed Frank Church to the Foreign Relations Committee. At the end of 1978, Sparkman retired, and Church, with twenty-two years of experience on the committee, became the chairman.

Superficially, one would have thought that Church and Carter would have similar and complementary views on international affairs, for both were moralists concerning foreign policy. However, Church and Carter had both run in several 1976 Democratic presidential primaries, and harbored some resentment against one another as a result of these contests. According to William Bader: "The White House Staff, the 'Georgia mafiosa' . . . hated Frank Church for political reasons. Church had beat Carter in four out of five primaries."[81] Rosalynn Carter believed that Democratic party liberals, presumably including Frank Church, had launched a movement known as "ABC (Anybody but Carter)" during the last three weeks of the campaign.[82] Despite whatever ill will existed between Carter and Church, Carter indicated a desire to work closely with the Foreign Relations Committee and its chairman by meeting with the members of the committee before his inauguration, an unprecedented action for a president-elect.[83]

Following the 1978 elections, two significant changes took place within the committee itself. First, three conservative Republicans—Jesse Helms, Richard Lugar, and S. I. Hayakawa—joined the committee. The other three Republican members were Jacob Javits (the ranking Republican member), Charles Percy, and Howard Baker. The nine Democratic members of the committee, in descending order of seniority, were Frank Church (chairman), Claiborne Pell, George McGovern, Joseph Biden, Jr., John Glenn, Richard Stone, Paul Sarbanes, Edmund Muskie, and Edward Zorinsky. Senators Biden and Lugar were also members of the Senate Intelligence Committee, which reviewed the verification procedures of the treaty.

The second important change within the committee was the decision to do away with the former bipartisan staff and to create a minority staff appointed by the Republican members. To some extent, the minority staff was supposed to challenge and question the majority staff. As was the case with congressional staff overall, the staff of the Foreign Relations Committee had grown significantly in the late 1960s and 1970s. In 1965, there were nine professional staff members; by 1979 the number had grown to thirty. Both the addition of the three conservative Republican members and the creation of a minority staff heightened partisan division within the committee.

On the same day that President Carter signed the SALT II Treaty, the staff director of the Foreign Relations Committee sent a memorandum to the members of the committee outlining a proposed schedule of the hearings.[84] This proposal called for twenty days of hearings, four days for the committee's markup (rewriting or adding attachments), and a target date of September 25 to submit the committee's report to the Senate. By way of comparison, the committee held seven days of hearings in 1972 during its consideration of the SALT I agreements, and held sixteen days of hearings, two days of markup, and three days of executive session briefings during its consideration of the Panama Canal treaties. As it turned out, the schedule outlined by the staff director could not be kept because of events that were only indirectly related to SALT II.

On July 9, the Foreign Relations Committee began hearings on the treaty. These hearings were held for a total of twenty-seven days from July through October. The public hearing record filled five volumes of 2,266 pages with the testimony of eighty-eight witnesses.[85] In addition, the committee held thirteen executive sessions, and the transcripts of these sessions totaled more than 1,200 pages. Six witnesses testified only in executive session, bringing the total number of witnesses who testified before the committee to ninety-four.[86]

The Senate Armed Services Committee

Opponents of the SALT II Treaty were anxious to have a formal, public forum in which to review and criticize the treaty. Senator Jackson, a member of the Senate Armed Services Committee, convinced the chairman of the committee, John Stennis, to hold hearings on the treaty. In addition to Stennis and Jackson, the other Democratic members of the committee (in descending order of seniority) were Howard Cannon, Harry Byrd, Sam Nunn, John Culver, Gary Hart, Robert Morgan, J. James Exon, and Carl Levin. The Republican members of the committee were John Tower (the ranking minority member), Strom Thurmond, Barry Goldwater, John Warner, Gordon Humphrey, William Cohen, and Roger Jepsen. The committee held hearings on sixteen days, and the testimony of twenty-nine witnesses filled 1,610 pages of four volumes.[87]

Henry Jackson and Richard Perle used the committee as a forum in which to criticize the SALT II Treaty. According to one protreaty public interest–group lobbyist, Perle was "absolutely unstinting in his opposition and his ability to use the [Senate] Armed Services Committee for his purposes."[88] Jackson's and Perle's files contain a number of memoranda concerning their preparations for the hearings. One memo, entitled "An Outline for the SASC Hearings: What We Hope to Establish," notes, "It should be our purpose in the hearings to demonstrate that pivotal administration arguments are not supported by evidence and/or logic, that the treaty is unequal and unverifiable, that it is flawed with loopholes and ambiguities."[89] Another memo reviews the strengths and weaknesses of various Carter administration witnesses.[90] Harold Brown was viewed as "probably the administration's stongest witness." The newly appointed director of the Arms Control and Disarmament Agency, retired general George Seignious, was portrayed as "a weak witness—if he claims that he is only recently involved we help make the point that it is Warnke's treaty." Clearly, Jackson and Perle wanted to characterize the treaty as Warnke's: "Even though retired, Warnke should be called as the principal architect of the treaty."

Both the supporters and the opponents of the treaty worked with the individual witnesses who bolstered their respective cases. Larry Smith, the staff member who was working closely with senators Culver and Hart on the committee, coordinated the questions that the supporters were going to ask administration witnesses.[91] Senator Jackson's office coordinated the testimony of the witnesses opposed to the treaty. A memo of October 1979 from Jackson's office noted:

> Nitze is best speaking from his own experience—in this case as a SALT nego-tiator during the last administration. There are several issues that he wishes to address, including: (1) a comparison of his force ratios . . . with Harold Brown's . . .; (2) the administration's lack of candor in relating the Soviet position on MX deployment; [and] (3) the irrelevance of the 10 RV [reentry vehicle] (fractionation) limit to the survivability of Minuteman.[92]

This memo also noted: "Ed [Rowny] wants a chance at least to paraphrase the assessments he made for the JCS and their views as expressed in the memo-randa they refuse to turn over. I will prepare a couple of questions that will give him an opportunity to lay that out."[93] The Armed Services Committee's hearings on the treaty provided the forum for opponents to express their criticisms publicly.

The Senate Intelligence Committee

The Senate Intelligence Committee was created to oversee executive branch intelligence operations and to consider matters related to the intelli-gence capabilities of the United States. Consequently, the Senate Foreign Relations Committee requested that the Intelligence Committee review the verification issues related to the SALT II Treaty. The request was made for three specific reasons: (1) the issues involved were of a highly sensitive nature; (2) verification was clearly going to be a significant issue in the debate over SALT, and it therefore deserved the most thorough and profes-sional treatment; and (3) the Intelligence Committee was set up to deal with these issues.[94]

Several members of the Intelligence Committee were also members of either the Foreign Relations Committee (Biden and Lugar) or the Armed Services Committee (Jackson). According to William Miller, the staff direc-tor of the Intelligence Committee in 1979: "About one-third of the Senate reviewed the material collected by the Intelligence Committee, and nine or ten of these considered it very closely . . . . Senator [Robert] Byrd was one of those who was rigorous in reviewing the material."[95] The question of verifica-tion became an important one in the debate over SALT II, and the Senate Intelligence Committee played an important role in addressing this issue. On October 5, the committee issued its unclassified report consisting of five pages.[96]

THE SENATE'S ACTION ON THE TREATY

After the president submits a treaty to the Senate for its advice and consent, it is referred to the relevant committees, which hold hearings and issue a report. The full Senate may act on the treaty in several different ways. First, the Senate may advise and consent to the ratification of a treaty as it is submitted without proposing any changes. Second, it may reject a treaty. Third, the Senate may attach specific stipulations in its resolution of ratification.

The Senate may attach several different types of conditions, including amendments, reservations, understandings, and declarations.[97] An amendment changes the actual text of the treaty and therefore the "terms of the contract" between or among the signatories. Therefore, a treaty that is amended by the Senate would have to be resubmitted to the president and the other parties to the treaty.

A reservation is "a limitation, qualification, or contradiction of the obligations in the treaty, especially as they relate to the party making the reservation."[98] A reservation may have such a significant effect on the terms of a treaty that the president would have to notify the other signatories, who, in turn, could file a reservation of their own or refuse to proceed with the treaty. During the hearings on the SALT II Treaty, there was some question as to the legal status of reservations. In his testimony to the Foreign Relations Committee, Eugene V. Rostow argued that "a reservation has the same legal effect as a letter from my mother."[99] To remove any doubts about the legal status of reservations, the committee drafted the resolution of ratification to require that the Soviet Union explicitly accept all reservations adopted by the U.S. Senate.

Understandings or interpretations may be part of the resolution of ratification in order to explain, elaborate, or clarify certain aspects of the treaty. If an interpretation does not affect the terms of the treaty, then it has no legal effect; however, the president informs the other negotiating parties of any such interpretations. These understandings are commonly used to clarify the meanings of treaties. Similar to sense of the Senate resolutions, declarations are "statements of the Senate's position, opinion or intentions on matters relating to issues raised by the treaty in question, but not to its specific provisions."[100]

A number of different amendments to the SALT II Treaty were considered by the Senate Foreign Relations Committee. The opponents of the treaty drafted amendments that were designed to make the treaty unacceptable to the Soviet Union. A number of these so-called killer amendments were presented by conservative senators. Other amendments were presented for other reasons. Senator Garn recalled: "I didn't expect any of my amendments to be accepted in the Senate. . . . I wanted to use them as an educational process rather than expecting them to be accepted."[101]

The Foreign Relations Committee concluded its hearings and began its markup sessions on the treaty on October 15. The committee held sixteen public sessions and six executive sessions during markup and considered thirty-six conditions to the SALT II Treaty. The committee divided these conditions into three categories. Category I conditions were those that did not require formal notification to the Soviet Union.[102] Category II provisions were those that "would be formally communicated to the Soviet Union as official statements of the position of the United States Government in ratifying the Treaty, but which do not require their agreement."[103] Category III provisions were those that would require the explicit agreement of the Soviet government in order for the treaty to enter into force.

Twenty-three of the thirty-six proposed conditions were adopted; of these, thirteen were Category I conditions, five were Category II conditions, and two were Category III conditions. Clearly, the latter were the most important conditions since they required the explicit approval of the Soviet Union. The first of these conditions was a reservation adopted by the committee by a vote of fourteen to zero which stipulated that the agreed statements and common understandings contained in the SALT II Treaty and protocol would be of the same legal status as the treaty. The second Category III condition adopted by the committee was a reservation that the letter given by General Secretary Brezhnev to President Carter concerning the capabilities and production of the Backfire bomber would be legally binding on the Soviet Union.

On October 5, 1979, the Senate Intelligence Committee issued a unanimous report that concluded, "Overall, the Committee finds that the SALT II Treaty enhances the ability of the United States to monitor those components of Soviet strategic weapons forces which are subject to the limitations of the Treaty."[104] Considering the fact that the Intelligence Committee included such hard-line members as Henry Jackson, Jake Garn, Richard Lugar (who voted against the treaty in the Foreign Relations Committee), and Malcolm Wallop, the unanimous approval of the Intelligence Committee's report significantly strengthened the claim of the Carter administration that the treaty was adequately verifiable.

On November 9, 1979, after four months of hearings and what Foreign Relations Committee members characterized as one of the most exhaustive examinations of any treaty ever to be submitted to the U.S. Senate, that committee, by a vote of nine to six, voted to recommend the ratification of the treaty to the full Senate. Seven Democrats (Church, McGovern, Biden, Sarbanes, Muskie, Pell, and Zorinsky) and two Republicans (Percy and Javits) voted for the treaty. Two Democrats (Glenn and Stone) and four Republicans (Helms, Hayakawa, Baker, and Lugar) voted against it.

On December 17, 1979, nineteen undecided senators sent President Carter a letter in which they raised a number of concerns over certain provisions of the SALT II Treaty including those concerning heavy missiles, limitations on the basing modes of the MX, and the exclusion in the treaty itself of restrictions concerning the Soviet Backfire bomber. [105] In addition, the senators expressed their concern over the "precedential effect" of the three-year protocol to the treaty and its limitations on cruise missiles. This letter raised some serious issues and, importantly, indicated the nineteen senators who were undecided as of mid-December.

Three days later over the objections of Chairman Stennis, the Senate Armed Services Committee adopted a report denouncing the treaty as "not in the national security interests of the United States." According to reports, Henry Jackson and Richard Perle were the principal authors of the report. [106] The report specifically cited the following areas of concern: (1) certain inequalities such as the Soviet advantage in throw weight, the Soviet possession of modern, large ballistic missiles, the exclusion of the Soviet Backfire bomber, the inclusion of Western theater nuclear forces, and the potential precedents established by the protocol to the treaty; (2) loopholes concerning new types of ICBMs; (3) the verification of the treaty; and (4) ambiguities contained in the treaty. [107]

Ten senators voted in favor of releasing the report and seven senators voted "present," in effect indicating their opposition to the release of the report. [108] Although the report was released in December 1979, Majority Leader Byrd did not allow it to be filed officially with the clerk of the Senate until a year later. One Senate aide noted, "People in the White House were absolutely crushed by the vote in the Senate Armed Services Commitee," and in an interview, Anne Wexler confirmed that those in the White House viewed this vote as a major setback. [109]

Interestingly, Sam Nunn voted with six other members who were opposed to the committee's release of the report. By that time, although he never made a formal commitment on SALT II, Nunn was reportedly leaning toward supporting the ratification of the treaty. [110]

Estimates vary as to the effect of the Senate hearings on the fate of the SALT II Treaty. In retrospect, Perle remarked, "The treaty was dead after the hearings." [111] Larry Smith estimated that after the hearings the full Senate vote stood at fifty-seven in favor of the treaty, twenty-seven opposed, and sixteen undecided. Senator Cranston, known as one of the best vote counters in the Senate, estimated that shortly before the treaty was signed, the tally stood at twenty firmly against, ten leaning against, forty leaning heavily toward ratification, ten leaning slightly toward ratification, and twenty undecided.[112]

CONCLUSION

Jimmy Carter, Hamilton Jordan, Jody Powell, Gerald Rafshoon, and Carter's other advisers from Georgia were very good at running elections, as Carter's nearly miraculous election in 1976 showed. During the presidential campaign and once in office, the members of the new administration prided themselves on being Washington "outsiders." In the aftermath of Vietnam and Watergate, the American public viewed not being from Washington as a virtue. Seen from another angle, however, not being from Washington meant that the administration had no experience in the arcane and often parochial ways of Washington. Initially, the members of the Carter administration believed that they could operate the way they wanted to, without regard to what they considered the stuffiness and pretension of official Washington.

The Carter administration had some early successes in dealing with the Congress, not so much because of the administration's adept dealing with Congress, but rather because the administration went around Congress and appealed to the American people. In the debate over the Panama Canal treaties, the members of the Carter administration did what they did best: in essence, they ran a political campaign to get the treaties ratified. Influential citizens from key states were invited to attend briefings and encouraged to contact their senators to vote for the treaties.

Buoyed by their success with the Panama Canal treaties, the members of the administration decided to adopt the same approach once the SALT II Treaty was signed. But the domestic and international contexts were quite different in 1979 than earlier. The administration had used a great deal of its political capital by 1979, and this capital had not been replenished. Indeed, the minor slights and personality conflicts between administration officials and members of Congress had exacerbated relations between the White House and Capitol Hill. In addition, Jimmy Carter and two of his principal foreign policy officials, Cyrus Vance and Harold Brown, were not inclined toward, nor did they enjoy, meeting informally with members of Congress.

The Carter administration did not formally begin its campaign to ratify the SALT II Treaty until it was signed in June 1979, but the treaty opponents had been working for several years against the treaty. A political campaign takes time, money, and personnel to run. The members of the administration could devote their attention and the resources of the executive branch to the ratification of the treaty, but there were many other issues that demanded their attention. And there were legal restrictions against the use of federal funds to lobby for a particular program such as the SALT II Treaty.

At the time that President Carter signed the treaty and submitted it to the Senate for its advice and consent, it appeared that public opinion favored the treaty and the Senate opposed it, just the opposite of the case with the Panama Canal treaties. Despite this fact, the administration adopted a ratification strategy based on the Panama Canal treaties model. As three Senate commit-tees conducted hearings on the treaty during the summer of 1979, at the other end of Pennsylvania Avenue the White House sought to win public support for the treaty.

On Capitol Hill, a group of protreaty Senators led by Alan Cranston, John Culver, Gary Hart, and Joseph Biden and staff members Larry Smith, Charles Stevenson, and Jan Kalicki sought to increase support for the treaty. The antitreaty senators were led by Henry Jackson, Jake Garn, Jesse Helms, and John Tower and staff members Richard Perle, John Carbaugh, and James Lucier. Both sides sought to use the hearings as a forum in which to prove their respective cases. Because this treaty concerned defense issues, rather than simply foreign policy issues, the Senate Armed Services Committee's hearings and critical report were significant. In other cases in which the Foreign Relations Committee and the Armed Services Committee had held differing views, the report of the former was often given greater weight because other treaties dealt primarily with foreign policy rather than defense issues.

On the assumption that the same factors would apply, by the end of the summer, it appeared that the treaty proponents had won the battle. In its lead editorial of August 20, 1979, the *Los Angeles Times* predicted that "it appears probable that the agreement will be ratified by the Senate."[113] Politi-cally conservative publications such as *Business Week* supported ratifica-tion.[114] If the Senate had voted on SALT II in middle to late August, the treaty would have been ratified. But such a vote was not taken because the Senate Foreign Relations Committee had not completed its hearings and report on the treaty.

NOTES

1. Jimmy Carter, interview with Michael Charlton, *From Deterrence to Defense: The Inside Story of Strategic Policy* (Cambridge: Harvard University Press, 1987), 72.

2. Howard Baker, "Press Conference on SALT II," unpublished transcript, June 27, 1979.

3. John Glenn, "SALT: A Congressional Perspective," unpublished press release, May 17, 1979, 1.

4. Michael Foley, *The New Senate: Liberal Influence on a Conservative Institution, 1959–1972* (New Haven: Yale University Press, 1980).

5. I. M. Destler, "Congress," in Joseph S. Nye, Jr., ed., *The Making of America's Soviet Policy* (New Haven: Yale University Press, 1984), 54.

6. Joshua Muravchik, "The Senate and National Security: A New Mood," in David M. Abshire and Ralph N. Nurnberger, eds., *The Growing Power of Congress* (Beverly Hills: Sage Publications, 1981), 251–52.

7. Ibid., 200–1.

8. Thomas P. O'Neill, Jr., with William Novak, *Man of the the House: The Life and Political Memoirs of Speaker Tip O'Neill* (New York: Random House, 1987), 310–11.

9. Ibid., 308.

10. Jimmy Carter, quoted in Robert Shogan, *Promises to Keep: Carter's First Hundred Days* (New York: Crowell, 1977), 207.

11. Jimmy Carter, *Keeping Faith: Memoirs of a President* (New York: Bantam Books, 1982), 65.

12. Charles O. Jones, *The Trusteeship Presidency: Jimmy Carter and the United States Congress* (Baton Rouge: Louisiana State University Press, 1988), 96.

13. Memo from Madeleine Albright to Zbigniew Brzezinski, "Overview of 95th Congress," October 20, 1978, in "FG 6–1–1/Aaron, David: 1/20/77–12/31/79," Box FG–23, WHCF–Subject File, Federal Government–Organizations, Jimmy Carter Library.

14. Carter, *Keeping Faith,* 108.

15. This was also the view of those congressional staffers interviewed by Eric L. Davis, "Legislative Liaison in the Carter Administration," *Political Science Quarterly* 94, no. 2 (Summer 1979): 292.

16. Larry Smith, interview with author, Washington, DC, October 20, 1987, and Alan Platt, interview with author, Washington, DC, October 23, 1987.

17. Sen. William Proxmire, interview with author, Washington, DC, June 4, 1987.

18. Davis, "Legislative Liaison in the Carter Administration," 290–92.

19. William Bader, "Congress and the Making of U.S. Security Policies," *Adelphi Paper* 173 (Spring 1982): 18.

20. William Perry, interview with author, Menlo Park, Calif., January 15, 1988.

21. Alan Platt, *The U.S. Senate and Strategic Arms Policy, 1969–1977* (Boulder, Colo.: Westview Press, 1978).

22. Letter from Paul Warnke to Vice President Mondale, May 7, 1977, in Henry M. Jackson Papers, Accession no. 3560–6, Box 61, Folder 12, University of Washington Libraries.

23. Ralph Earle II, interview with author, Washington, DC, October 23, 1987.

24. Muravchik, "The Senate and National Security," 1.

25. John F. Bibby, Thomas E. Mann, and Norman J. Ornstein, *Vital Statistics on Congress 1980* (Washington: American Enterprise Institute, 1980), 71–73; Jones, *The Trusteeship Presidency,* 62–63.

26. Charles O. Jones, *The United States Congress: People, Place, and Policy* (Homewood, Ill.: Dorsey Press, 1982), 58.

27. See, for example, Mark M. Lowenthal, *SALT Verification,* report no. 78–142F (Washington: Library of Congress, Congressional Research Service, July 1978), and Harry L. Wrenn, *SALT II: Major Policy Issues,* issue brief no. IB79074 (Washington: Library of Congress, Congressional Research Service, July 1979).

28. U.S. Congress, Congressional Budget Office, *SALT II and the Costs of Modernizing U.S. Strategic Forces* (Washington: Government Printing Office, September 1979).

29. Bibby, Mann, and Ornstein, *Vital Statistics on Congress,* 74.

30. William Bader, interview with author, Arlington, Va., October 20, 1987.

31. Strobe Talbott, *Endgame: The Inside Story of SALT II* (New York: Harper and Row, 1979), 215–16.

32. James McGregor Burns, "Jimmy Carter's Strategy for 1980," *Atlantic Monthly,* March 1979, 41–46.

33. Richard Burt, "Carter Will Submit Treaty on Missiles," *New York Times,* January 15, 1979.

34. Unidentified Senate aide, quoted in Rudy Abramson, "GOP Liberals, Moderates Hold Fate of Arms Pact," *Los Angeles Times,* May 11, 1979.

35. Richard Perle, "The Senator and American Arms Control Policy," in Dorothy Fosdick, ed., *Staying the Course: Henry M. Jackson and National Security* (Seattle: University of Washington Press, 1987), 194–95.

36. John Newhouse, *War and Peace in the Nuclear Age* (New York: Alfred A. Knopf, 1989), 259.

37. Rowland Evans quoted by Harrison W. Fox, Jr., and Susan Webb Hammond, *Congressional Staffs: The Invisible Force in American Lawmaking* (New York: The Free Press, 1977), vii.

38. Dorothy Fosdick's father was Harry Emerson Fosdick, one of the most respected Protestant preachers of the twentieth century and a prominent pacifist. Given Senator Jackson's hardline positions on foreign and defense policy, it was more than a little ironic that Fosdick's daughter was his principal adviser during his Senate career.

39. Henry Kissinger, interview with Michael Charlton, *From Deterrence to Defense,* 43 (emphsis in original).

40. Jimmy Carter, telephone interview with author, April 12, 1988, transcript, 2.

41. Author's confidential interview.

42. Alan Platt, interview with author, Washington, DC, October 23, 1987.

43. Perle denies that he wanted a position in the Carter administration, but other sources indicated that he wanted to go into the executive branch; Alan Platt and Barry Blechman, interviews with author, Washington, DC, October 23, 1987; Richard Perle, telephone interview with author, November 10, 1988.

44. Nancy Ramsey, interview with author, Washington, DC, June 5, 1987.

45. Muravchik, "The Senate and National Security," 255.

46. "List of Staff Available for Work on SALT," in Henry M. Jackson Papers, Accession no. 3560–6, Box 61, Folder 12, University of Washington Libraries.

47. Jody Powell, *The Other Side of the Story* (New York: William Morrow and Company, 1984), 252–62.

48. "Statement by Senator Henry M. Jackson," press release, May 9, 1979, in Henry M. Jackson Papers, Accession no. 3560–6, Box 13, Folder 15, University of Washington Libraries.

49. Larry Smith, interview with author,.

50. Ibid.; Alan Cranston, interview with author, Washington, DC, June 5, 1987; John Culver, interview with author, Washington, DC, July 12, 1988.

51. Alan Cranston, interview with author. The members of the group were senators Cranston (chairman), Dale Bumpers, John Chafee, Frank Church, John Culver, John Durkin, John Glenn, Gary Hart, Daniel Inouye, Edward Kennedy, Patrick Leahy, Carl Levin, Charles Mathias, Robert Morgan, Edmund Muskie, Claiborne Pell, William Proxmire, David Pryor, James Sasser, Robert Stafford, and Paul Tsongas.

52. William Bader, interview with author.

53. The participants in the Dole group were senators William Armstrong, Henry Bellmon, Pete Domenici, Gordon Humphrey, Roger Jepson, Harrison Schmitt, Richard Schweiker, Alan Simpson, Strom Thurmond, Malcolm Wallop, and John Warner. The Roth group included senators Henry Bellmon, Rudy Boschwitz, Lawton Chiles, Dennis DeConcini, Walter Huddleston, John Melcher, Larry Pressler, James Sasser, and Alan Simpson.

54. Tab 1 of Memo from Matthew Nimetz to David Aaron, January 18, 1978, WHCF–Subject File, FO 6–1, Jimmy Carter Library.

55. Letter from George McGovern, Mark Hatfield, and William Proxmire to President Carter, March 2, 1979, reprinted in the *Congressional Record–Senate*, March 5, 1979, S 2044.

56. Richard Burt, "Liberal Senators Say Arms Pact Would Not Curb Weapons Race," *New York Times*, March 5, 1979.

57. Mark O. Hatfield, interview with author, Washington, DC, June 4, 1987.

58. Ronald Tammen, interview with author, Washington, DC, June 4, 1987.

59. Anne Wexler, interview with author, Washington, DC, October 28, 1988.

60. Mark Hatfield and William Proxmire, interviews with author, Washington, DC, June 4, 1987.

61. Ralph Earle II, interview with author, Washington, DC, October 23, 1987. In July, the Friends Committee on National Legislation estimated that twenty-nine were likely to vote for the treaty, thirteen were leaning toward support, twenty-eight were undecided, sixteen were leaning against, and fourteen were definitely against the treaty. *FCNL Washington Newsletter*, July 1979, 8.

62. William Perry, interview with author, Menlo Park, Calif., January 15, 1988.

63. "Baker: Senate Undecided on SALT II," *Washington Post*, January 15, 1979.

64. Comments on "Meet the Press," January 14, 1979, quoted in Destler, "Trade Consensus, SALT Stalemate: Congress and Foreign Policy in the 1970s," in Thomas E. Mann and Norman J. Ornstein, eds., *The New Congress* (Washington, DC: American Enterprise Institute for Public Policy Research, 1981), 345.

65. Steven V. Roberts, "Baker Is Inclining against Arms Pact," *New York Times*, April 12, 1979.

66. "Speech by Senator Howard Baker to the National Press Club," June 6, 1979, unpublished transcript, 3.

67. "Statement by Senate Republican Leader Howard Baker on the SALT II Treaty," June 27, 1979, unpublished transcript, 2.

68. Paul Warnke, interview with author, Los Angeles, May 20, 1987.

69. Howard Baker, *No Margin for Error: America in the Eighties* (New York: Times Books, 1980), 192.

70. Letter from President Carter to Sam Nunn, February 14, 1977, "Executive, FG 264,

1/1/78–12/31/78," Box FG–209, WHCF–Subject File, Federal Government–Organizations, Jimmy Carter Library.

71. Eugene V. Rostow, interview with author, Washington, DC, October 28, 1988.

72. Albert R. Hunt, "In the SALT Debate, Senator Sam Nunn's Role Could Prove Decisive," *Wall Street Journal*, March 22, 1979.

73. Memo from Frank Moore and Zbigniew Brzezinski to President Carter, January 23, 1979, WHCF, Foreign Affairs, Executive, FO 6–1, 11/21/78–2/10/79, Jimmy Carter Library.

74. Memo from Madeleine Albright to Zbigniew Brzezinski, July 30, 1979, "Executive, FO 6–1 (7/13/79–7/31/79)," Box FO–42, WHCF–Subject File, Foreign Affairs, Jimmy Carter Library.

75. Unidentified senator, quoted in Phil Gailey, "Nunn May Be Key in Senate's SALT Debate," *Washington Star*, April 27, 1979.

76. Ibid.

77. Sam Nunn, "SALT II," unpublished speech delivered to the Air Force Association, Warner Robins, Georgia, July 17, 1978, 1.

78. "Three Senate Experts Discuss the Pros and Cons of SALT II," *New York Times*, July 8, 1979.

79. Sam Nunn, "SALT II and Defense Spending," *Congressional Record–Senate*, September 7, 1979, S 12167.

80. Jimmy Carter, telephone interview with author, transcript, 3.

81. William Bader, interview with author.

82. Rosalynn Carter, *First Lady from Plains* (Boston: Houghton Mifflin, 1984), 132.

83. U.S. Congress, Senate, Foreign Relations Committee, *Meeting with President-Elect Carter*, 94th Cong., transition period, November 23, 1976.

84. Memo from William Bader to the Members of the Senate Committee on Foreign Relations, June 18, 1979, in Henry M. Jackson Papers, Accession no. 3560–6, Box 49, Folder 26, University of Washington Libraries.

85. U.S. Congress, Senate, Committee on Foreign Relations, *The SALT II Treaty*, hearings, 5 parts, 96th Cong., 1st sess., 1979.

86. U.S. Congress, Senate, Committee on Foreign Relations, *The SALT II Treaty*, report no. 96–14, November 19, 1979, 96th Cong., 1st sess., 52.

87. U.S. Congress, Senate, Committee on Armed Services, *Military Implications of the Treaty on the Limitation of Strategic Offensive Arms and Protocol Thereto (SALT II Treaty)*, hearings, 4 parts, 96th Cong., 1st sess., 1979.

88. Nancy Ramsey, interview with author.

89. Office of Senator Henry M. Jackson, "An Outline for SASC Hearings: What We Hope to Establish," n.d., in Henry M. Jackson Papers, Accession no. 3560–6, Box 61, Folder 12, University of Washington Libraries.

90. Office of Senator Henry M. Jackson, "SALT Hearings Witness List," n.d., in Henry M. Jackson Papers, Accession no. 3560–6, Box 61, Folder 12, University of Washington Libraries.

91. Larry Smith, interview with author.

92. Office of Senator Henry M. Jackson, "Memorandum on Nitze and Rowny Hearings,

October, 1979," n.d., in Henry M. Jackson Papers, Accession no. 3560–6, Box 61, Folder 12, University of Washington Libraries.

93. Ibid.

94. William Miller, interview with author, Washington, DC, October 21, 1987.

95. Ibid.

96. U.S. Congress, Senate, Select Committee on Intelligence, *Principal Findings on the Capabilities of the United States to Monitor the SALT II Treaty*, report, 96th Cong., 1st sess., October 5, 1979.

97. Senate Foreign Relations Committee Report, 34.

98. Ibid.

99. Testimony by Eugene Rostow, Senate Foreign Relations Hearings, pt. 2:393; also see pt. 4:13–14.

100. U.S. Congress, Library of Congress, Congressional Research Service, *Treaties and Other International Agreements: The Role of the United States Senate* (Washington: Government Printing Office, 1984), 109–11.

101. Sen. Jake Garn, interview with author, Washington, DC, June 3, 1987.

102. Senate Foreign Relations Committee Report, 18.

103. Ibid.

104. Senate Select Committee on Intelligence Report, 5.

105. Letter from Sam Nunn, Lawton Chiles, John Danforth, Harrison Schmitt, Edward Zorinsky, David Boren, Lloyd Bentsen, James Exxon, Dennis DeConcini, Alan Simpson, John Warner, Henry Bellmon, Rudy Boschwitz, Pete Domenici, John Heinz, Richard Stone, S. I. Hayakawa, Larry Pressler, and David Durenberger to Jimmy Carter, December 17, 1979.

106. Destler, "Congress," 52.

107. Senate Armed Services Committee Report, 16–17.

108. Rudy Abramson, "Divided Senate Panel Attacks Arms Pact," *Los Angeles Times*, December 21, 1979.

109. Ronald Tammen, interview with author, Washington, DC, June 4, 1987, and Anne Wexler, interview with author, Washington, DC, October 28, 1988.

110. *Congressional Quarterly, Weekly Report*, December 15, 1979.

111. Richard Perle, telephone interview with author.

112. Abramson, "GOP Liberals, Moderates Hold Fate of Arms Pact."

113. "The Shadow of Soviet Might," *Los Angeles Times*, August 20, 1979.

114. *Business Week*, August 13, 1979, 100.

CHAPTER SEVEN

The Domestic Implications of International Events

By the middle of August 1979, Carter administration officials were very confident that they had presented a persuasive case for the SALT II Treaty to the American people and the Senate. They were so confident, in fact, that most of the principal members of the administration went out of town on vacation. One senior National Security Council official who remained in Washington spent much of his time during the latter part of August requesting copies of cartoons that various cartoonists had drawn concerning SALT II.

At the end of August, the vacations of senior members of the administration were interrupted with disturbing news: U.S. intelligence agencies had discovered a Soviet military unit in Cuba that was labeled a "combat brigade." The discovery of the brigade and the handling of this issue by the administration and several prominent senators greatly influenced the debate over SALT II. Although floor debate on the treaty was originally scheduled to begin in early October, the controversy created by the discovery of the brigade delayed floor debate until November.

Then, in early November, a group of Iranian so-called students seized control of the U.S. embassy in Tehran and took sixty-six Americans hostage. While not directly related to the SALT II debate, this action raised questions in the minds of the public and members of the Senate about the verification of the SALT II Treaty and the overall competence of the Carter administration in the foreign policy area. Concerned about the growth and the militancy of Islamic fundamentalism, the Soviet Union invaded Afghanistan on December 25, 1979, an action that sealed the formal fate of the SALT II Treaty.

In this chapter, I will review the relationship between domestic and international politics and the development of these three external events—the Soviet combat brigade in Cuba, the Iranian hostage crisis, and the Soviet invasion of Afghanistan—as they related to the SALT II ratification debate.

DOMESTIC AND INTERNATIONAL POLITICS

The domestic politics of many nations have little or no effect on international politics; however, given the size and power of the United States, its domestic politics often affect global politics. For example, the election of Richard Nixon as president in 1968 had a substantial effect on international relations. Of course, the causal relationship can be reversed; that is, international events can have significant effects on the domestic politics of states, including, despite its size and power, the United States. The Arab-Israeli War of October 1973 and the subsequent Arab oil boycott had significant domestic implications for the United States, including increased oil and gasoline prices, higher inflation rates, increased fertilizer prices, the stimulation of the search for oil deposits within the United States, and the development of alternatives to petroleum and synthetic petroleum-based products.

Once important international events occur, they may quickly fade from view or they may grow in importance. The longevity of any such issue depends on its perceived importance to domestic political interests within the United States, including public opinion, interest groups, the Congress, and factions within the executive branch.

Domestic and international issues may either be linked to one another or not. There are several types of linkage. Some issues are inherently linked because of their natural relation to one another. For example, oil prices within the United States and the actions of OPEC are inherently linked. Policymakers may link two or more diverse issues for their own purposes. For example, Nixon and Kissinger linked progress in the SALT negotiations with the USSR to the Soviet Union's actions in the Vietnam War.[1] Of course, the use of linkage is not limited to members of the executive branch, as Sen. Henry Jackson and Rep. Charles Vanik demonstrated when they explicitly linked most favored nation treatment with free emigration in their amendment to the 1974 Trade Reform Act.

During the Carter administration, the issue of linkage became one of the most serious differences between Zbigniew Brzezinski and Cyrus Vance. President Carter recognized that "Brzezinski was much more inclined to want to link the arms control efforts with the inevitable competition between us and the Soviets on extending influence."[2] Vance recalled that Brzezinski

> was more concerned with sending signals to the Soviet Union and being tough than he was with success in arms control. I felt very strongly that continuing the momentum of arms control was essential. It was really of fundamental importance in the overall U.S.-Soviet relationship; arms control and progress thereof or lack of progress was usually reflective of the state of relations between the Soviet Union and the United States.[3]

Brzezinski's approach meant that the SALT II Treaty became hostage to Soviet international behavior, a fact that became quite clear during the fall of 1979. President Carter had neither the background nor the inclination to choose decisively between the views of his national security adviser and those of his secretary of state; consequently, policy drifted.

THE SOVIET COMBAT BRIGADE IN CUBA

Cuba holds a special interest for Americans; it is only ninety miles from the United States, and the two countries had close cultural, economic, and historical ties for many years prior to Fidel Castro's 1959 revolution. When Castro turned to the Soviet Union for help, it was almost as if one of the fifty states had left the fold. Both Republicans and Democrats opposed Castro's new government, and under the Eisenhower administration, plans were begun to attack Cuba and overthrow Castro. These plans culminated in the Bay of Pigs invasion, the single most embarassing foreign policy episode of the Kennedy administration. Eighteen months after this fiasco, the Kennedy administration regained stature as a result of its effective handling of the Cuban missile crisis. As a consequence of the volatile history of U.S.-Cuban relations, all administrations, particularly Democratic ones, have been sensitive about Cuba.

The Bay of Pigs and the Cuban missile crisis are not the only episodes concerning Cuba that have played a role in American foreign policy since the 1960s. In 1969–70, the Soviets built naval facilities at Cienfuegos, and the United States was concerned that the Soviets were building a base for Soviet nuclear submarines. Negotiations between the USSR and the United States resolved this potentially volatile incident.[4] In October 1978, Secretary of Defense Harold Brown alerted President Carter to intelligence information that the USSR was shipping MiG–23 fighter-bombers to Cuba, a development that, Brown pointed out, could have serious domestic political consequences for the administration. Vance discussed the aircraft with Soviet Ambassador Anatoly Dobrynin, and the Soviets gave assurances that these aircraft were not equipped with racks to carry nuclear bombs.[5] This incident undoubtedly sensitized members of the Carter administration to the potential for and dangers of a Cuban crisis.

In the 1970s, Cuban and Soviet forces cooperated in a number of areas of the world to support Marxist factions and governments. In 1974–75, Soviet planes transported Cuban soldiers to Angola to intervene on behalf of Marxists, and in 1977–78 the Soviets airlifted Cubans into the Horn of Africa to defend Ethiopia against a Somali invasion. In response to this latter intervention, Brzezinski advocated a strong countermove—the deployment of an aircraft carrier task force to the area—and the linkage of this action to other issues of U.S.-Soviet relations.[6] Vance, Brown, and the Joint Chiefs of Staff opposed Brzezinski, and the Special Coordinating Committee of the NSC concluded that "there should be no direct linkage between Soviet and Cuban actions in the Horn and bilateral activities involving either country and the United States."[7] Brzezinski believed that the failure of the United States to decisively oppose the Soviets was a serious error and stated on numerous occasions that "SALT lies buried in the sands of Ogaden."[8]

In early 1979, the Soviets and Cubans remained active on the international front. Early in 1979, they assisted the People's Democratic Republic of Yemen in its attack on the Yemen Arab Republic. In addition, there was evidence that Cuba and the Soviet Union were assisting the insurgents in Grenada and El Salvador. To many, including Brzezinski, it looked as if the Soviet Union and Cuba were on the move in the Western Hemisphere and the rest of the world.

In order to assess the intentions, capabilities, and objectives of Soviet and Cuban forces in Cuba and other parts of the world, in March 1979 Col. William Odom, Brzezinski's military assistant, drafted a request to the intelligence community, signed by Brzezinski, to conduct a special review of Soviet and Cuban military forces around the world and particularly of Soviet forces in Cuba.[9] This review, according to former Senate Foreign Relations Committee staff director William Bader, "had to do with Cuban 'out of area' operations in Angola, Ethiopia, and elsewhere."[10] Sen. Richard Stone, one of those who was most concerned about Soviet military activities in Cuba, recalled that Brzezinski and Odom made this request only "after we started pressuring, not on their own. It took pressure to get that stepped-up intelligence."[11]

In April, Brzezinski's staff sent a second request to the heads of other U.S. government intelligence agencies. According to David Aaron, the deputy NSC adviser, Brzezinski and the NSC staff "went around [CIA Director Stansfield] Turner. We didn't trust him. Our attitude was that the CIA did bad work."[12] This comment illustrates the ill will between Brzezinski and Turner, a situation that had existed since the first days of the administration when Brzezinski replaced the president's daily "intelligence briefing" by Admiral Turner with a "national security briefing" by himself. Thereafter, Turner's personal meetings with the president were reduced to one per month.[13]

The SALT II Treaty was signed on June 18, and the Senate debate on the agreement began in earnest soon after this. On July 12, almost a month after the treaty was signed and four months after the Brzezinski-Odom request for an intelligence review, the intelligence community released a coordinated report that a Soviet brigade organization, separate from known Soviet training units, had been in Cuba for several years.[14] However, this report did not refer to the unit as a "combat" brigade.

Five days later, on July 17, Senator Stone raised the issue of a Soviet combat brigade at a Foreign Relations Committee hearing convened to consider the SALT II Treaty.[15] On his way to the hearing, one of his aides told Stone that he had overheard a conversation among several executive branch officials in which they referred to a "Soviet combat brigade." The same morning Stone had met with John Carbaugh, an aide to Sen. Jesse Helms, one of the Senate's irreconcilable opponents to the SALT II Treaty. Carbaugh had heard reports of a Soviet combat unit in Cuba and passed these reports on to both Stone and ABC television.[16] According to Stone: "I had some sources that were giving me some disquieting information about activities going on inside of Cuba. We had hearings going on, and I was in a position to ask some military people questions. . . .The answers I got were not reassuring to me."[17] Specifically, Stone felt that Secretary of Defense Brown and the intelligence officials at the hearing gave "an unequivocal answer but not a flat denial" concerning the presence in Cuba of a Soviet combat brigade.[18] During the course of the heated hearings, Stone indicated that he would pass on his unresolved suspicions to the press.

In response to Stone's threat, Secretary Brown, Sen. Frank Church, and their staff members drafted a statement concerning the Soviet military unit. The statement, issued in the names of Senator Church (the chairman of the Foreign Relations Committee) and Sen. Jacob Javits (the ranking Republican on the committee), said that there was "no evidence of any substantial increase in the size of Soviet military presence in Cuba over the previous several years," and that "our intelligence does not warrant the conclusion that there are any other significant Soviet military forces in Cuba."[19]

On July 18, the *Washington Star* reported, "Sen. Richard Stone, D-Fla., yesterday said Soviet combat troops may be in Cuba in violation of the agreement that ended the Cuban missile crisis in 1962."[20] The next day, ABC diplomatic correspondent Ted Koppel reported that, according to unnamed congressional sources, "a brigade of Soviet troops, possibly as many as 6,000 combat-ready men, has been moved into Cuba within recent weeks."[21] Koppel also noted that the Carter administration denied this report. Members of the administration continued to refer to the Church-Javits statement of July 17 in responding to questions concerning the "combat brigade." Following the *Washington Star* and ABC reports, the brigade story faded from public attention.

By mid-August, it appeared that the SALT II Treaty was emerging from the Senate relatively unscathed, and consequently, members of the administration, legislators, and other government officials departed on their scheduled vacations, leaving a hot, humid Washington to thousands of visiting tourists. President Carter left for a cruise down the Mississippi River on a paddlewheel steamer, the *Delta Queen;* at the end of the month Vice President Mondale and David Aaron left for China; Cyrus Vance went to Martha's Vineyard; Zbigniew Brzezinski went to his vacation home in Vermont; newly appointed White House special counsel Lloyd Cutler, who had been given the responsibility for the SALT ratification effort, went to France for a canal cruise and tour of four-star restaurants; and Senator Church went to Idaho, not to vacation but to campaign since he faced a tough reelection campaign. Soviet Ambassador Anatoly Dobrynin was also out of town visiting his gravely ill mother and father in Moscow. As Deputy Secretary of State Warren Christopher recalled, the Soviet combat brigade episode "occurred during one of those long summer days when the government does not operate at its best."[22]

On August 16, in monitoring the communications between the as yet unidentified Soviet military unit and military command centers in Havana, the National Security Agency heard Soviet military personnel request permission for the Soviet unit to use Cuban military maneuvering areas for exercises. The next day, a U.S. KH–11 satellite took photographs of the Soviet unit, which consisted of an estimated two thousand to three thousand troops equipped with tanks, artillery, and armored personnel carriers. This indicated that the unit was configured for combat and not simply training.[23] On August 22, the CIA's National Foreign Assessment Center issued an intelligence finding that the Soviet military unit was a "combat brigade." This report was published in the *National Intelligence Digest*, a highly classified, closely read report that is circulated among some four hundred senior government officials. CIA Director Turner noted: "Because the subject was sensitive, the CIA took the unusual step of checking with the staff of the National Security Council before publishing. Approval was given."[24] President Carter was informed of the CIA's finding the next day.

One week after the publication of the CIA's report, Clarence Robinson, Jr., the senior military editor of *Aviation Week and Space Technology*, called Richard Baker, a member of Under-Secretary of State David Newsom's staff, and asked him to comment on information that clearly came from the CIA report as published in the *National Intelligence Digest*.[25] Baker was immediately aware of the source of the information and the significance of the call, for he was a member of a working group that had been considering what to do about a possible leak of the August 22 report. Baker told Robinson that he had no comment on the information and called Newsom, who in turn called the secretary of state. According to Newsom:

> Secretary Vance's primary concern was the impact on the SALT agreement, already encountering heavy weather in Congress. His first thought was to reach the Soviets. Given their interest in SALT, he hoped they would find common cause and make such adjustments as necessary to minimize the issue. His second concern was to ensure that key members of Congress knew of and saw the matter in perspective before they read about it in the press.[26]

Newsom was given the responsibility of contacting the Soviets and key members of the Congress about new information concerning the brigade.

Senator Stone and Senator Church

Two senators, both Democrats but from opposite ends of the ideological spectrum, played key roles in the debate over the Soviet combat brigade in Cuba: Richard Stone and Frank Church.

Stone was first elected to the Senate in 1974 as a conservative Democrat. Although he had little background in international relations, Stone was given a seat on the Foreign Relations Committee. Reflecting the interests of his Florida constituents, Stone had two principal concerns in foreign affairs, the Middle East and Cuba. Stone had a number of contacts in the Cuban émigré community in Florida and paid attention to their reports of Soviet military activities in Cuba. He had been particularly concerned about reports in 1978 that the Soviets had delivered MiG–23s to the Cubans. He was also concerned about reports that Soviet naval visits had included nuclear submarines.[27]

Prior to the 1978 debate on the Panama Canal treaties, Stone was highly critical of both the treaties and Panama, to which he publicly referred as a "left-leaning, rickety, tin-horn dictatorship."[28] Subsequently, Stone came to believe that defeat of the treaties would cause major problems for the United States in Latin America that "no amount of military force could suppress."[29] Stone faced a problem with his constituents; namely, he had initially strongly opposed the treaties and then reversed himself. To justify this reversal, Stone wrote to President Carter and asked for a reassurance that the United States would not back down from its military commitments in the Caribbean. President Carter responded, "In particular, it has and will be the policy of the United States to oppose any efforts, direct or indirect, by the Soviet Union to establish military bases in the Western Hemisphere."[30] Thus reassured, Stone voted for the ratification of the Panama Canal treaties, despite a number of conservative groups that sought to pressure him to change his mind.

Following the Panama Canal votes, Stone paid close attention to the reports he received from his constituents and sources within the intelligence community concerning Soviet activities in Cuba. He was up for reelection in 1980 and, given his votes in favor of the Panama Canal treaties, he needed to bolster his support and credibility with conservatives in Florida. Thus, he was the first to raise the issue of the Soviet brigade on July 17 in the Foreign Relations Committee's hearings, and although this issue quickly faded from the headlines, he continued to press the administration for information and stepped-up intelligence on Cuba. On July 19, Stone requested from Vice President Mondale and David Aaron a report on Soviet military forces in Cuba, and on July 24, he wrote to President Carter asking about the Soviet military presence in Cuba. On July 27, Secretary of State Vance, responding to Stone's letter to the president, repeated almost verbatim the statement that senators Church and Javits had released on July 17.[31] Stone immediately rejected Vance's reassurances, labeling his response a "whitewash." For Senator Stone, the Cuban issue was one of both national and his own electoral security.

Frank Church was interested in Cuba both because of his position as chairman of the Senate Foreign Relations Committee and because he was up for reelection. In addition, Cuba was an important symbolic issue to his constituents in Idaho. For Church, the Cuban combat brigade episode of 1979 shared a number of similarities with the Cuban missile crisis of seventeen years before.

Frank Church was first elected to the Senate by Idaho voters in 1956. Idaho was a conservative state and many of his constitutents were uncomfortable with Church's liberal, internationalist ideas. To try to allay these concerns during his 1962 reelection campaign, Church visited the U.S. base at Guantanamo, Cuba, where he received a tour and a briefing. Upon his return to the United States, Church sent a detailed campaign newsletter to his constituents saying that he was fully informed of developments in Cuba and that as a member of the Foreign Relations Committee and as a personal friend of President Kennedy, he would know if there was any military threat to the United States from Cuba. Church concluded that, based on his special knowledge, there was nothing to be concerned about.

This newsletter arrived in his constituents' mailboxes on October 22, 1962, the same day that President Kennedy publicly announced that the Soviets were attempting to clandestinely deploy missiles to Cuba. When Kennedy made his speech, Church was in Idaho campaigning and as soon as Kennedy had finished speaking, Church told his wife, "The campaign is over."[32] However, Church decided he had one possibility of snatching victory from almost sure defeat. He called Attorney General Robert Kennedy and explained his predicament: "I am embarrassed even to be calling you at a time like this. I will understand fully if there is nothing you can do for me, but just today I assured the people of my state that we have nothing to worry about in Cuba. What can I do?"[33] The White House sent an Air Force plane to fly Church back to Washington for consultations with the president. Once he was briefed by the White House staff, he went to a television studio and delivered a live report on the crisis to the people of Idaho. Church had managed to convert a potential disaster for his campaign into an asset, and he went on to win the election.

Following his election to the Senate, Church was assigned a seat on the Foreign Relations Committee and became chairman of the committee in 1978.

Church was prominent within the Democratic party and briefly ran in several of the 1980 presidential primaries. He did well enough to defeat Jimmy Carter in four primaries, which perhaps contributed to the relationship between the two men that Church's son described as "rigidly impersonal and strained."[34] Despite any personal tension between the two men, Church was a staunch supporter of Carter's programs in the Senate. He served as the floor manager for the ratification of the Panama Canal treaties in 1978, and this, coupled with Church's earlier involvement with anti-Vietnam efforts and his chairmanship of a special committee that investigated the CIA, stimulated intense opposition from conservatives. By the summer of 1979, two political campaign committees had been established: the Committee for a Positive Change and the Anybody But Church Committee, which was sponsored by the National Conservative Political Action Committee (NCPAC). Church was concerned that the archconservative Sen. Jesse Helms planned to go to Idaho to campaign against him.[35]

In August 1977, Church and his wife had visited Cuba and spent three days with Fidel Castro. With Castro as their tour guide, they visited cooperative farms and housing projects, and went skin diving. At the end of the visit, Church and Castro held a joint press conference at Havana Airport. Castro called Church an "important, courageous politician" who was "capable, serious and intellectual . . . a man you could talk to."[36] In July 1979, NCPAC widely distributed throughout Idaho a leaflet showing a picture of Church and Castro and containing several of Castro's complimentary comments about Church. Church's opponent, Steven Symms, showed broadcast news clips of Church and Castro driving around Cuba in a Soviet jeep and smoking Cuban cigars. When the Senate recessed in August, Church returned to Idaho, not to relax, but to campaign, perhaps for his political life.

The Brigade Issue Becomes Public
The State Department was concerned that the news of the "Soviet combat brigade" would soon appear in the press, particularly given the call to Under-Secretary Newsom's office by the editor of *Aviation Week and Space Technology* on August 29. There were other factors that influenced the Carter administration to contact members of Congress with the new information concerning the brigade. First, the administration's reputation and standing with the Congress was not good. Executive-congressional relations had not been cordial from the beginning of the administration, and several major errors on the part of the administration had made a bad situation worse. For example, when President Carter decided to formally recognize the People's Republic of China in December 1978, key members of Congress including Howard Baker, Frank Church, John Glenn, Jacob Javits, and Clement Zablocki "were irritated by the lack of

consultation and by the fact that they were called to the White House one hour before the announcement to be informed, not consulted."[37] For members of Congress to find out about the brigade in the newspaper would only worsen executive-congressional relations further.

Second, the State Department had been in communication with Senator Stone and had informed him of the status of the brigade. As Newsom later told a reporter, "We had already informed Senator Stone, but since we had started down the path of Congressional consultation, the broader relationship we have with the Chairman of the Senate Foreign Relations Committee and with some other members of Congress required us to notify a whole set of people."[38] Consequently, on August 29, a group consisting of the secretary of state, Newsom, Marshall Shulman (Vance's principal adviser on Soviet affairs), Robert Berry of the Bureau of European Affairs, Peter Tarnoff (the head of the executive secretariat), and Hodding Carter (the department's press spokesman) drafted a statement that "confirmed the presence in Cuba of what appears to be a Soviet combat brigade."[39]

On August 30, Under-Secretary Newsom telephoned key members of the Congress, including the majority and minority leaders of the Senate and the chairmen and ranking minority members of the House Foreign Affairs Committee and the Senate Foreign Relations Committee. Newsom read the new statement to these men, and none reacted particularly strongly. Newsom then called the two senators who were most directly interested in the Cuban issue at that time. Newsom reached Senator Stone in Florida, and he did not react very strenuously; after all, this was simply a confirmation of what he had been saying publicly for the previous month and a half.

When he reached Church, Newsom recalled, Church "reacted sharply to the information. His first words were, 'That will sink SALT.'"[40] That night at dinner, Church told his staff aide, Peter Fenn, "You won't believe this, but there's a Soviet combat brigade in Cuba, exactly the opposite of what the administration told us thirty days ago."[41] One staff member believed that the circumstances of the 1979 Cuban episode were so similar to those of 1962 that they reawakened "tribal memories" in Church's mind.[42] Unfortunately, Church's foreign policy aides were not with him in Idaho and could not, therefore, offer their advice.

Church called Secretary Vance and told him that the information concerning the brigade should be made public and that if no one else was going to release it, he would. According to Newsom, Vance replied, "We'll trust you to use your judgment on that, Senator."[43] After an unsuccessful attempt to talk with President Carter about the brigade issue, Church called a press conference and announced the administration's confirmation that a Soviet combat brigade was in Cuba. Church also called for the removal of the troops from Cuba. The fact that Church, one of the Senate's most liberal members, called attention to the brigade was newsworthy, and all of the major newspapers and networks reported this story. On Thursday, August 31, the day after Church's press conference, both the State Department and Senator Stone held their own press conferences. Perhaps because of the long Labor Day weekend, public and media reaction was somewhat mild.

Congress reconvened on Tuesday, September 5, and in order to allay congressional concerns and to set the stage for his discussions about the combat brigade with the Soviets, Secretary Vance decided that he should make a statement concerning the Soviet troop issue. In his press conference, Vance noted that the United States "would not be satisfied with the status quo," a statement that President Carter had approved the day before.[44]

On the same day as Vance's press conference, the Senate Foreign Relations Committee called witnesses to testify about the brigade. At these hearings, Vance repeated his statement that the status quo would not be acceptable. He also asserted that the issues of the Soviet troops and SALT II should not be linked, that SALT dealt with "matters of fundamental importance," which were of a higher priority than the "very serious matter" of the Soviet troops. Vance also indicated that Soviet troops had been in Cuba since the 1970s, an assertion that was strongly challenged by President Ford and Henry Kissinger. Ford has stated, "To my very best knowledge, and I double-checked it with the people who were in the NSC when I was there, there was no evidence that it [the brigade] was, or had been, in Cuba during my administration."[45]

Following the testimony by administration witnesses, Senator Church commented, "There is no likelihood whatever that the Senate will ratify the SALT Treaty as long as Soviet combat troops are in Cuba."[46] Senate Minority Leader Howard Baker said that the presence of the brigade was unacceptable and that "SALT cannot be considered in isolation of this reality." Sen. S. I. Hayakawa, a member of the Foreign Relations Committee, commented: "We should immediately suspend further consideration of the ratification of SALT II until after all Soviet combat troops have been withdrawn from Cuba. To fail to draw the line now is to invite greater problems in the future."[47]

Interest in the brigade issue grew to the point that President Carter and his advisers decided that he should deliver a nationally televised address on the subject to clarify the facts and to reassure the public. On the evening of September 7, the president outlined the "facts relating to this issue:" There were two thousand to three thousand Soviet combat troops in Cuba; these troops had been in Cuba "for some time"; and the United States was pursuing this issue with the Soviet Union and consulting with the Congress.[48]

While the president and the secretary of state were attempting to reassure the public and downplay the importance of the brigade, in an interview published in the *Washington Post,* Zbigniew Brzezinski took a far more militant approach. He noted that "the posturing of Cuba as a nonaligned country is fundamentally ridiculous" and that "Castro is a puppet of the Soviet Union and we view him as such." Brzezinski went on to note that the Soviet Union supplied Cuba with "jet fighters, transports, submarines, missile patrol boats, attack helicopters and antisubmarine patrol boats" and that Cuba was converting its military forces "from a primarily defensive role to one capable of offensive operations far from Cuban shores."[49] These remarks were hardly consistent with those of the president and the secretary of state.

The Soviet Response

Because long-time Soviet ambassador to the United States Anatoly Dobrynin was in Moscow when the brigade issue became important, for protocol reasons, Under-Secretary Newsom, rather than Secretary Vance, met with Soviet chargé d'affaires Vladillian Vasev to seek an explanation for the presence of the brigade in Cuba. Vasev questioned the legal basis for the United States' raising the issue and said he would report the U.S. concerns to Moscow. On September 5, Vasev delivered the Soviet government's reply to the issues that Newsom had raised.

On September 9, Dobrynin returned to Washington and met the next day with Secretary Vance. A public version of the earlier Soviet reply was published in *Pravda* on September 10. Referring to the U.S. contention that Soviet combat forces had recently arrived in Cuba as "totally groundless," the article pointed out: "For about 17 years there has been a training center in Cuba, where Soviet military personnel help Cuban servicemen learn about Soviet military technology which is used by the Cuban Army. Neither the number nor the functions of the said Soviet personnel have changed throughout all these years."[50] The article also criticized members of Congress for making "alarm-spreading statements" and noted, "It is not by chance that all this outcry is being used by circles in the U.S. that are trying to prevent ratification of the SALT II treaty and, in any case, to complicate its ratification." This linkage with SALT II became a dominant theme in subsequent Soviet commentaries on the brigade issue.

Over the next several weeks, eight Soviet-American meetings on the subject of the brigade were held: six between Vance and Dobrynin and two between Vance and Soviet Foreign Minister Andrei Gromyko. In addition, there was one exchange on the hotline between President Carter and Chairman Brezhnev and a secret meeting between Senate Majority Leader Robert Byrd and Ambassador Dobrynin. In his discussions, Vance sought to obtain a public Soviet commitment to disband the brigade, to reassign the unit's personnel to training duties, and to distribute the unit's tanks and artillery to the Cubans. But the Soviets were adamant that the brigade had been in Cuba since 1962 and that the crisis over it had been artificially created. In an address to the United Nations General Assembly, Foreign Minister Gromyko stated: "This propaganda [about the Soviet combat brigade] is totally without foundation in reality and is indeed based on falsehoods. The Soviet Union and Cuba have already so declared. And our advice on this score is simple: the artificiality of this entire question must be honestly admitted and the matter closed."[51]

As the discussions between Secretary Vance and Soviet officials were taking place, the *New York Times* quoted Brzezinski as saying that the "Soviet combat brigade in Cuba stems from a Soviet 'pattern of disregard' for American interests" and that the United States might be forced to retaliate if the Soviets did not cooperate in finding a resolution to the crisis.[52] Brzezinski called attention to Soviet and Cuban military activities around the world, activities that he claimed threatened American interests. In an interview with National Public Radio on September 28, Brzezinski compared the brigade crisis to the Berlin crisis of 1961, one of the most serious Soviet-American conflicts of the entire post–World War II period.[53] Unnamed White House sources, whom many assumed to be Brzezinski, indicated that the United States was considering various moves to retaliate against the presence of the brigade, including the sale of weapons to China and a campaign of "interference" by the United States in Eastern Europe. Such actions, if implemented, would be considered by Soviet leaders as serious threats to Soviet vital interests.[54] Clearly, Brzezinski's statements during the Cuban brigade crisis worked at cross-purposes to the discussions that Secretary Vance was having with the Soviets and contributed to the schism between Vance and Brzezinski.

By the end of September, the negotiations between the United States and the Soviet Union had not achieved any meaningful progress, and the president and his advisers decided to do two things: to address the nation and to convene a group of prominent Americans, consisting of sixteen former Republican and Democratic government officials including McGeorge Bundy, Clark Clifford, Henry Kissinger, John McCloy, John McCone, Dean Rusk, and Brent Scowcroft.[55] Some believed that the appointment of such a blue-ribbon panel was inadvisable because it could establish a direct parallel in the minds of the public and members of Congress between the brigade crisis and the Cuban missile crisis when President Kennedy had appointed a similar, ad hoc advisory group. Members of the Carter administration, however, believed that the group was needed. According to Vance: "We were moving in a direction that was unproductive, and we had to cool things down at that point. The group of 'wise men' helped to do that."[56]

Two days after meeting with his blue-ribbon panel, President Carter delivered an address to the nation concerning the brigade issue and the SALT II Treaty. Noting that "this Soviet brigade in Cuba is a serious matter," the president indicated various military, intelligence, and economic measures that the United States was taking in response. He then said: "The greatest danger to American security tonight is certainly not the two to three thousand Soviet troops in Cuba. The greatest danger to all the nations of the world. . .is the breakdown of a common effort to preserve the peace, and the ultimate threat of nuclear war. I renew my call to the Senate of the United States to ratify the SALT II Treaty."[57] He concluded: "Politics and nuclear arsenals do not mix. We must not play politics with the security of the United States. We must not play politics with the survival of the human race. We must not play politics with SALT II. It is much too important for that—too vital to our country, to our allies, and to the cause of peace."[58]

Reactions to the president's speech varied widely. The Soviet news agency TASS commented, "President Carter's speech confirms that he and those around him intend to use the myth which they created themselves as a threat to the United States on the part of the U.S.S.R. and Cuba for further boosting the course toward a step-up of the arms race, militarization of budgets, and the heightening of tension in various parts of the world."[59] Despite this criticism, the dispatch was judged to be relatively mild. The response from American conservatives could hardly be considered mild. Minority Leader Baker commented, "We stood toe-to-toe with the Soviet Union and unlike 1962, we blinked instead of the Russians."[60] Senator Stone called the president's response "inadequate," and Sen. Henry Jackson commented, "The President's response to the discovery of Soviet combat troops in Cuba is inadequate, even by his own previously stated criteria."[61] Majority Leader Byrd, who had followed the SALT II debate very closely and who had met personally with Dobrynin during the discussions over the combat brigade, wrote a detailed, strong defense of the treaty on October 1, the same day as the president's speech. Labeling the entire episode a "pseudo-crisis," Byrd argued that "the Cuban question should not overshadow the SALT II Treaty—a treaty that represents the work of nearly seven years of negotiations by three administrations, Republican and Democratic."[62] Despite the president's and Byrd's pleas, the majority of the Senate apparently agreed with the administration's critics, for on the day after Carter's speech, the Senate adopted a resolution stipulating that the SALT II Treaty could not be ratified until the president assured the Senate that Soviet troops in Cuba were not engaged in a combat role.

The Results of the Soviet Combat Brigade Episode

The furor created over the Soviet combat brigade influenced the SALT II ratification debate in a number of significant ways. First, at least one important senator, Russell Long, came out against ratification of the treaty as a result of the brigade affair.[63] Second, this crisis reversed the momentum of the Carter administration's SALT ratification effort. At the end of August, *New York Times* reporter Richard Burt, who was known to be critical of SALT II, wrote an article entitled "SALT II's Chances Seem Good But SALT III Will Be Tougher."[64] Five weeks later, no one believed that "SALT II's chances were good."

A third result of the brigade episode was to heighten the differences between Secretary of State Vance and NSC adviser Brzezinski. According to Brzezinski, the Soviet combat brigade

> was the only crisis during the Carter Administration that was handled by the State Department. It was a Policy Review Committee meeting, with Vance in the chair, that decided how to handle this, and I decided to let it play out. After it was over, I went and told the President what had happened and why, and he said, 'never again' was it to be handled that way. Carter said that the Special Coordinating Committee [of the NSC] is the crisis organ of the Administration, and that I should be in the chair.[65]

The differences between the two advisers became sharper and culminated in Vance's resignation over the attempted rescue of the American hostages in Iran in April 1980.

Fourth, the debate over the Soviet brigade in Cuba prominently underscored the question of verification. Opponents of the SALT II Treaty asked, "If the United States cannot even keep track of a few thousand Soviet soldiers, how can it possibly keep track of thousands of Soviet missiles?" Supporters of the treaty noted that "the problem of finding a unit of 2,000 to 3,000 Soviet soldiers on a Caribbean island of 10 million people and 190,000 Soviet-equipped Cuban troops was a 'jigsaw puzzle' of excruciating difficulty."[66] In the aftermath of the crisis, the Senate Intelligence Committee conducted a classified study of the Soviet brigade and concluded that intelligence methods for counting numbers of submarines, intercontinental ballistic missiles, and long-range bombers were different from, and in some ways less complicated than, the methods used to count and classify conventional military forces.[67] This report, however, was highly classified and was not completed in time to affect the SALT II ratification debate.

Disclosures in the late 1980s concerning the number of Soviet forces in Cuba since the Cuban missile crisis underscore the difficulty of accurately

keeping track of Soviet conventional forces in Cuba. In 1963 Secretary of
Defense Robert McNamara testified that approximately seventeen thousand
Soviet troops and technicians remained in Cuba.[68] At a 1989 meeting of
American and Soviet policymakers who had participated in the Cuban missile crisis, the Soviets disclosed that, in fact, forty thousand Soviet troops and
advisers remained in Cuba after the crisis.[69] It is not surprising that the
United States could not keep track of a few thousand troops if it was off by
twenty-three thousand in its estimate of Soviets who remained in Cuba
following the missile crisis.

Fifth, the brigade episode resulted in the worsening of U.S.-Soviet relations. The Soviets believed that the crisis had been manufactured in order to
scrap the SALT II Treaty. In mid-September 1979, former U.S. ambassador
Raymond Garthoff told Georgi Arbatov, the director of the Institute for the
Study of the U.S.A. and Canada in Moscow: "This was no devious effort of
the U.S. But even Arbatov could not conceive that this was just an accident
of American politics. Arbatov replied that there were elements within the
Carter Administration who wanted to cause trouble in U.S.-Soviet relations.
Brzezinski and others, he said, wanted to cause this difficulty."[70] Valentin
Berezhkov, former first secretary of the Soviet embassy in Washington, told
an interviewer:

> I think there was a re-evaluation of the Treaty, resulting in the determination
> that it would not be good to go into the election campaign supporting the
> Treaty. The question was how to jettison the Treaty without losing face, and
> putting blame on the U.S.S.R. . . . Senator Church was looking for some-
> thing that would allow him to back out of supporting SALT. Church and
> Carter both jumped at the information of the brigade as a good thing.[71]

A sixth and very important result of the brigade imbroglio was to delay
the Senate's consideration of the SALT II Treaty. The original schedule for
consideration of the treaty called for the hearings to be completed by September 18 and for the Foreign Relations Committee's report to be filed by
September 25.[72] J. Brian Atwood, the assistant secretary of state for congressional affairs, estimated that if the treaty had made it to the floor, debate would have lasted at least a month.[73] Steven Baker, who was Senator
Byrd's principal aide working on SALT II, estimated that floor debate
would have lasted as long as six weeks.[74] Prior to the raising of the brigade
issue, a vote in the Senate on SALT II could have been taken as early as
late October; however, because of the delay caused by the brigade issue, a
vote could not be taken until December at the earliest. As it turned out,
this delay was critical.

The Significance of the Brigade Issue

Virtually everyone saw the Soviet combat brigade crisis as an unmitigated disaster. Deputy Secretary of State Warren Christopher characterized it as "a kind of self-inflicted wound."[75] White House counselor Hedley Donovan watched "the Executive and Congress together create a superfluous crisis, in a world sufficiently dangerous with real problems."[76] White House assistant Anne Wexler saw it as "a screw-up from beginning to end."[77] Both William Perry and Gen. Edward Meyer considered it "a tempest in a teapot,"[78] and a British newspaper described it as "a self-inflicted technical knock-out."[79]

Although there was unanimous agreement that the crisis had been handled badly, there was great disagreement as to who was at fault. The interpretations of who was responsible for the "mangling" (rather than managing)[80] of the Soviet combat brigade episode resembled the plot of the Japanese play *Roshomon*. President Carter believed the brigade crisis "was not a matter of discovery; it was a matter of great distortion on the part of a couple of senators, primarily for political reasons. The most important one was Frank Church."[81] After the crisis was over, Church told his son that "he had erred badly by seizing this issue in the way he had," and he told one of his principal foreign policy advisers that his behavior in this crisis was the "worst political mistake of his career."[82] Brzezinski attributed the failure to the incompetent handling of the crisis by Vance and the State Department and to the moderate approach to the Soviet Union that the department advocated. When asked, in retrospect, what he would have done differently about the Soviet combat brigade, Vance replied, "I would have used a different word than 'unacceptable,' and I certainly would have . . . pressed harder to make sure that I was getting accurate information from the intelligence community."[83] The Soviets saw the episode as a "red herring and [believed] that someone was behind it to embarrass them and sabotage SALT II."[84]

In his assessment of the brigade episode, former Under-Secretary of State David Newsom noted that it "had an impact out of all proportion to the circumstances . . . there certainly was no basis for comparison with the missiles of 1962, the submarines of 1970, or the MiG–23s of 1978."[85] In the end, the brigade played a central role in the failure of the ratification of the SALT II Treaty, but this episode alone did not defeat the treaty. Other external events only tangentially related to SALT II also played a role.

THE IRANIAN HOSTAGE CRISIS

Iran has been a significant factor in American foreign policy on a number of occasions since World War II. In January 1942, Great Britain and the

Soviet Union signed a treaty with Iran in which they promised "to respect the territorial integrity of Iran" and to withdraw their military forces "not later than six months" after hostilities between the Allies and Germany had ceased.[86] At the Tehran conference, Churchill, Roosevelt, and Stalin reaffirmed the desire of the Allies to maintain the independence and territorial integrity of Iran. Despite these agreements, at the end of the war the Soviet Union refused to withdraw its troops from northern Iran and supported separatists who demanded autonomy for Azerbaijan. President Truman demanded that the Soviets keep their wartime promises and withdraw, which they did. This ended one of the first skirmishes of the cold war, but it was not the last significant international incident involving the United States and Iran.

In 1952, a popular Iranian politician, Mohammed Mossadegh, who had devised the nationalization of the Iranian oil industry, challenged the shah's authority. The shah first dismissed him and then was forced to reinstate him as prime minister because of popular pressure. Mossadegh increasingly depended on the Communist Tudeh party, and the United States was fearful that his continued leadership would result in Iran's becoming part of the Soviet bloc. Consequently, the United States and Great Britain devised a plan to overthrow Mossadegh and place the shah back in control.[87] The plan was successful, and the shah was grateful for the American help he received.

Following the successful coup, one of the first visitors to Iran was the American vice president, Richard Nixon. The shah and Nixon got along well, and both leaders wanted a close strategic relationship between the United States and Iran; however, President Eisenhower was not particularly interested in such a relationship. When Nixon emerged from political obscurity to become president in 1969, he was in the position to pursue the objective he and the shah had discussed fifteen years earlier.[88] The need for an American presence in the Persian Gulf region was heightened by the decision of Great Britain in January 1968 to remove its military forces previously stationed east of Suez.

When they came into office, Nixon and his national security adviser, Henry Kissinger, sought to create a tripolar balance of power with the United States, the Soviet Union, and the People's Republic of China as the three dominant powers. In 1972, Nixon visited Beijing in February and Moscow in May. Following his Moscow summit meeting, Nixon flew directly to Tehran where he met with the shah and agreed to increase the number of U.S. military advisers and technicians living in Iran and to allow Iran to purchase essentially whatever American military technology it wanted, short of nuclear weapons. As the shah himself told an interviewer in April 1973, "We are getting anything and everything non-atomic that the U.S. has."[89] American arms transfers to Iran supported the Nixon-Kissinger approach to Persian

Gulf security. According to this approach, Iran and Saudi Arabia were the "twin pillars" of western security in the region. Of course, because of the increasing demand for oil, Saudi Arabia was important; however, in strictly military terms Iran was the more important of the two pillars.

As numerous observers have noted, the shah attempted to develop and modernize his country too quickly. Beneath the veneer of modernization—a technologically advanced military, modern buildings, new social progams— was the bedrock of fundamental Islamic beliefs. However, because most western diplomats and journalists had their contacts within the cosmopolitan elements of Iranian society, the depth and magnitude of the opposition to the shah's programs went largely unnoticed until the eve of the revolution.

The shah was disturbed by the election of Jimmy Carter in 1976 and would have preferred the reelection of Gerald Ford. Carter was an unknown, and his emphasis on human rights and the need to significantly reduce U.S. arms transfers were anathema to the shah. Despite their differences, Carter and the shah met in Washington in November 1977 and in Tehran at the end of December 1977. At the latter meeting, Carter referred to Iran as "an island of stability in one of the more troubled areas of the world," a remark that would come to haunt Carter.[90] Just one week after Carter's visit to Tehran, there was a large demonstration in the religious city of Qom, and police killed a number of students, an event that can be seen in retrospect to have marked the beginning of the revolution that culminated in the departure of the shah in mid-January 1979 and the return of the Ayatollah Khomeini to Iran on February 1, 1979, after more than fourteen years of exile.

Two weeks after the ayatollah's return to Iran, a group of Iranians attacked the American embassy in Tehran. According to the U.S. ambassador, "A murderous barrage of automatic weapon fire opened up on the embassy from all sides."[91] The embassy staff retreated into the interior of the embassy and began to destroy important documents and codes. The group that entered the embassy consisted of both attackers and rescuers. The rescuers were led by Ibrahim Yazdi, the newly appointed foreign minister. With Yazdi's help, the attackers were expelled from the embassy, and Khomeini sent an emissary to apologize for the attack. The actions of the new Iranian government led U.S. officials to believe that Khomeini wanted to maintain normal diplomatic relations with the United States.

In late February, twenty U.S. Air Force employees who manned two intelligence sites in northeastern Iran in order to monitor Soviet missile tests at Tyuratom were taken prisoner by the Iranians. According to President Carter, "after a frightening interval of several days," the hostages were released.[92] The loss of the two "Tacksman" radar sites became an issue in the SALT II ratification debate later in 1979. Sen. John Glenn and others argued that the loss of these sites crippled the American capability to monitor Soviet missile tests. The Carter administration argued that the loss of the two sites reduced but did not eliminate the American capability to monitor Soviet missile tests and that the United States could rely on other means of monitoring Soviet missile tests including flying U–2 spy planes along the Turkish-Soviet border. In addition, Secretary Brown noted that it takes twenty to thirty flight tests to develop a new missile over several years, and that the United States would be able to monitor effectively any Soviet violation of the SALT II missile flight test limitations.[93] Other supporters of the treaty contended that "while the Iranian bases were particularly useful in providing data for monitoring the limitations on new types, such developments can still be satisfactorily verified without them."[94]

When he left Iran in January 1979, the shah indicated that he wanted to come to the United States. President Carter extended the shah an invitation, but when he left Iran, the shah and his entourage accepted Anwar Sadat's invitation to go to Egypt. The shah stayed there for almost two weeks and then accepted King Hassan's invitation to visit Morocco. In February, the shah decided that he wanted to go to the United States, but by that time, President Carter and Secretary Vance had changed their minds about inviting him. The president reasoned: "As long as there is a country where the Shah can live safely and comfortably, it makes no sense to bring him here and destroy whatever slim chance we have of rebuilding a relationship with Iran. It boils down to a choice between the Shah's preferences as to where he lives and the interests of our country."[95] Brzezinski argued that it was not likely that the United States would be able to rebuild a relationship with Iran for some time and "if we turned our backs on the fallen Shah, it would be a signal to the world that the U.S. is a fair-weather friend."[96] When King Hassan let the shah know that it was time for him to move on, he went next to the Bahamas and then to Mexico.

Several prominent Americans attempted to pressure President Carter to allow the shah to come to the United States. In April, Carter wrote in his diary: "David Rockefeller . . . came in to spend some time with me. . . . The main purpose of this visit, apparently, is to try to induce me to let the Shah come into our country. Rockefeller, Kissinger and Brzezinski seem to be adopting this as a joint project."[97] But Carter did not invite the shah, unconvinced that "the Shah or we would be better off with him playing tennis several hours a day in California instead of in Acapulco."[98]

But, at the beginning of October, the president was presented with new information that totally changed the circumstances: the shah was seriously ill. By mid-October, a team of doctors had diagnosed the shah's illness as obstructive jaundice. In addition, he had a cancerous spleen, a cancerous tumor in his neck, and possibly lymphoma. The doctors examining the shah indicated that he needed to be in a large medical center equipped with advanced medical technology. Such a facility was not available in Mexico, and the doctors recommended that he be admitted to the United States for treatment as soon as possible. News of the shah's cancer came as a complete surprise to U.S. government officials; it was, according to Gary Sick of the National Security Council, "without question, one of the best-kept state secrets of all time."[99] In light of these new circumstances, President Carter and all of his advisers unanimously agreed that the shah should be admitted to the United States, and on October 23, the shah flew to New York for medical treatment. The officials of the new Iranian government were also surprised (and skeptical) to learn of the shah's cancer and were displeased that he had been admitted to the United States.

At 10:30 A.M. Tehran time on November 4, 1979, an estimated three thousand Iranians stormed the American embassy. This attack was similar to the attack of nine months earlier but initially appeared more benign since the attackers were not armed. Those in the embassy retreated to the chancery, and in keeping with Department of State standard operating procedures, immediately established telephone contact with the department's operations center in Washington. The assumption was that the government of Iran would handle this crisis the same way that it had the previous February, and, in fact, the Iranian foreign minister, Ibrahim Yazdi, who had rescued the Americans in the earlier attack, assured chargé d'affaires Bruce Laingen that the attack was comparable to a sit-in at an American university and that the situation would be resolved "within 48 hours."[100] The next day, Yazdi and other moderates of the new government were surprised when Ahmed Khomeini, the ayatollah's son, climbed over the embassy fence and congratulated the students for their action, a clear sign that the ayatollah approved of the action and that the Iranian government was not going to intervene to resolve the crisis as it had done in February. In protest, Prime Minister Bazargan resigned from the government, and it became clear that the situation would not be resolved in the promised forty-eight hours.

In fact, it took fourteen months to resolve the hostage crisis and during those 444 days, the American government and public became fixated on the crisis. In the period from 1972 through 1977, the three major television networks devoted an average of five minutes per year to material concerning Iran.[101] Diplomatic historian Gaddis Smith believes that, following the capture of the American hostages, there was "more extensive coverage on television and in the press than any other event since World War II, including the Vietnam war."[102] A popular, late-night news program hosted by Ted Koppel, "Nightline," was originally created to present the news of each day concerning the hostage crisis. In retrospect, Cyrus Vance believes that it was a mistake "not to have played down the crisis as much as possible, particularly after it became evident that freeing the hostages would be a long, slow process."[103]

As the crisis dragged on, pressure mounted for a military solution. Brzezinski was the foreign policy official who most strongly supported such an operation, and Vance was at the other end of the spectrum opposing the military approach. Significantly, when Secretary Vance was out of town on April 11, a meeting of the National Security Council was held and a mission to rescue the hostages was approved. When told of the decision, Vance returned to Washington "stunned and angered that such a momentous decision had been made" in his absence.[104] So strongly did Vance oppose military action that he informed the president that he would resign whether or not the rescue mission succeeded. True to his word, Vance announced his resignation following the tragic failure of the rescue mission and the deaths of eight American servicemen.

The hostage crisis continued throughout the remainder of the Carter administration. It was, according to Zbigniew Brzezinski, the administration's "worst setback."[105] The crisis dominated the attention of the president and his closest advisers for months; they would meet daily for hours to discuss the crisis. However, the administration had begun a number of other important initiatives that bracketed the hostage crisis: the Camp David agreements, energy legislation, the normalization of relations with the People's Republic of China, and SALT II. The hostage crisis significantly weakened Jimmy Carter domestically. It was no coincidence that the same week the hostages were taken California's Gov. Jerry Brown and Sen. Edward Kennedy both announced that they were challenging President Carter for the Democratic presidential nomination.

The Iranian revolution and subsequent hostage crisis influenced the SALT II ratification in two ways. First, the loss of the two intelligence-gathering sites raised the specific issue of verification of the treaty, particularly of the ability of the United States to monitor the provisions of the agreement dealing with ICBM modernization. Second, the takeover of the U.S. embassy in Tehran and the seemingly unending humiliation of the hostages and the United States at the hands of the Iranian "students" called into question in the minds of many Americans the competence of President Carter and his administration in the field of foreign policy.

THE SOVIET INVASION OF AFGHANISTAN

For a number of reasons, Soviet (and before them, Russian) government officials have long been interested in Iran and Afghanistan. Central Asians living in the USSR are ethnically and culturally related to many of the groups who live in Iran and Afghanistan. As Soviet military power grew, so too did the Soviet desire to extend its power and influence in these areas. The Soviet refusal to leave Azerbaijan at the end of World War II was one indicator of the USSR's desire to extend its influence into the region. By the 1970s, the military power of the Soviet Union was at an all-time high level. In addition, Soviet leaders became concerned about the spread of Islamic fundamentalism, particularly in light of the fact that approximately 20 percent of the population in the Soviet Union is Moslem.

The Soviet Union showed great interest in Afghanistan throughout the 1970s. In April 1978, radical leftists in the Afghan army overthrew the civilian government of President Mohammed Daoud in a violent coup. Within days, the leader of a pro-Communist faction, Nur Mohammed Taraki, who was quite open about his support for the Soviet Union, emerged as the most important leader in Kabul, simultaneously holding the positions of president, prime minister, and general secretary of the Communist party. Throughout 1978 and the first eight months of 1979, Taraki appeared to be losing control of the countryside and the army. Religious insurgents called for the overthow of the Taraki government, a call that was heeded in September when Taraki was killed in a coup. He was replaced by Foreign Minister Hafizullah Amin, whom the Soviets undoubtedly hoped would be more successful in fighting the resistance groups than Taraki had been. Contrary to Soviet desires, however, Amin demonstrated some independence from the USSR.

The Soviets were clearly concerned about the growing power of Islamic fundamentalism throughout the Middle East and Persian Gulf regions. Following their takeover of the government of Iran, Khomeini and his followers criticized Soviet meddling in the domestic politics of Afghanistan, and important figures such as Ayatollah Shariatmadari publicly supported the Afghan resistance fighters who were opposing the Soviet-supported Taraki regime. [106] In November 1979, a group of conservative Moslems took over the Grand Mosque in Mecca, Saudi Arabia—the holiest shrine of Islam. Although this event was clearly unrelated to the takeover of the American embassy in Tehran at the beginning of the month, Khomeini held the United States and its ally Saudi Arabia responsible for the shocking act. Khomeini's attack stimulated a mob in Islamabad, Pakistan, to attack and burn the U.S. embassy there on November 21. In the course of the attack, two Americans and two Pakistani embassy employees were killed. [107] Two weeks later, the U.S. embassy in Libya was attacked and burned.

Soviet-Iranian relations had deteriorated during the summer and fall of 1979. The Soviet Union insisted on reaffirming the provisions of a 1921 Soviet-Iranian treaty that allowed for Soviet intervention into Iran if a third party threatened to attack the Soviet Union from Iran or if the USSR considered its border to be threatened. Iranian officials considered this treaty a vestige of the past and abrogated the treaty on November 5, the day after the takeover of the U.S. embassy. This is not to suggest that the two events were related, but rather to demonstrate that the new "Islamic Republic" was hostile toward both the United States and the Soviet Union.

It may very well be that Iranian actions increased Soviet fears of the spread of Islamic fundamentalism and influenced the USSR to invade Afghanistan in late December. When Soviet forces entered Kabul on December 27, it was clear that the prospects for improved Soviet-American relations and the ratification of the SALT II Treaty lessened significantly. President Carter sent Brezhnev what he called "the sharpest message" of his presidency on the hot line telling him that the invasion of Afghanistan was "a clear threat to the peace" and "could mark a fundamental and long-lasting turning point in our relations."[108] Although Carter did not want to scrap the SALT II Treaty, he recognized the reality of the situation: that it meant "the immediate and automatic loss of any chance for early ratification of the SALT II treaty."[109] Consequently, on January 3, 1980, Carter wrote to Majority Leader Byrd requesting that the treaty be withdrawn from active Senate consideration. Despite this action, the treaty was placed as the the first item of business for the Senate in 1980.

NOTES

1. Dan Caldwell, *American-Soviet Relations: From 1947 to the Nixon-Kissinger Grand Design and Grand Strategy* (Westport, Conn.: Greenwood Press, 1981).

2. Jimmy Carter quoted by Michael Charlton, *From Deterrence to Defense: The Inside Story of Strategic Policy* (Cambridge: Harvard University Press, 1987), 79.

3. Cyrus Vance, interview with author, New York City, July 14, 1988.

4. Henry A. Kissinger, *White House Years* (Boston: Little, Brown, 1979), 632–52; Raymond Garthoff, *Détente and Confrontation: American-Soviet Relations from Nixon to Reagan* (Washington: Brookings, 1985), 76–83.

5. Cyrus Vance, *Hard Choices: Critical Years in American Foreign Policy* (New York: Simon and Schuster, 1983), 132–33.

6. David B. Ottaway, "Why the Outcry over Cuba's African Role?," *Washington Post*, January 5, 1978.

7. Zbigniew Brzezinski, *Power and Principle: Memoirs of the National Security Adviser 1977–1981* (New York: Farrar, Straus and Giroux, 1983), 184.

8. Ibid., 189.

9. Don Oberdorfer, "The 'Brigada': Unwelcome Sight in Cuba," *Washington Post*, September 9, 1979.

10. William Bader, interview with author, Arlington, Va., October 20, 1987.

11. Richard Stone, interview with author, Washington, DC, October 27, 1988.

12. David Aaron, interview with Gloria Duffy, in Gloria Charmian Duffy, "Crisis Politics: The Carter Administration and Soviet Troops in Cuba, 1979" (Ph.D. diss., Columbia University, 1985), 126. I would like to thank Dr. Duffy for providing me with a copy of her dissertation.

13. Brzezinski, *Power and Principle*, 64.

14. Don Oberdorfer, "Cuban Crisis Mishandled, Insiders and Outsiders Agree," *Washington Post*, October 16, 1979.

15. U.S. Congress, Senate, Committee on Foreign Relations, *The SALT II Treaty*, hearings, 5 parts, 96th Cong., 1st sess., 1979, pt.2:178–80.

16. Oberdorfer, "Cuban Crisis Mishandled," 14.

17. Richard Stone, interview with author.

18. Stone, quoted in Oberdorfer, "Cuban Crisis Mishandled," 14.

19. U.S. Congress, Senate, Committee on Foreign Relations, "Statement Issued by Senator Frank Church (D-Idaho), Chairman of the Senate Foreign Relations Committee, and Senator Jacob Javits (R-New York), Ranking Minority Member," Committee on Foreign Relations Media Notice, July 17, 1979; reprinted in "Soviet Troops in Cuba Possible, Stone Says," *Miami Herald*, July 18, 1979.

20. "How Many Russians in Cuba?," *Washington Star*, July 18, 1979.

21. Ted Koppel, quoted in Oberdorfer, "Cuban Crisis Mishandled," 14.

22. Warren Christopher, telephone interview with author, May 2, 1988.

23. Robert C. Toth and John H. Averill, "New Cuba Crisis Began with U.S. Preoccupied," *Los Angeles Times*, September 7, 1979.

24. Stansfield Turner, *Secrecy and Democracy: The CIA in Transition* (New York: Harper and Row, 1985), 232.

25. David D. Newsom, *The Soviet Brigade in Cuba: A Study in Political Diplomacy* (Bloomington: Indiana University Press, 1987), 22.

26. Ibid., 31

27. Richard Stone, interview with author.

28. Quoted in Newsom, *The Soviet Brigade*, 13.

29. Ibid.

30. Letter from President Jimmy Carter to Sen. Richard Stone, reprinted in U.S. Congress, Senate, Committee on Foreign Relations, *Hearings and Markup on the Panama Canal Treaties*, 95th Cong., 2d sess., 1978, 6:101.

31. Letter from Cyrus Vance to Richard Stone, U.S. Congress, Senate, Committee on Foreign Relations, *The SALT II Treaty*, hearings, pt. 1:615.

32. F. Forrester Church, *Father and Son: A Personal Biography of Senator Frank Church of Idaho by His Son* (New York: Harper and Row, 1985), 57.

33. Ibid.

34. Ibid., 134.

35. William Bader, interview with author.

36. Quoted in Church, *Father and Son*, 139.

37. Vance, *Hard Choices*, 119.

38. Elizabeth Drew, "Profile: David Newsom," *New Yorker*, June 16, 1980, 76.

39. Newsom, *The Soviet Brigade*, 32–33.

40. Ibid., 34.

41. Quoted in Duffy, "Crisis Politics," 168.

42. Ibid., 171.

43. Newsom, *The Soviet Brigade*, 34.

44. Oberdorfer, "Cuban Crisis Mishandled," 1.

45. Gerald R. Ford, interview with author, Rancho Mirage, Calif., June 15, 1988, 2.

46. Robert C. Toth, "Soviets' Cuba Force 'Very Serious Matter'—Vance," *Los Angeles Times*, September 6, 1979.

47. Ibid., 6.

48. "Text of Televised Remarks by President Carter, September 7, 1979," *Washington Post*, September 8, 1979.

49. *Washington Post*, September 8, 1979.

50. "Who Needed This and Why?" *Pravda*, September 10, 1979, 1; translated in *Foreign Broadcast Information Service/U.S.S.R.*, September 11, 1979; cited in Duffy, "Crisis Politics," 206.

51. Don Shannon, "Gromyko Calls Cuba Troop Charges False," *Los Angeles Times*, September 26, 1979.

52. Bernard Gwertzman, "Brzezinski Cautions Soviets on Cuba Unit," *New York Times*, September 23, 1979.

53. Oswald Johnson and Don Irwin, "Carter Plans Action on Cuba Troop Issue," *Los Angeles Times*, September 29, 1979.

54. Dan Caldwell, ed., *Soviet International Behavior and U.S. Policy Options* (Lexington, Mass.: Lexington Books, 1985).

55. The other members of the group were: George W. Ball, Roswell Gilpatric, W. Averell Harriman, Nicholas deB. Katzenbach, Sol Linowitz, David Packard, William Rogers, James Schlesinger, and William Scranton; see Vance, *Hard Choices*, 363.

56. Cyrus Vance, interview with author.

57. "Text of President Carter's Speech to the Nation, October 1, 1979," Office of the White House Press Secretary, reprinted in Newsom, *The Soviet Brigade*, 85.

58. Ibid.

59. Dan Fisher, "Soviets Call Moves 'Gunboat Diplomacy,'" *Los Angeles Times*, October 3, 1979.

60. Robert G. Kaiser, "Carter Speech May Have Cost SALT Some Ground in the Senate," *Washington Post*, October 3, 1979.

61. "Statement by Senator Henry Jackson on President Carter's Response to Soviet Combat Forces in Cuba," October 2, 1979, in Henry M. Jackson Papers, Accession no. 3560, Box 13, Folder 36, University of Washington Libraries, 1.

62. Robert C. Byrd, "SALT and a 'Pseudo-Crisis,'" *Washington Post*, October 1, 1979.

63. "Vance, Dobrynin Confer Again on Soviet Troops in Cuba but No Details Are Given," *Los Angeles Times*, September 13, 1979.

64. Richard Burt, "SALT II's Chances Seem Good But SALT III Will Be Tougher," *New York Times*, August 26, 1979.

65. Zbigniew Brzezinski, interview with Gloria Duffy, in Duffy, "Crisis Politics," 294; also see Weekly Report no. 112, October 12, 1979, in Brzezinski, *Power and Principle*, 566.

66. Don Oberdorfer, "Soviet Cuba Force Reported a Decade Ago," *International Herald Tribune*, September 11, 1979.

67. Duffy, "Crisis Politics," 279–80.

68. U.S. Congress, House, Committee on Armed Services, "Testimony of Secretary of Defense Robert McNamara," *Hearings on Military Posture and Authorization of Appropriations*, January 30, 1963, 255.

69. Dan Fisher, "U.S. Far Off on Troop Estimates in Cuba Crisis," *Los Angeles Times*, January 30, 1989.

70. Raymond Garthoff, interview with Gloria Duffy, in Duffy, "Crisis Politics," 252.

71. Valentin Berezhkov, interview with Gloria Duffy, in ibid., 256.

72. Memorandum from Bill Bader to Members, Committee on Foreign Relations, June 18, 1979, in Henry M. Jackson Papers, Accession no. 3560–6, Box 49, Folder 26, University of Washington Libraries.

73. J. Brian Atwood, interview with author, Washington, DC, July 12, 1988.

74. Steven J. Baker, "Conclusion: Sharing Responsibility," in Hoyt Purvis and Steven J. Baker, eds., *Legislating Foreign Policy* (Boulder, Colo.: Westview Press, 1984), 207.

75. Warren Christopher, interview with author.

76. Hedley Donovan, *Roosevelt to Reagan: A Reporter's Encounters with Nine Presidents* (New York: Harper and Row, 1985), 155.

77. Anne Wexler, interview with author, Washington, DC, October 28, 1988.

78. William Perry, interview with author, Menlo Park, Calif., January 15, 1988, and Gen. Edward Meyer, telephone interview with author, October 21, 1987.

79. Quoted in the *Washington Post*, October 16, 1979.

80. Ray Cline, former CIA deputy director, called the administration's handling of the incident "mangling"; see Gloria Duffy, "Crisis Mangling and the Cuban Brigade," *International Security* 8, no. 1 (Summer 1983): 67.

81. Jimmy Carter, telephone interview with author, April 12, 1988. For Church's account of the episode, see Frank Church, "Carter on the Sinking of SALT: That's Not the Way I Remember It," *Washington Post*, November 19, 1982.

82. Forrester Church, *Father and Son*, 141; Bader, interview with author.

83. Cyrus Vance, interview with author.

84. Peter Tarnoff, interview with author, New York City, July 14, 1988.

85. Newsom, *The Soviet Brigade*, 50.

86. Herbert Feis, *From Trust to Terror: The Onset of the Cold War, 1945–1950* (New York: W. W. Norton, 1970), 63.

87. Kermit Roosevelt, *Countercoup: The Struggle for the Control of Iran* (New York: McGraw-Hill, 1979).

88. Gary Sick, *All Fall Down: America's Tragic Encounter with Iran* (New York: Penguin Books, 1986), 8–9.

89. Shah of Iran, interview with Arnaud de Borchgrave, *International Herald Tribune*, April 14, 1973.

90. Jimmy Carter, *Keeping Faith: Memoirs of a President* (New York: Bantam Books, 1982), 437.

91. William H. Sullivan, *Mission to Iran: The Last U.S. Ambassador* (New York: W. W. Norton, 1981), 258.

92. Carter, *Keeping Faith*, 451, 454.

93. Testimony of Secretary of Defense Harold Brown, U.S. Congress, Senate, Committee on Foreign Relations, *The SALT II Treaty*, hearings, 96th Cong., 1st sess., 1979, pt. 2:239–50.

94. Herbert Scoville, Jr., "Verification of Soviet Strategic Missile Tests," in William C. Potter, ed., *Verification and SALT: The Challenge of Strategic Deception* (Boulder, Colo.: Westview Press, 1980), 174; also see Herbert Scoville, Jr., "SALT Verification and Iran," *Arms Control Today* (February 1979).

95. President Carter, quoted in Hamilton Jordan, *Crisis: The Last Year of the Carter Presidency* (New York: G. P. Putnam's Sons, 1982), 29.

96. Ibid.

97. Carter, *Keeping Faith*, 452.

98. Ibid., 453.

99. Sick, *All Fall Down*, 213.

100. Yazdi, quoted in ibid., 229.

101. Arnold Raphel, "Media Coverage of the Hostage Negotiations—From Fact to Fiction," U.S. Department of State, Foreign Service Institute, *Executive Seminar in National and Inernational Affairs*, 24th session (1981–82), 14; quoted in Gaddis Smith, *Morality, Reason and Power: American Diplomacy in the Carter Years* (New York: Hill and Wang, 1986), 181.

102. Smith, ibid., 198.

103. Vance, *Hard Choices*, 380.

104. Ibid., 409.

105. Brzezinski, *Power and Principle*, 354.

106. Alvin Z. Rubinstein, *Soviet Policy toward Turkey, Iran, and Afghanistan: The Dynamics of Influence* (New York: Praeger, 1982), 104.

107. Harold H. Sauders, "Diplomacy and Pressure, November 1979–May 1980," in Warren Christopher, ed., *Americans Hostage in Iran: The Conduct of a Crisis* (New Haven, Conn.: Yale University Press, 1985), 90–91.

108. Carter, *Keeping Faith*, 472.

109. Ibid., 473.

CHAPTER EIGHT

Conclusions:
Outcome, Implications,
and Lessons

At the beginning of the SALT II debate in June 1979, Sen. Daniel Patrick Moynihan exclaimed, "If there's one flaw in the American Constitution—I'll concede one—it is that two-thirds is an unnatural vote for any democratic assembly."[1] In this chapter, I will consider four important questions. First, could the SALT II Treaty have been ratified by that "democratic assembly," the United States Senate? Second, why was SALT II not ratified? Third, should the "unnatural vote," the two-thirds majority required for the ratification of treaties by the Constitution, be amended and if so, then how should should treaties be ratified? Fourth, what lessons can be drawn from this experience for other cases of treaty ratification?

COULD THE SALT II TREATY HAVE BEEN RATIFIED?

The answer to the question of whether or not the SALT II Treaty could have been ratified is time-dependent. Prior to the signing of the treaty, most senators were undecided about the agreement. For example, a poll of senators in the spring of 1979 found that approximately forty were "generally favorably disposed to arms control agreements, but who were undecided on SALT II because of the Soviet military build-up and activities in the world."[2]

Once the treaty was signed by the U.S. president and the Soviet premier, senators began to take firm positions on its ratification. In July 1979, the month after the treaty was signed, the Friends Committee on National Legislation found that forty-two senators were either "likely to vote for SALT II" or "leaning toward" voting for the treaty; twenty-eight were undecided; and thirty were either firmly against or leaning against SALT II.[3] The undecided senators were the ones who would have determined the fate of the treaty, had a vote on SALT II taken place. By mid-August, it appeared that a sufficient number of the undecideds had made up their minds to support the treaty to guarantee ratification.

But in the following months, both the "discovery" of the Soviet combat brigade in Cuba and the Iranian hostage episode raised serious questions in the minds of many senators about the competence of the Carter administration and had an effect on the level of support for SALT II. In mid-November, the principal pro-SALT interest group, Americans for SALT, found that forty-seven senators were for or leaning for the ratification of the treaty; three were critical from an arms control perspective; sixteen were undecided; and thirty-four were against or leaning against.[4] Because it only takes thirty-four negative votes to defeat a treaty, it is unlikely that the treaty had much of a chance of ratification even before the Soviets invaded Afghanistan. By mid-December, Americans for SALT estimated that fifty senators were in favor or leaning for the treaty, thirty-three were against or leaning against, and seventeen were undecided.[5] The Conservative Caucus estimated that fifty-seven were in favor, thirty-one opposed, and twelve undecided. Senator Cranston estimated that, just prior to the invasion of Afghanistan, the votes were fifty-eight in favor or leaning in favor, thirty-one against, and eleven undecided.[6]

Many of the vote estimate counts seemed to reflect the ideological biases of the estimators. For example, Gen. Edward Rowny noted: "SALT II was dead in the water in the late summer or early fall [of 1979], and the removal [of the treaty from the Senate] from active consideration by Carter after Afghanistan was just an easy way for him to recognize the obvious: SALT II didn't have a chance."[7] Another prominent SALT opponent, Eugene Rostow, recalled, "We had the treaty beaten by mid-August [1979]."[8] The treaty supporters' estimates were very different. William Perry, the deputy secretary of defense, believed as late as mid-December (prior to the invasion of Afghanistan) that the treaty would be ratified.[9]

As noted in chapter 7, President Carter withdrew the treaty from Senate consideration following the Soviet invasion of Afghanistan. After the United States had retaliated for the Soviet invasion in a number of ways, there was a debate within the administration about whether the president should activate consideration of the treaty in the Senate. Secretary Vance urged the president to request the Senate to vote on the treaty, and Senator Cranston believed that the treaty could have been ratified even after the Soviet invasion of Afghanistan.[10] The staff director of the Senate Committee on Foreign Relations, William Bader, believed that the treaty could have been ratified by February or March of 1980.[11]

In retrospect, both the supporters and the opponents of the treaty appear to have been too optimistic for their respective cases. The treaty was clearly not defeated by mid-August, as Rowny and Rostow have claimed, nor could the treaty have been ratified after the Soviet invasion of Afghanistan.

WHY WAS SALT II NOT RATIFIED?

As the research presented in this book demonstrates, there were a number of reasons why the SALT II Treaty was not ratified. These reasons can be considered in four principal categories: (1) President Carter and his administration, (2) public opinion and interest groups, (3) the Senate and executive-congressional relations, and (4) external events.

President Carter and His Administration

Several observers who have analyzed the SALT II Treaty ratification debate have concluded that the main reason the treaty was not ratified was because of the handling of the treaty by President Carter and his advisers. One former Arms Control and Disarmament Agency official concluded that "the Carter Administration made a series of political misjudgments and mistakes, largely prior to the June 1979 signing of SALT II, which undermined congressional and public confidence in the executive branch's stewardship of the strategic issues and which, cumulatively, significantly hurt the treaty's chances for ratification."[12] There is some truth to this criticism.

Jimmy Carter's personality had a clear and undeniable effect on the SALT II Treaty ratification debate. During the 1976 election campaign, President Carter saw and presented himself to the American people as an outsider to Washington politics. Carter believed that his lack of experience with national and international affairs was an advantage rather than a disadvantage, and once elected, he did little to woo the Washington community of present and past government officials, legislators, lobbyists, and journalists to support his programs.

According to former NSC staff member, Gary Sick, Carter "seemed to believe that if a decision was correct it would sell itself, and his disregard for the potentially dangerous political consequences of his programs at times appeared to border on recklessness."[13] As a consequence of this aspect of Carter's personality, he was unwilling to spend much time meeting with members of Congress on an informal basis to cultivate relationships that could have perhaps helped him win congressional support of his programs.

Carter made a number of errors in appointments to his administration. His errors were of four types. First, the president appointed some policymakers who had conflicting views that were in many respects mutually exclusive. Second, he appointed some people who should not have been appointed to positions in his administration. Third, he did not appoint several prominent individuals to his administration whom he should have appointed. Fourth, he appointed several advisers too late.

At various times in American history, the weaknesses of presidents have partially been compensated for by presidential advisers. Edward House, Harry Hopkins, Henry Kissinger, and others had abilities that enabled them to complement and ably assist the respective presidents they served. Because President Carter had little background in foreign affairs, he particularly needed someone to assist him in this complex area. To the detriment of his leadership, for the most important foreign policy positions in his administration Carter selected two men who had very different views of the best ways of dealing with the United States' primary adversary, the Soviet Union. Broadly speaking, national security adviser Zbigniew Brzezinski favored a policy of competition and confrontation with the Soviet Union, while Secretary of State Cyrus Vance supported a policy of negotiation and moderation. Unfortunately, President Carter failed to choose one approach or the other during the course of his administration. A number of former Carter administration officials interviewed for this book noted that Carter would have been far better off to choose one approach or the other and to proceed on the basis of that approach rather than trying to follow two mutually exclusive policies throughout his four years in office.

In retrospect, a number of the policies supported by Brzezinski appear to have slowed down or damaged the prospects for the ratification of the SALT II Treaty. Brzezinski was principally responsible for linking SALT II to Cuban and Soviet activities in Africa in 1978; pushing for the United States to normalize relations with the People's Republic of China in late 1978; and pressing the American intelligence community to investigate Soviet activities in Cuba and elsewhere in the spring and summer of 1979. Although some former members of the Carter administration believe that Brzezinski was privately opposed to SALT II, most of the former officials interviewed for this book believed that Brzezinski thought it was more important to seek to limit the expansion of Soviet influence in the world than to ratify the SALT II Treaty. In contrast, Vance believed that the control of nuclear weapons was so important that SALT II should not be be linked to other, secondary issues on the agenda of American-Soviet relations. For his part, Brzezinski believed that foreign policy "events bore out my grimmer assessments of the Soviet role [in the world],"[14] a claim that may have become a self-fulfilling prophecy rather than a description of reality.

As the president's assistant for national security affairs, Brzezinski occupied the key position between the president and his advisers. He was responsible for drafting summaries of NSC meetings for the president, yet there was concern among department secretaries that their views were not accurately summarized.[15] According to CIA Director Stansfield Turner: "We all felt very nervous when we ended an SCC [Special Coordinating Committee meeting] because we never knew what Zbig sent to the president. He never showed us the memos he sent to the president, and there was always a concern whether views were accurately represented."[16] This heightened the natural bureaucratic paranoia and competition that exists in any administration.

The division at the top of the Carter administration was characteristic of the administration at lower levels. In order to achieve his heartfelt goal of nuclear arms control, President Carter appointed a man known for his strong support of arms control, Paul Warnke, as director of the Arms Control and Disarmament Agency and the chief American negotiator at the SALT II talks. This appointment stimulated a great deal of controversy and opposition to the Carter administration in general and to SALT II in particular, and several close observers believe that the appointment was a mistake.[17]

In order to placate conservatives such as Sen. Henry Jackson, the administration tolerated several prominent critics within its agencies. According to former ACDA official Barry Blechman, the administration had its "worst enemies right in its midst—Rowny and Odom—these guys were open lines to all their opponents, and there was no understanding [by Carter administration officials] that this was serious business."[18] A senior member of the administration believed that General Rowny "was being disloyal to the Chiefs and [that] he was playing his own political game. On the basis of this, the question was shouldn't he be fired? In the end, it was decided that if we did [fire him], it would raise more problems that if we didn't. . . .We made a big mistake by not firing Ed Rowny, as we should have."[19] Just prior to the signing of SALT II, General Rowny retired from the army and became one of the leading opponents of the ratification of the treaty. What distinguished General Rowny from literally hundreds of other retired officers who opposed the SALT II Treaty was his service on the SALT II delegation, which President Carter or Defense Secretary Brown could have ended when they entered office in January 1977.

President Carter made several other appointments that should not have been made. Frank Moore, the director of the Office of Congressional Relations, received universally bad marks from members of Congress and their staffers. One former senior Senate staff member called Moore "the worst White House Congressional liaison I ever dealt with."[20] John Isaacs, a veteran pro–arms control lobbyist, believes that in order to win the Senate's approval of SALT II, the administration should have "hired a better lobbying team for Congress. Carter hired all those nice Georgia boys, which is fine, but they didn't know about Congress."[21]

Perhaps as damaging to the administration as some appointments that were made were several appointments that were not made. The most important of those candidates who were not appointed to positions in the Carter administration was Paul Nitze. For four decades, Nitze had been centrally involved in the planning and implementation of U.S. defense policy. He had advised every president since Truman and had been an early supporter of Jimmy Carter in the 1976 election. However, when Carter and Nitze met, they did not get along, and following an unpleasant meeting at Carter's home in Plains, Georgia, the two did not meet again until Nitze went to the White

House as a member of the executive committee of the most important group opposing SALT II, the Committee on the Present Danger.[22] Nitze's opposition to SALT II was not inevitable and perhaps could have been prevented by appointing him to a senior position in which he would not directly deal with the president. Ironically, this was the type of position to which both Rowny and Nitze were appointed during President Reagan's second term of office.[23]

President Carter appointed several advisers too late. It was clear to many that an overall "SALT ratification czar" would be needed in order to obtain ratification, but this appointment was not made until mid-August 1979 when the president named the respected Washington attorney Lloyd Cutler to this position. Cutler, however, was appointed at least a year too late; hearings on SALT II were already well under way and opponents to the treaty had been working for more than a year. Several senior members of the administration were critical of Cutler's appointment on the grounds that he was not familiar with the ways that Congress operated, national security issues, or the substance of SALT II. In addition to Cutler, the president appointed former *Time* magazine senior editor Hedley Donovan as a senior White House adviser.[24] This appointment was designed to broaden the base of Carter's advisers, but like the Cutler appointment, it came too late.

There was a sense in the Senate that even those Carter administration officials who were in favor of SALT II were not totally convinced of its value. An arms control official recalled, "Harold Brown did not go out around the country and explain the administration's defense policy until the fall of 1980" and "getting Vance to go out and make a speech was like pulling teeth."[25] Sen. John Culver recalled: "A lot of Carter's advisers were more worried about how acceptable they were here or there than winning their own fight [on SALT II]. . . . There wasn't enough hot blood in some of those veins—a lot of brains—but not enough hot blood or passion."[26] Brzezinski was more than willing to fill the public relations vacuum that was created by Brown's and Vance's reticence, and he held a number of press conferences and made a number of speeches reflecting his particular views. A number of Brzezinski's public relations efforts were inconsistent with the president's main priorities, including the ratification of SALT II.

Related to, but separate from, the personnel problems of the Carter administration were the substantive problems concerning the SALT II Treaty. Reflecting his deeply held personal values and convictions, President Carter made human rights the dominant theme of his administration's approach to foreign policy during his first several years in office. This emphasis attracted considerable public and congressional support within the United States; however, it alienated a number of American allies, such as the Shah of Iran, and adversaries of the United States, such as Leonid Brezhnev.

The administration's timing was critical in several areas of arms control. The decision to lay aside the SALT II agreement negotiated by the Nixon and Ford administrations and to present the "comprehensive proposal" calling for deep cuts in March 1977 was a major error. According to Senator Cranston: "Instead of seeking to conclude a treaty that was almost complete, Carter created almost a new treaty. This got things off to a bad start and destroyed the bipartisan opportunity that was there to have a Democratic president complete the work of two previous Republican presidents. This upset a good opportunity."[27] The new proposal was unfortunate because it further alienated the Soviets from Carter and caused a delay in the negotiations. Further delays were caused by the debates over cruise missiles, the Backfire bomber, and verification procedures of the treaty. In addition, the United States's recognition of the People's Republic of China caused a delay of three to six months. As Lloyd Cutler noted: "The treaty was signed too late. In the first two years [of Carter's administration], he would have had a much better chance of getting sixty-seven votes."[28]

The administration's sequencing of the Panama Canal treaties and the SALT II Treaty also contributed to the outcome of the debates. A number of moderate Republican and conservative Democratic senators believed that they could vote for one or the other of the agreements, and the conservative Democrat, Sen. Richard Stone, told President Carter, "You don't ask a vulnerable politician to walk the plank twice."[29] The Panama treaties came first, and the Carter administration put the pressure on, and a number of these moderate and conservative senators voted in favor of them. The Carter administration essentially spent its political capital on Panama, leaving little in reserve for the SALT II ratification effort.

Timing was also important during the SALT II debate itself. The treaty was signed in June and withdrawn from Senate consideration in January, a total of six and one-half months. Former NSC official under Nixon and Ford, William Hyland, has commented, "The [Carter] administration's handling of the ratification process was badly botched; no president should have allowed the Senate to dally over such a critical treaty."[30]

Despite all of the problems related to Jimmy Carter's personality and his administration, the research conducted for this book indicates that, had the Senate voted on the treaty in mid-August, it would have been ratified. What then intervened to block ratification?

Public Opinion and Interest Groups

Following the end of U.S. involvement in the Vietnam War, American public opinion favored a return to "domestic priorities" and a turn away from international commitments. This move toward the isolationist end of the pendulum of opinion and away from the internationalist end is characteristic of American public opinion throughout history. By the time Jimmy Carter entered office in 1977, the turn away from international involvements—the Vietnam syndrome—had ended, and Americans were becoming more concerned about the principal orientation of U.S. foreign policy since 1947: the containment of the Soviet influence throughout the world. Yet Carter was unaware of this change because his chief adviser on public opinion, Patrick Caddell, was telling him that Americans were concerned about the danger of World War III and the issue of peace about the same time that public opinion was, in fact, moving in the opposite direction.

This change in public opinion coincided with the rise of a number of conservative interest groups in the United States. Many of these had existed for years; others were founded in the 1970s to combat a perceived decline of support for strong American defense and foreign policies. At least one, the Committee on the Present Danger, was founded as a direct response to the election of Jimmy Carter. Some of these conservative groups were well financed and staffed; they were certainly better financed than their liberal, pro–arms control counterparts. Despite the resources of these groups, it would be an exaggeration to claim that they were able to turn public opinion around in a conservative direction. (The Committee on the Present Danger—the group that both proponents and opponents of SALT II most often cited as the most influential anti-SALT interest group—had a full-time staff of three professionals and four secretaries, and a budget of $300,000 in 1979.)

The conservative interest groups encouraged the rightward trend in public opinion and were able to take advantage of it for four major reasons. First, these groups began campaigning against SALT II long before it was signed, in contrast to the Carter administration which did not begin its full-scale ratification campaign until after the treaty was initialed. Second, the conservative groups took full advantage of new technologies for contacting and influencing public and congressional opinion. In 1980, Richard Viguerie sent out more than seventy million computer-based, direct-mail appeals, which raised more than $20 million for conservative congressional candidates.[31] Third, many of the conservative, anti-SALT groups coordinated their efforts and thereby made more efficient use of their resources. For example, the Committee on the Present Danger identified the attentive public as its target audience, and the American Security Council targeted the mass public as its audience.[32] These organizations also exchanged address lists for various mailings and solicitations of funds. Fourth, the conservative groups adopted an effective media campaign highlighted by the success of the popular anti-SALT film, *The SALT Syndrome*, which one scholar judged to be the single most important influence on public opinion about SALT.[33]

Clearly, the conservative interest groups won the battle against the pro-SALT moderate and liberal groups. Why was this the case? Because public opinion had shifted in a more conservative direction, the pro-SALT groups were fighting an uphill battle. In addition, as political scientist Miroslav Nincic has argued persuasively, the shift in public opinion may have resulted from "the politics of opposites," meaning that "other things being equal, the public will tend to prefer assertiveness in dovish presidents while seeking a more conciliatory stance in hawkish chief executives . . ."[34] Throughout Carter's term, public support for his Soviet policy increased when he became more assertive and tended to decrease when he became more conciliatory.[35]

The Senate

Given the constitutional requirement for a two-thirds majority vote in favor of treaties, the ultimate fate of the SALT II Treaty lay with the Senate. The Carter administration sought to influence public opinion in the hope that the influential citizens invited to the White House to hear a briefing on the treaty would then contact their senators to vote in favor of it. This was the strategy that the administration had used to gain the ratification of the Panama Canal treaties, and it had worked (although the Panama treaties were barely ratified).

The members of the Carter administration used the Panama Canal treaties ratification campaign as the template for the SALT II Treaty ratification campaign. This was an unfortunate error, for the situations were reversed in these two cases. In the Panama case, the Senate favored the treaties, and the public opposed them. It therefore made good sense for the Carter administration to target the public as the audience for its ratification campaign. In the SALT II case, the public favored the treaty, and the Senate did not. Rather than using the Panama strategy, it would have been far better for the members of the administration to devote their time, effort, and resources to convincing the Senate rather than the public of the need for the SALT II Treaty.

President Carter and his administration also erred in trying to win over certain members of the Senate, most notably Henry Jackson. From the early days of his administration, Jimmy Carter sought Jackson's support, yet as Carter himself later recalled, it was very unlikely that Jackson would vote in favor of any SALT II Treaty.[36]

Quite rightly, Carter emphasized the need to gain the support of prominent, moderate senators, including Majority Leader Robert Byrd and Armed Services Committee member Sam Nunn. Both Byrd and Nunn carefully reviewed the advantages and disadvantages of the treaty. Senator Byrd announced his support of the treaty at the end of October, following the Soviet combat brigade episode. Senator Nunn appeared to be leaning in favor of the treaty after Carter agreed to a significant increase in defense spending.

Sen. Howard Baker would have been crucial had the Senate voted on SALT II. His support of the Panama Canal treaties had made their ratification possible. Although some observers believe that Baker could not have voted for SALT II given his support of the Panama treaties, others believe that he could have been convinced to vote in favor of SALT II if the administration had negotiated with him more seriously on the issues about which he was concerned, particularly Soviet heavy missiles.[37] Given the international events of late August through December 1979, the question of Baker's support became moot; however, it does raise an important issue, namely, the crucial role that the majority and minority leaders of the Senate play in the ratification of treaties.

External Events: Cuba, Iran, and Afghanistan

Because of the unpredictable nature of international events, foreign policy successes or failures are often the result, to use Dean Acheson's phrase, of "plain dumb luck."[38] Acheson believed that this was the principal explanation for the Kennedy administration's success in the Cuban missile crisis. Many observers believe the same factor accounts for the Carter administration's failure to ratify SALT II.

The Senate would likely have ratified the treaty had a vote been taken before the end of August. However, following the discovery of the Soviet combat brigade in Cuba and the politicization of this issue by Senator Stone and Senator Church, the vote on SALT II was significantly delayed. The takeover of the U.S. embassy in Tehran during the first week in November raised more questions in the minds of the public about the Carter administration's competence in the foreign policy area, and the Soviet invasion of Afghanistan drove the final nail in the coffin of SALT II.

It is conceivable that SALT II could have been ratified even after these three developments, but only if the treaty was not linked to Soviet international behavior in the minds of senators and the public. Several members of the Carter administration (most notably Zbigniew Brzezinski), however, had worked hard to link the arms control issue to Soviet foreign policy. As J. Brian Atwood, former assistant secretary of state for congressional affairs during the Carter administration, recalled, "I found it somewhat ironic that Brzezinski would be saying that the issue involving the Horn of Africa had defeated SALT when in my view, it was his handling of that issue—linkage—that caused the biggest problem."[39]

In assessing all of these reasons, the underlying shift in public opinion was the most important factor. However, even despite this shift and the errors committed by President Carter and his appointees, the administration was able to gain significant support for the SALT II Treaty during the summer of 1979. But the three external events precluded a positive vote on the treaty.

THE CONSTITUTIONAL QUESTION

Article II, section 2, of the U.S. Constitution grants the president the power "by and with the Advice and Consent of the Senate, to make treaties, provided two thirds of the Senators present concur . . ." Several contentious treaty debates in the history of the United States have caused Americans to question whether this provision is still advisable. This question was raised in the aftermath of the debate over the Treaty of Versailles and again during and after the SALT II Treaty debate.

Under the Articles of Confederation, the president acted as the agent of the Senate in the negotiation of treaties, and a two-thirds vote by the Senate was required to approve any treaty. At the Constitutional Convention, there was much debate about who should negotiate treaties and the provisions for ratifying them. Some at the convention wanted the Senate to retain its power to negotiate treaties, and a number of delegates wanted both houses of Congress to approve treaties. The New England states were concerned about fishing rights, and the southern states were anxious to retain control over the Mississippi River. The small states were anxious not to be dominated by the large states, and the votes of the small states were needed to ratify the Constitution. As a result, the convention acceded to the wishes of the small states and recommended that the president negotiate treaties with the advice of the Senate and that the Senate approve treaties by a two-thirds vote.[40] However, this was a contentious issue as evidenced by the fact that a motion to substitute a simple majority vote for the two-thirds requirement failed by one vote.

Critics of the two-thirds majority point out that this requirement is undemocratic and is one "which no other modern democracy has seen fit to adopt; it was simply one of those regional bargains out of which the Constitution was so largely confounded."[41] Other critics have charged that the requirement "has impeded and threatens to impede further the conduct of U.S. foreign relations, most especially in the field of arms control."[42] As the United States's population has grown, so too has the disparity between the largest and smallest states. In 1987, the least populated state, Wyoming, had a population of 490,000 compared to the most populated state, California, which had 27,663,000 people.[43] Yet each of these two states, along with the other forty-eight, had two senators. Assuming that the senators from the seventeen smallest states voted as a block, it is theoretically possible for thirty-four senators representing 7.1 percent of the total U.S. population to block a treaty. It is calculations such as these, plus the frustrating experiences of the executive and congressional branches in dealing with treaties in the post–World War II era, that have led a number of scholars and policymakers to suggest alternative means of ratifying treaties.

A Parliamentary System of Government

Given the close ties between the thirteen American colonies and Great Britain, it is not surprising that some of the delegates to the Constitutional Convention favored a parliamentary system of government. But the Constitution created a system of government incorporating the separation of powers rather than the selection of executive officers solely from the legislative branch. However, the latter, parliamentary system has continued to attract the support of prominent Americans throughout U.S. history.

Woodrow Wilson was perhaps the most prominent of those who have favored a parliamentary system for the United States. In his doctoral dissertation, *Congressional Government*, published in 1885, Wilson's admiration for the parliamentary system was quite evident.

Down to the present day, a number of American politicians and political scientists have continued to advocate the parliamentary system. James Mac-Gregor Burns has suggested that the terms of the president and members of the House of Representatives be simultaneous. Former longtime senator J. William Fulbright has argued that a parliamentary system for the United States would decrease the power of special interests, make for more democratic and less expensive elections, and result in more informed presidents. In Fulbright's view:

> Perhaps the greatest difference between a president and a prime minister is that a prime minister in a parliamentary system must meet his peers and critics face to face. His presence in the House is not a state occasion filled with the trappings of ceremony and pomp associated with a president's visit to Congress. It is this power of parliament to continually require the prime minister to explain and justify his policies to an informed body of colleagues that is crucial.[44]

Following his disappointing experience in trying to gain the Senate's ratification of the SALT II Treaty, Lloyd Cutler wrote an article in which he outlined a number of reforms for the U.S. government which, if adopted, would result in a parliamentary type of system. Arguing that "the separation of powers between the legislative and executive branches, whatever its merits in 1793, has become a structure that almost guarantees stalemate today,"[45] Cutler contends that there are a number of reasons that make parliamentary reforms more important today than in the past: it is far more difficult today to obtain a broad consensus; foreign policy has become more important as the nations of the world have become increasingly interdependent; the power of political parties has declined significantly; and authority in Congress has become fragmented.

The only way "to form a government," according to Cutler, is to amend the Constitution to provide for the election of a "trio of candidates" in each congressional district consisting of the president, the vice president, and a member of the House of Representatives. In addition, Cutler suggests that the president be allowed (or required) to select 50 percent of his cabinet from members of his party in the House and Senate, who would retain their congressional seats while serving in the cabinet. Other potential reforms could include granting the president the power to dissolve Congress and to call for new elections, and granting the power to the Congress by a two-thirds vote to call for new presidential elections.

A Single Six-Year Term for the President

At the Constitutional Convention a single six-year term of office for the president was discussed and eventually dismissed. However, in 1826 this reform was proposed to the Congress as a constitutional amendment and has been reintroduced more than 160 times since then.[46] Given this proposal's popularity and longevity, one scholar has labeled it "the reform that just won't die."[47] Fifteen presidents have endorsed this proposal, as have a number of former government officials and business and civic leaders. In 1985, the Committee for a Single Six-Year Term began a campaign designed to gain public acceptance of the proposal.[48] The members of the committee were impressive; the cochairmen were Herbert Brownell and Griffin Bell, the attorneys general in the Eisenhower and Carter administrations respectively, and members included William Simon, former Nixon administration secretary of the treasury, and Carter's secretary of state, Cyrus Vance.

In the preface to his memoirs, Cyrus Vance notes: "We all desire a strong and effective foreign policy but there are structural and human constraints that hobble us in achieving this objective. Perhaps the most important of these is the president's four year term."[49] Vance believes that a single six-year term would free the president from the pressures of campaigning and result in better decisions. Vance argues, "In short, the six-year term would provide a needed matrix of continuity and stability for our foreign policy."[50]

Change the Two-Thirds Requirement

A two-thirds majority requirement is, as Senator Moynihan has pointed out, an "unnatural majority," and this majority has been changed in the past for actions other than treaty ratification. For example, in 1975 the Senate passed a filibuster reform that called for a vote of three-fifths in place of two-thirds. With this reform as a precedent, a bipartisan group, the Committee on the Constitutional System, in 1987 called for the replacement of the two-thirds requirement for treaty ratification either by a reduction to three-fifths of the Senate or by requiring a simple majority vote of both houses of Congress.[51]

When asked about his evaluation of the two-thirds treaty-ratification requirement, President Carter responded: "I think it [the two-thirds requirement] is one of the major defects in the United States Constitution, perhaps the most serious one. I think we should have a 50 percent vote of the Senate [to approve treaties]."[52]

A Majority Vote of Both Houses

Partially because of the difficulty of obtaining a two-thirds vote of approval from the Senate, President Carter and his advisers considered concluding SALT II as an executive agreement rather than a treaty.[53] According to the Arms Control and Disarmament Act of 1961, the executive branch may not take action to "obligate the United States to disarm or to reduce or to limit the . . . armaments of the United States" except by treaty or "unless authorized by further affirmative legislation by the Congress of the United States."[54] The SALT I agreements included one treaty—the Anti-Ballistic Missile Treaty—and one executive agreement—the Interim Agreement on Offensive Forces. The former chief negotiator at the SALT I negotiations and director of the Arms Control and Disarmament Agency, Gerard Smith, supports this approach: "If a majority vote of both House of Congress is sufficient to make war, it should be sufficient to make agreements having peaceful purposes."[55] The precedent and the legal mechanism therefore exist for the president to conclude arms control agreements that are approved by simple majority votes of the House and the Senate.

Maintain the Status Quo

Despite these reforms and others presented by various individuals and groups, there is still strong support for the existing system. When asked about his view of the two-thirds requirement, President Ford replied:

> I have always felt that an administration that tried to bypass the two-thirds majority for the ratification process would be going down the wrong path. It would be a signal, an indication of weakness. . . . The minute an administration, Democratic or Republican, tries to circumvent that two-thirds requirement, in my judgment, it is an indication of weakness and I tend to distrust the effort, whatever it might be. So I am pretty hard-line on that, and I just think any administration that does not have enough faith in what they are doing—

that they go down the [executive agreement] path rather than the treaty path—is getting in very, very murky waters."[56]

Various study groups have also been hesitant to recommend changing the two-thirds requirement for treaty ratification. The Atlantic Council of the United States' Working Group concluded that "the present situation does not call for any constitutional amendments or any major changes in our institutions of government."[57] The American Assembly of Columbia University and the Commission on Public Understanding about the Law of the American Bar Association concluded its review of the Constitution by specifically rejecting the proposal to accept a three-fifths majority requirement to ratify treaties.[58]

Any public policy—domestic or international—can be evaluated by assessing its desirability and its feasibility. In the case of constitutional reform, a number of measures appear to be highly desirable. For example, given low voter-turnout rates and the decreasing power of political parties, a number of the reforms calling for a move toward a parliamentary system look attractive. However, it is very unlikely that any of these reforms would be adopted. In addition, there could be serious unintended consequences of such reforms should they be adopted. Therefore, it is likely that future presidents will have to cope with the two-thirds requirement for the ratification of treaties.

THE LESSONS OF THE SALT II TREATY RATIFICATION DEBATE

The SALT II Treaty ratification debate lasted six and a half months, one of the longest periods of time in American history that the Senate has actively considered a treaty. What lessons can be learned from this case?

1. *Conclude existing negotiations before presenting dramatic, new proposals.* In retrospect, members of the Carter administration believe that the decision to present the comprehensive proposal in March 1977 during Secretary Vance's trip to Moscow was a mistake. Vance has commented: "The President and Zbig—and to a degree Harold [Brown]—were in favor of deep cuts, but [it was] primarily the President. My own view was we were better to move in smaller steps and do it more rapidly building on Vladivostok . . . and Paul Warnke felt the same way."[59] The counselor of the State Department under Vance believed that the SALT II Treaty was delayed several years as a result of the March 1977 proposal and that the proposal was a significant mistake.[60]

A new administration feels the necessity of reviewing previous arms control efforts. But in politics, time is not a free good, and the time required for such reviews has often been purchased at a dear price. When Richard Nixon came into office in January 1969, Henry Kissinger conducted a major review of the strategic balance before engaging the Soviets in the first strategic arms limitation negotiations. This review took ten months to complete, so the SALT I negotiations did not begin until November 1969, and during this period, the United States was testing multiple, independently targetable, reentry vehicles (MIRVs). It is possible that effective controls could have been placed on MIRVs had the SALT negotiations begun at the beginning rather than the end of 1969. It is also possible that President Carter could have completed a SALT II agreement along the lines of the Vladivostok Accord had he not presented the comprehensive proposal.

2. *Once an arms control agreement is signed, the president should press for its timely consideration by the Congress.* Those Carter administration officials interviewed for this book believe almost unanimously that the administration allowed the Congress too much time to consider the SALT II Treaty. According to David Aaron: "It took us too long to get a vote, and we got pecked to death by goslings. The opponents were praying for a miracle and they got it with [the Soviet invasion] of Afghanistan."[61] In the end, the length of time that the administration allowed the Senate precluded the formal ratification of the treaty.

3. *Defense policy and weapons deployment decisions should be made with explicit attention to arms control considerations.* Strategists developed the conceptual foundations of arms control in the early 1960s and policymakers built on these foundations in the aftermath of the Cuban missile crisis. Since that time, strategists, scholars, policymakers, and journalists have too often thought of arms control and defense policy as two separate endeavors, when they are, in fact, integrally related to one another. Rephrasing Clausewitz, arms control can be defense policy by other means.

President Carter's defense policy decisions had deep and profound implications for his arms control policy. Since the time of the first significant arms control agreement, the Limited Test Ban Treaty, the approval of the Joint Chiefs of Staff and the Congress for arms control agreements has been bought with weapons modernization. In order to get the Joint Chiefs and Senator Jackson to accept the Limited Test Ban Treaty, President Kennedy had to accept a "safeguards program" calling for significantly increased nuclear testing underground. To obtain the support of the JSC and Senator Jackson for the SALT I agreements, President Nixon agreed to a speed-up of the Trident submarine program, the development of cruise missiles, and the building of the B–1 bomber. As SALT II was being negotiated, it was clear that President Carter was going to have to pay a price for JCS and senatorial acceptance. When Carter unilaterally canceled the B–1 bomber program on the grounds that it cost too much, he was in effect unintentionally and unwittingly approving the MX program. It would have been impossible to ratify

SALT II without either the B–1 or the MX; this was simply not possible politically.

4. *While there is a legitimate place for disagreement and dissent at the highest levels of foreign policy decision making, there cannot be a division on fundamental issues of policy such as the U.S. strategy for dealing with the Soviet Union.* Throughout the cold war, the United States had a coherent, widely understood strategy, supported on a bipartisan basis, for dealing with the Soviet Union—containment. With the fractionalization of communism and the rise of nationalistically oriented communist movements, the application of containment became more difficult. Nixon and Kissinger sought to establish a richer, more differentiated approach to dealing with the Soviet Union, but this grand design and strategy failed to win the support of the Congress and the American public.[62]

Jimmy Carter had little experience in international affairs before he was elected president. He therefore had to rely on others for foreign policy advice, and he selected Zbigniew Brzezinski and Cyrus Vance as his two principal foreign policy advisers. Rather than choosing between Brzezinski's and Vance's very different and mutually exclusive views of U.S.-Soviet relations, Carter attempted to meld the two approaches, with results that were disappointing to Carter himself, to the Congress, and to the American people.

5. *The executive branch should work closely with the Congress to develop arms control policies and proposals that are acceptable to informed members of Congress.* This lesson would on the surface appear to be self-evident; however, the Carter administration failed to work with the Congress effectively despite attempts to do so. Secretary Vance estimated that he spent about a quarter of his time on congressional matters and that for every hour of congressional testimony, he spent five to six hours of preparation.[63] Vance, Secretary of Defense Brown, ACDA Director Seignious, and his predecessor, Paul Warnke, discussed SALT issues in nearly fifty different congressional hearings from January 1977 through July 1979. During the same period, there were more than 140 individual briefings on SALT for senators and another 100 briefings for senators' staff members.[64] In addition, Ambassador Ralph Earle II testified more than forty times, and during one of his visits to Washington from the negotiations in Geneva, he saw fifty-nine senators in forty-two days.[65] These were significant attempts to communicate and consult with the Congress and were far more extensive than during the SALT I negotiations.

The major problem area concerned the relationship between the White House and Capitol Hill. President Carter, Vance, and Brown had not served in the Congress and did not fully understand the mores and traditions of the Congress. The only high-level member of the Carter administration to have served in the Congress was Vice President Walter Mondale, and the president did not involve him in the SALT II ratification campaign until very late in the game, after the takeover of the U.S. embassy in Iran. By then, the game was all but over and Mondale, no matter how extensive his contacts on the Hill, could not reverse the situation.

Carter and his advisers had a barely concealed disdain for members of Congress, and they paid dearly for this attitude during the SALT II debate and during other legislative battles. The director of the White House Office of Congressional Relations, Frank Moore, was notoriously ineffective, although the abilities of several of his subordinates, including Robert Beckel and Dan Tate, partially compensated for his ineffectiveness.

Very late in the process, Lloyd Cutler was brought into the White House as counselor, but Cutler did not have a very good understanding of Congress. At one point during the fall of 1979, he asked a State Department official if he could address the Senate on the floor, a prerogative reserved solely for senators and former presidents.[66] After his first meeting with Majority Leader Byrd, someone asked Cutler what he had learned, and he replied, "That you don't call him 'Bob.'"[67] The experience of SALT II suggests that it is vital for the president to have an adviser in the White House who has close access to him and who also has a knowledge of and contacts on Capitol Hill. Curiously, although Vice President Mondale had extensive experience in the Senate, he did not play a central role in developing and implementing the administration's ratification strategy, because Carter's closest advisers chose not to include Mondale in their planning.

6. *There may be problems that are so important that progress on their resolution should not be linked to other issues.* At the time of the SALT II debate, a number of issues were portrayed as extremely significant, so important that if unresolved, some claimed, SALT II could not be ratified. More than a decade later, however, the significance of many of these issues has paled considerably. For example, looking back on the SALT II debate in 1987, Senator Garn noted that at the time of the debate, he considered the discovery of the Soviet combat brigade in Cuba to be very important, but that, in retrospect, it was not very important.[68] Yet, as this study has demonstrated, the delay caused by the discovery of the brigade was a major reason that the treaty was not ratified.

Many people assume that it was the Soviet invasion of Afghanistan that caused the death of SALT II. J. Brian Atwood has pointed out:

> One can argue plausibly that Soviet actions alone doomed the ratification effort. But, given our divergent world interests, unpopular Soviet behavior is inevitable during any ratification timetable. If we responded to Soviet aggression in context, we would have no *need* to link SALT. And, if we described

arms control accurately, as a restraint on Soviet strategic forces, we would have no *desire* to link SALT. In my view, Soviet actions alone did not doom SALT. . . . It is more likely a victim of self-inflicted linkage.[69]

Zbigniew Brzezinski sought to link Soviet behavior in Africa and other parts of the world to SALT II, and Cyrus Vance attempted to decouple SALT II from other secondary issues. Linkage did not deter the Soviets from invading Afghanistan, so the effectiveness of this tactic is open to question.

The Significance of the Ratification Failure

So what? What difference does it make that the Carter administration failed to formally ratify the SALT II Treaty, especially since the Reagan administration observed the terms of the treaty until late in the second term?

The failure to ratify the SALT II Treaty significantly set back American-Soviet relations and the efforts to control strategic nuclear arms for almost a decade. Given the rapid pace of development of modern strategic weapons, this delay was important, in economic terms if in no other ways. Of course, the ratification of the SALT II Treaty alone would not have slowed the pace of defense expenditures and technological developments; that requires political will and that will was lacking until the latter part of President Reagan's eight years in office.

The SALT II Treaty was perhaps best described by JCS Chairman Gen. David Jones as a "modest, but useful" agreement. Had it been ratified, the stage would have been set for the next step; indeed, a statement on the points to be addressed in SALT III was appended to the SALT II Treaty. Opportunities forfeited never come back in the same form, and the failure to ratify the SALT II Treaty and the lack of political will that this represented resulted in the deterioration of U.S.-Soviet relations, the stalling of arms control, and the delay of our ability to shape our future in a desired direction. That was a costly price.

NOTES

1. Interview with Daniel P. Moynihan, "Face the Nation," transcript (Washington: CBS News, June 17, 1979), 5.

2. *Congressional Quarterly*, April 15, 1979.

3. Friends Committee on National Legislation, *FCNL Washington Newsletter*, July 1979, 8.

4. Unpublished list compiled by Americans for SALT, cited in Theodore James Koontz, "The SALT II Debate: An Analysis of Senatorial Decision Making," Ph.D. diss., Harvard University (Ann Arbor, Mich.: University Microfilms, 1985), 62.

5. Unpublished memo, Americans for SALT, December 10, 1979.

6. Letter from Alan Cranston to Dan Caldwell, June 30, 1987.

7. Edward Rowny, interview with author, Washington, DC, June 3, 1987.

8. Eugene Rostow, interview with author, Washington, DC, October 28, 1988.

9. William Perry, interview with author, Menlo Park, Calif., January 15, 1988.

10. Cyrus Vance, interview with author, New York City, July 14, 1988, and Alan Cranston, interview with author, Washington, DC, June 5, 1987.

11. William Bader, interview with author, Arlington, Va., October 20, 1987.

12. Alan Platt, "The Politics of Arms Control and the Strategic Balance," in Barry Blechman, ed., *Rethinking the U.S. Strategic Posture* (Cambridge: Ballinger, 1982), 156.

13. Gary Sick, *All Fall Down: America's Tragic Encounter with Iran* (New York: Penguin Books, 1986), 262.

14. Zbigniew Brzezinski, *Power and Principle: Memoirs of the National Security Adviser 1977–1981* (New York: Farrar, Straus and Giroux, 1983), 29.

15. Cyrus Vance, interview with author.

16. Stansfield Turner, interview with author, McLean, Va., July 13, 1988.

17. John Isaacs, interview with author, Washington, DC, June 2, 1987, and J. Brian Atwood, interview with author, Washington, DC, July 12, 1988.

18. Barry Blechman, interview with author, Washington, DC, October 23, 1987.

19. Senior member of the Carter administration, confidential interview with author.

20. Former senior Senate staff member, confidential interview with author.

21. John Isaacs, interview with author.

22. Strobe Talbott, *The Master of the Game: Paul Nitze and the Nuclear Peace* (New York: Alfred A. Knopf, 1988), 148–49.

23. Following their terms of service as the chief American negotiators at the START and INF talks, Rowny and Nitze were each appointed Special Adviser to the President and Secretary of State for Arms Control Matters.

24. Hedley Donovan, *Roosevelt to Reagan: A Reporter's Encounters with Nine Presidents* (New York: Harper and Row, 1985).

25. Barry Blechman, interview with author.

26. John Culver, interview with author, Washington, DC, July 12, 1988.

27. Alan Cranston, interview with author.

28. Lloyd Cutler, interview with author, Washington, DC, October 27, 1988.

29. William Bader, interview with author.

30. William G. Hyland, *Mortal Rivals: Superpower Relations from Nixon to Reagan* (New York: Random House, 1987), 225.

31. Paul A. Dawson, *American Government: Institutions, Policies, and Politics* (Glenview, Ill.: Scott, Foresman and Company, 1987), 214.

32. Charles Kupperman, interview with author, Washington, DC, June 5, 1987.

33. David Carl Kurkowski, "The Role of Interest Groups in the Domestic Debate on SALT II," Ph.D. diss., Temple University (Ann Arbor, Mich.: University Microfilms, 1982).

34. Miroslav Nincic, "The United States, the Soviet Union, and the Politics of Opposites," *World Politics* 40, no. 4 (July 1988): 469.

35. Ibid., 465.

36. Jimmy Carter, telephone interview with author, April 12, 1988.

37. Alton Frye, interview with author, Washington, DC, July 12, 1988.

38. Dean Acheson, "Dean Acheson's Version of Robert Kennedy's Version of the Cuban Missile Affair: Homage to Plain Dumb Luck," *Esquire* 71 (February 1969).

39. J. Brian Atwood, interview with author.

40. Robert A. Dahl, *Congress and Foreign Policy* (New York: W. W. Norton, 1964), 224.

41. Ibid.

42. Benjamin S. Loeb, "Amend the Constitution's Treaty Clause," *Bulletin of the Atomic Scientists* (October 1987): 38.

43. "New Estimates of State Populations," *New York Times*, December 30, 1987.

44. J. William Fulbright with Seth P. Tillman, *The Price of Empire* (New York: Pantheon Books, 1989).

45. Lloyd N. Cutler, "To Form a Government," *Foreign Affairs* 59, no. 1 (Fall 1980): 127.

46. David Broder, "A Frail Amendment," *Washington Post*, February 11, 1979.

47. Bruce Buchanan, "The Six-Year One Term Presidency: A New Look at an Old Proposal," *Presidential Studies Quarterly* 18, no. 1 (Winter 1988): 129.

48. Griffin Bell, Herbert Brownell, William Simon, and Cyrus Vance, "For a One-Term Six Year Presidency," *New York Times*, December 31, 1985.

49. Cyrus Vance, *Hard Choices: Critical Years in America's Foreign Policy* (New York: Simon and Schuster, 1983), 13.

50. Ibid.

51. Stuart Taylor, Jr., "Citing Chronic Deadlock, Panel Urges Altering Political Structure," *New York Times*, January 11, 1987; also see Committee on the Constitutional System, *A Bicentennial Analysis of the American Political Structure: Report and Recommendations of the Committee on the Constitutional System* (Washington: Committee on the Constitutional System, 1987), 12.

52. Jimmy Carter, telephone interview with author, transcript, 7.

53. Ibid., 8.

54. Public Law 87–297, 75 Stat. 631, Sec. 33.

55. Gerard Smith, "There Is No Other Way," *Arms Control Today* 11, no. 1 (January 1981): 5.

56. Gerald R. Ford, interview with author, Rancho Mirage, Calif., June 15, 1988, transcript, 5–6.

57. Edmund S. Muskie, Kenneth Rush, and Kenneth W. Thompson, *The President, the Congress and Foreign Policy: A Joint Project of the Association of Former Members of Congress and the Atlantic Council of the United States* (Lanham, Md.: University Press of America, 1986), 3.

58. The American Assembly of Columbia University and the Commission on Public Understanding about the Law of the American Bar Association, *The U.S. Constitution Today: Final Report of the Seventy-third American Assembly* (New York: The American Assembly, 1987), 9.

59. Cyrus Vance, interview with author.

60. Matthew Nimetz, interview with author, New York City, July 15, 1988.

61. David Aaron, interview with author, San Francisco, January 16, 1988.

62. Dan Caldwell, *American-Soviet Relations: From 1947 to the Nixon-Kissinger Grand Design and Grand Strategy* (Westport, Conn.: Greenwood Press, 1981).

63. Vance, *Hard Choices*, 14.

64. U.S. Congress, Senate, Committee on Foreign Relations, *The SALT II Treaty*, hearings, 96th Cong., 1st sess., 1979, pt. 1:94–95.

65. Ralph Earle II, interview with author, Washington, DC, October 23, 1987.

66. Author's confidential interview. During the SALT II debate, President Ford considered the possibility of exercising his right to address the Senate as a former president; Ford, interview with author, transcript, 4.

67. Author's confidential interview.

68. Jake Garn, interview with author, Washington, DC, June 3, 1987.

69. J. Brian Atwood, "The SALT II Treaty: A Victim of Self-Inflicted Linkage" (Address to the Harvard Club of Boston, December 17, 1980), 16.

Selected Bibliography

I. INTERVIEWS

David Aaron, San Francisco, January 16, 1988

J. Brian Atwood, Washington, DC, July 12, 1988

William Bader, Arlington, Virginia, October 20, 1987

Hans Binnendijk, Arlington, Virginia, October 19, 1987

Barry Blechman, Washington, DC, October 23, 1987

Landon Butler, Washington, DC, October 21, 1987

Jimmy Carter, telephone interview, April 12, 1988

Michael Chanin, Washington, DC, October 28, 1988

Warren Christopher, telephone interview, May 2, 1988

Alan Cranston, Washington, DC, June 5, 1987

John Culver, Washington, DC, July 12, 1988

Lloyd Cutler, Washington, DC, October 27, 1988

Ralph Earle II, Washington, DC, October 23, 1987

Gerald R. Ford, Rancho Mirage, California, June 15, 1988

Alton Frye, Washington, DC, July 12, 1988

Jake Garn, Washington, DC, June 3, 1987

Mark Garrison, telephone interview, February 4, 1988

Mark O. Hatfield, Washington, DC, June 4, 1987

J. Brian Hehir, Malibu, California, August 8, 1988

William Hyland, New York City, July 14, 1988

Karl Inderfurth, Washington, DC, October 22, 1987

John Isaacs, Washington, DC, June 2, 1987

Bruce Jentleson, telephone interview, February 2, 1989

Curtis Kammen, Washington, DC, July 13, 1988

Spurgeon Keeny, Washington, DC, October 19, 1987

William Kincade, Washington, DC, July 13, 1988

Michael Krepon, Washington, DC, October 19, 1987

Joseph Kruzel, Atlanta, Georgia, September 24, 1987

Charles Kupperman, Washington, DC, June 5, 1987

Ray McCrory, Washington, DC, July 13, 1988

Edward Meyer, telephone interview, October 21, 1987

William Miller, Washington, DC, October 21, 1987

Roger Molander, Washington, DC, October 22, 1987

Eric Newsom, Washington, DC, October 21, 1987

Matthew Nimetz, New York City, July 15, 1988

Richard Perle, telephone interview, November 10, 1988

William Perry, Menlo Park, California, January 15, 1988

Alan Platt, Washington, DC, October 23, 1987

William Proxmire, Washington, DC, June 4, 1987

Gerald Rafshoon, Washington, DC, October 27, 1988

Nancy Ramsey, Washington, DC, June 5, 1987

Eugene Rostow, Washington, DC, October 28, 1988

Edward Rowny, Washington, DC, June 3, 1987

George Seignious II, Washington, DC, October 21, 1987

Walter Slocombe, Washington, DC, June 3, 1987

Larry Smith, Washington, DC, October 20, 1987

Charles Stevenson, Washington, DC, October 21, 1987

Richard Stone, Washington, DC, October 27, 1988

Ronald Tammen, Washington, DC, June 4, 1987

Peter Tarnoff, New York City, July 14, 1988

James Timbie, Washington, DC, June 4, 1987

Stansfield Turner, McLean, Virginia, July 13, 1988

Victor Utgoff, Arlington, Virginia, July 11, 1988

Cyrus Vance, New York City, July 14, 1988

Paul Warnke, Los Angeles, California, May 20, 1987

Roy Werner, Anaheim, California, August 5, 1987

Anne Wexler, Washington, DC, October 28, 1988

II. BOOKS AND ARTICLES

Abshire, David M., and Ralph N. Nurnberger, eds. *The Growing Power of Congress.* Beverly Hills: Sage Publications, 1981.

Adelman, Kenneth L. "Rafshooning the Armageddon: The Selling of SALT." *Policy Review* 9 (Summer 1979): 85–102.

Almond, Gabriel A. *The American People and Foreign Policy.* New York: Praeger, 1960.

American Assembly of Columbia University and the Commission on Public Understanding about the Law of the American Bar Association. *The U.S. Constitution Today: Final Report of the Seventy-third American Assembly.* New York: American Assembly, 1987.

The Americas in a Changing World: A Report of the Commission on United States–Latin American Relations. New York: Quadrangle, 1974.

Art, Robert J., and Stephen E. Ockenden. "The Domestic Politics of Cruise Missile Development, 1970–1980." In *Cruise Missiles: Technology, Strategy and Politics,* edited by Richard Betts. Washington, DC: Brookings Institution, 1981.

Aspin, Les. "The Verification of the SALT Agreement." *Scientific American* (February 1979): 38–45.

Bader, William. *Congress and the Making of US Security Policies.* Adelphi Paper, no. 173, 14–21. London: International Institute for Strategic Studies, 1982.

Baker, Howard. *No Margin for Error: America in the Eighties.* New York: Times Books, 1980.

Ball, Desmond. *Can Nuclear War Be Controlled?* Adelphi Paper, no. 169. London: International Institute for Strategic Studies, 1981.

———. *Developments in U.S. Nuclear Policy under the Carter Administration.* ACIS Working Paper, no. 21. Los Angeles: Center for International and Strategic Affairs, University of California, 1980.

Barlow, Jeffrey G. *SALT II: The Basic Arguments.* Backgrounder, no. 98. Washington, DC: The Heritage Foundation, September 5, 1979.

———. *SALT II Treaty Ambiguities: The Backfire Bomber and the SS–20.* Backgrounder, no. 102. Washington, DC: The Heritage Foundation, October 29, 1979.

Barnet, Richard J. "The Search For National Security." *The New Yorker,* April 27, 1981.

Barnhart, Michael, ed. *Congress and United States Foreign Policy: Controlling the Use of Force in the Nuclear Age.* Albany, N.Y.: State University Press, 1987.

Bauer, Raymond A., Ithiel de Sola Pool, and Lewis Anthony Dexter. *American Business and Public Policy: The Politics of Foreign Trade.* Chicago: Aldine, 1972.

Bennet, Douglas J., Jr. "Congress in Foreign Policy: Who Needs It?" *Foreign Affairs* 57, no. 1 (Autumn 1978): 40–50.

Bennett, Paul. *Strategic Surveillance: How America Checks Soviet Compliance with SALT.* Cambridge: Union of Concerned Scientists, 1979.

Bennett, Ralph Kinney. "The Fatal Illusions of SALT II." *Reader's Digest* (May 1979): 97–102.

Berry, Jeffrey M. *Lobbying for the People: The Political Behavior of Public Interest Groups.* Princeton: Princeton University Press, 1977.

Bertram, Christoph. *Beyond SALT II.* Adelphi Paper, no. 141. London: International Institute for Strategic Studies, 1978.

Bibby, John F., Thomas E. Mann, and Norman J. Ornstein. *Vital Statistics on Congress 1980.* Washington, DC: American Enterprise Institute, 1980.

Blacker, Coit D., and Gloria Duffy, eds. *International Arms Control: Issues and Agreements.* 2d ed. Stanford: Stanford University Press, 1984.

Blechman, Barry M. "Do Negotiated Arms Limitations Have a Future?" *Foreign Affairs* 59, no. 1 (Fall 1980): 102–25.

———, ed. *Rethinking the U.S. Strategic Posture.* Cambridge: Ballinger, 1982.

Boyer, Paul. "From Activism to Apathy: The American People and Nuclear Weapons, 1963–1980." *The Journal of American History* 70, no. 4 (March 1984): 821–44.

Brauch, Hans Guenter, and Duncan L. Clarke, eds. *Decisionmaking for Arms Limitation: Assessments and Prospects.* Cambridge: Ballinger, 1983.

Brennan, Donald G., ed. *Arms Control, Disarmament, and National Security.* New York: George Braziller, 1961.

Brown, Harold. *Thinking about National Security: Defense and Foreign Policy in a Dangerous World.* Boulder, Colo.: Westview Press, 1983.

Brzezinski, Zbigniew. *Alternative to Partition: For a Broader Conception of America's Role in Europe.* New York: McGraw-Hill, 1965.

———. "The Balance of Power Delusion." *Foreign Policy*, no. 7 (Summer 1972): 54–59

———. *Between Two Ages: America's Role in the Technetronic Era.* New York: Viking Press, 1970.

———. *Game Plan: How to Conduct the U.S.-Soviet Contest.* New York: Atlantic Monthly Press, 1986.

———. *The Permanent Purge.* Cambridge: Harvard University Press, 1956.

———. *Power and Principle: Memoirs of the National Security Adviser 1977–1981.* New York: Farrar, Straus and Giroux, 1983.

———. "Recognizing the Crisis." *Foreign Policy*, no. 17 (Winter 1974–75): 16–17.

———. *The Soviet Bloc: Unity and Conflict.* Cambridge: Harvard University Press, 1967.

———. "U.S. Foreign Policy: The Search for Focus." *Foreign Affairs* 51, no. 4 (July 1973): 708–27.

———, Francois Duchêne, and Kiichi Saeki. "Peace in an International Framework." *Foreign Policy*, no. 19 (Summer 1975): 3–17.

———, and Samuel P. Huntington. *Political Power: USA/USSR.* New York: Viking Press, 1964.

Buchanan, Bruce. "The Six-Year One Term Presidency: A New Look at an Old Proposal." *Presidential Studies Quarterly* 18, no. 1 (Winter 1988): 129–42.

Buchanan, Patrick J. "How to Defeat the Treaty." *Public Opinion* (November–December 1978): 41–48.

Buchheim, Robert W., and Dan Caldwell. "The Standing Consultative Commission: Description and Appraisal." In *Conflict and Arms Control*, edited by Paul Viotti, 134–45. Boulder, Colo.: Westview Press, 1984.

Bull, Hedley. *The Control of the Arms Race.* New York: Praeger, 1961.

Burns, James MacGregor. *The Deadlock of Democracy.* Englewood Cliffs, N.J.: Prentice-Hall, 1963.

——. "Jimmy Carter's Strategy for 1980." *Atlantic Monthly* 243, no. 3 (March 1979): 41–46.

Burt, Richard. "SALT II and Offensive Force Levels." *Orbis* 18, no. 2 (Summer 1974): 465–81.

——. "The Scope and Limits of SALT." *Foreign Affairs* 56, no. 4 (July 1978): 751–70.

——, ed. "A Strategic Symposium: SALT and U.S. Defense Policy." *The Washington Quarterly* 2, no.1 (Winter 1979).

Caldwell, Dan. *American-Soviet Relations: From 1947 to the Nixon-Kissinger Grand Design and Grand Strategy.* Westport, Conn.: Greenwood Press, 1981.

——, ed. *Henry Kissinger: His Personality and Policies.* Durham, N.C.: Duke University Press, 1983.

——, ed. *Soviet International Behavior and U.S. Policy Options.* Lexington, Mass.: Lexington Books, 1985.

Califano, Joseph A., Jr. *Governing America: An Insider's Report from the White House and the Cabinet.* New York: Simon and Schuster, 1981.

Carnesale, Albert, and Richard N. Haass, eds. *Superpower Arms Control: Setting the Record Straight.* Cambridge: Ballinger, 1987.

Carter, Jimmy. *Keeping Faith: Memoirs of a President.* New York: Bantam Books, 1982.

——. *Why Not the Best?* New York: Bantam Books, 1975.

Carter, Rosalynn. *First Lady from Plains.* Boston: Houghton Mifflin, 1984.

Charlton, Michael. *From Deterrence to Defense: The Inside Story of Strategic Policy.* Cambridge: Harvard University Press, 1987.

Church, F. Forrester. *Father and Son: A Personal Biography of Senator Frank Church of Idaho by His Son.* New York: Harper and Row, 1985.

Clarke, Duncan L. *Politics of Arms Control: The Role and Effectiveness of the U.S. Arms Control and Disarmament Agency.* New York: The Free Press, 1979.

Cohen, Bernard C. *The Political Process and Foreign Policy: The Making of the Japanese Peace Settlement.* Princeton: Princeton University Press, 1957.

————. *The Public's Impact on Foreign Policy*. Boston: Little, Brown, 1973.

Cohen, Stuart A. "SALT Verification: The Evolution of Soviet Views and Their Meaning for the Future." *Orbis* 24 (Fall 1980): 657–84.

Colby, William E. "Verifying SALT." *Worldview* 22 (April 1979): 4–7.

Committee on the Constitutional System. *A Bicentennial Analysis of the American Political Structure: Report and Recommendations of the Committee on the Constitutional System*. Washington, DC: Committee on the Constitutional System, 1987.

Committee on the Present Danger. *Common Sense and the Common Danger*. Washington, DC: Committee on the Present Danger, 1976.

————. *Does the Official Case for the SALT II Treaty Hold up Under Analysis?* Washington, DC: Committee on the Present Danger, March 1979.

————. *How the Committee on the Present Danger Will Operate—What It Will Do and What It Will Not Do*. Washington, DC: Committee on the Present Danger, November 10, 1976.

————. *Public Attitudes on SALT II: The Results of a Nationwide Scientific Poll of American Opinion*. Washington, DC: Committee on the Present Danger, March 1979.

————. *What Is the Soviet Union Up To?* Washington, DC: Committee on the Present Danger, April 1977.

————. *Where We Stand on SALT*. Washington, DC: Committee on the Present Danger, July 1977.

Cranston, Alan. *The Killing of the Peace*. New York: Viking Press, 1960.

Cutler, Lloyd. "To Form a Government." *Foreign Affairs* 59, no. 1 (Fall 1980): 126–43.

————, and Roger Molander. "Is There Life after Death for SALT?" *International Security* 6, no. 2 (Fall 1981): 3–20.

Dahl, Robert A. *Congress and Foreign Policy*. New York: W. W. Norton, 1964.

Dangerfield, Royden J. *In Defense of the Senate: A Study in Treaty Making*. Norman: University of Oklahoma Press, 1933.

Davis, Eric L. "Congressional Liaison: The People and the Institutions." In *Both Ends of the Avenue: The Presidency, the Executive Branch, and Congress in the 1980s*, edited by Anthony King. Washington, DC: Brookings Institution, 1983.

————. "Legislative Liaison in the Carter Administration." *Political Science Quarterly* 94, no. 2 (Summer 1979): 287–301.

Davis, Jacquelyn K., Patrick Friel, and Robert L. Pfaltzgraff, Jr. *SALT II and U.S.-Soviet Strategic Forces*. Cambridge: Institute for Foreign Policy Analysis, 1979.

Dawson, Paul A. *American Government: Institutions, Policies, and Politics*. Glenview, Ill.: Scott, Foresman and Company, 1987.

Deibel, Terry L. *Presidents, Public Opinion and Power: The Nixon, Carter and Reagan Years*. Headline Series, no. 280. New York: Foreign Policy Association, 1987.

DeMause, Lloyd, and Henry Ebel, eds. *Jimmy Carter and American Fantasy: Psychohistorical Explorations*. New York: Two Continents/Psychohistory Press, 1977.

Destler, I. M. "Trade Consensus, SALT Stalemate: Congress and Foreign Policy in the 1970s." In *The New Congress*, edited by Thomas E. Mann and Norman J. Ornstein, 329–62. Washington, DC: American Enterprise Institute for Public Policy Research, 1981.

———. "Treaty Troubles: Versailles in Reverse." *Foreign Policy*, no. 33 (Winter 1978–79): 45–65.

———, Leslie H. Gelb, and Anthony Lake. *Our Own Worst Enemy: The Unmaking of American Foreign Policy*. New York: Simon and Schuster, 1984.

Dexter, Lewis A. "What Do Congressmen Hear: The Mail." *Public Opinion Quarterly* 20 (Spring 1956): 17–27.

Divine, Robert A. *Blowing on the Wind: The Nuclear Test Ban Debate, 1954–1960*. New York: Oxford University Press, 1978.

Donley, Michael B., ed. *The SALT Handbook*. Washington, DC: Heritage Foundation, 1979.

Donovan, Hedley. "The Enigmatic President." *Time*, May 6, 1985.

———. *Roosevelt to Reagan: A Reporter's Encounters with Nine Presidents*. New York: Harper and Row, 1985.

Drew, Elizabeth. "An Argument over Survival." *The New Yorker*, April 4, 1977.

———. "Profile: David Newsom." *The New Yorker*, June 16, 1980.

Duffy, Gloria. "Crisis Mangling and the Cuban Brigade." *International Security* 8, no. 1 (Summer 1983): 67–87.

———. "Crisis Prevention in Cuba." In *Managing U.S.-Soviet Rivalry: Problems of Crisis Prevention*, edited by Alexander L. George, 285–318. Boulder, Colo.: Westview Press, 1983.

———. "Is the SALT Era Over?" In *The Arms Race in the 1980s*, edited by David Carlton and Carlo Shaerf, 114–23. New York: St. Martin's Press, 1982.

Edwards, John. *Super-Weapon: The Making of MX*. New York: Norton, 1982.

Erikson, Robert, Norman Luttbeg, and Kent L. Tedin. *American Public Opinion*. 2d ed. New York: Wiley, 1980.

Esposito, Lori. "The Selling of SALT." *Foreign Service Journal* (February 1982): 20–35.

Feis, Herbert. *From Trust to Terror: The Onset of the Cold War, 1945–1950*. New York: W. W. Norton, 1970.

Flanagan, Stephen J. "Congress, the White House and SALT." *Bulletin of the Atomic Scientists* (November 1978).

———. "The Domestic Politics of SALT II: Implications for the Foreign Policy Process." In *Congress, the Presidency and Foreign Policy*, edited by John Spanier and Joseph Nogee, 44–76. Elmsford, N.Y.: Pergamon Press, 1981.

———. "SALT II." In *Superpower Arms Control: Setting the Record Straight*, edited by Albert Carnesale and Richard N. Haass, 105–38. Cambridge: Ballinger, 1987.

Foley, Michael. *The New Senate: Liberal Influence on a Conservative Institution, 1959–1972.* New Haven: Yale University Press, 1980.

Ford, Gerald R. *A Time to Heal.* New York: Berkley Books, 1979.

———. *The Vladivostok Negotiations and Other Events.* IGCC Policy Papers, no. 2. San Diego: Institute on Global Conflict and Cooperation, University of California, 1986.

Fosdick, Dorothy, ed. *Staying the Course: Henry M. Jackson and National Security.* Seattle: University of Washington Press, 1987.

Fox, Harrison W., Jr., and Susan Webb Hammond. *Congressional Staffs: The Invisible Force in American Lawmaking.* New York: The Free Press, 1977.

Franck, Thomas M., and Edward Weisband. *Foreign Policy by Congress.* New York: Oxford University Press, 1979.

Friedrich, Carl J., and Zbigniew Brzezinski. *Totalitarian Dictatorship and Autocracy.* Cambridge: Harvard University Press, 1956.

Frye, Alton. *A Responsible Congress: The Politics of National Security.* New York: McGraw-Hill, 1975.

Fulbright, J. William, with Seth P. Tillman. *The Price of Empire.* New York: Pantheon Books, 1989.

Furlong, William L., and Margaret E. Scranton. *The Dynamics of Foreign Policymaking: The President, the Congress and the Panama Canal Treaties.* Boulder, Colo.: Westview Press, 1984.

Gaddis, John Lewis. *Strategies of Containment: A Critical Appraisal of Postwar American National Security Policy.* New York: Oxford University Press, 1982.

Garn, Jake. "The SALT II Verification Myth." *Strategic Review* 7 (Summer 1987): 16–24.

———. "The Suppression of Information Concerning Soviet SALT Violations by the U.S. Government." *Policy Review*, no. 9 (Summer 1979): 11–32.

Garthoff, Raymond L. *Détente and Confrontation: American-Soviet Relations from Nixon to Reagan.* Washington, DC: Brookings Institution, 1985.

Gelb, Leslie H. "The Future of Arms Control: A Glass Half Full." *Foreign Policy*, no. 36 (Fall 1979): 21–32.

Glad, Betty. *Jimmy Carter: In Search of the Great White House.* New York: W. W. Norton, 1980.

Graham, Daniel O. *Shall America Be Defended?* New Rochelle, N.Y.: Arlington House, 1979.

Gray, Colin S. "The End of SALT? Purpose and Strategy in U.S.-U.S.S.R. Negotiations." *Policy Review*, no. 2 (Fall 1977): 31–45.

———. "SALT II: The Real Debate." *Policy Review,* no. 10 (Fall 1979): 7–22.

———. "SALT II and the Strategic Balance." *British Journal of International Studies* (October 1975): 183–208.

Graybeal, Sidney, and Michael Krepon. "Making Better Use of the SCC." *International Security* 10, no. 2 (Fall 1985): 183–99.

Haass, Richard. *Congressional Power: Implications for American Security Policy.* Adelphi Paper, no. 153. London: International Institute for Strategic Studies, 1979.

Hadley, Arthur T. *The Nation's Safety and Arms Control.* New York: Viking Press, 1961.

Haig, Alexander M., Jr. "Judging SALT II." *Strategic Review* 8, no. 1 (Winter 1980): 11–17.

Hamilton, Alexander, James Madison, and John Jay. *The Federalist Papers,* no. 10. New York: New American Library, 1961.

Hamilton, Lee H., and Michael H. Van Dusen. "Making the Separation of Powers Work." *Foreign Affairs* 57, no. 1 (Autumn 1978): 17–39.

Hayakawa, S. I. "SALT." *Journal of International Relations* (Winter 1977): 289–98.

Heginbotham, Stanley J. "Constraining SALT II: The Role of the Senate." In *Congress and United States Foreign Policy: Controlling the Use of Force in the Nuclear Age,* edited by Michael Barnhart, 98–121. Albany, N.Y.: State University of New York Press, 1987.

———. "The President's Double Bind: The Politics and Alliance Diplomacy of Arms Control." In *Defending Peace and Freedom: Toward Strategic Stability in the Year 2000,* edited by Brent Scowcroft, 69–96. Lanham, Md.: University Press of America, 1988.

Hehir, J. Brian. "Limited but Substantial Achievements.'" *Commonweal* (March 2, 1979): 108–10.

Hogan, Michael J. *The Panama Canal in American Politics: Domestic Advocacy and the Evolution of Policy.* Carbondale: Southern Illinois University Press, 1986.

Holloway, David. *The Soviet Union and the Arms Race.* New Haven: Yale University Press, 1983.

Holsti, Ole R., and James N. Rosenau. *American Leadership in World Affairs: Vietnam and the Breakdown of Consensus.* Boston: Allen and Unwin, 1984.

Hoover, Robert A. *The MX Controversy: A Guide to Issues and References.* Claremont, Calif.: Regina Books, 1982.

———, and Lauren H. Holland. *The MX Decision: A New Direction in U.S. Weapons Procurement Policy?* Boulder, Colo.: Westview, 1985.

Hughes, Barry B. *The Domestic Context in American Foreign Policy.* San Francisco: W. H. Freeman, 1978.

Humphrey, Gordon J., et al. *SALT II and American Security.* Cambridge: Institute for Foreign Policy Analysis, 1980.

Hyland, William G. *Mortal Rivals: Superpower Relations from Nixon to Reagan.* New York: Random House, 1987.

Iklé, Fred Charles. "What It Means to be Number Two." *Fortune,* November 20, 1978.

Jackson, William D. "Soviet Images of the U.S. as Nuclear Adversary, 1969–1979." *World Politics* 33, no. 4 (July 1981): 614–38.

———. "The Soviets and Strategic Arms: Toward and Evaluation of the Record." *Political Science Quarterly* 94, no. 2 (Summer 1979): 243–62.

Johansen, Robert C. "Arms Bazaar." *Harper's,* May 1979, 21–29.

Johnson, U. Alexis, with Jef Olivarius McAllister. *The Right Hand of Power.* Englewood Cliffs, N.J.: Prentice-Hall, 1984.

Jones, Charles O. "Keeping Faith and Losing Congress: The Carter Experience in Washington." *Presidential Studies Quarterly* 14 (Summer 1984).

———. *The Trusteeship Presidency: Jimmy Carter and the United States Congress.* Baton Rouge: Louisiana State University Press, 1988.

———. *The United States Congress: People, Place, and Policy.* Homewood, Ill.: Dorsey Press, 1982.

Jordan, Hamilton. *Crisis: the Last Year of the Carter Presidency.* New York: G. P. Putnam's Sons, 1982.

Jorden, William J. *Panama Odyssey.* Austin: University of Texas Press, 1984.

Kaplan, Morton A., ed. *SALT: Problems and Prospects.* Morristown, N.J.: General Learning Press, 1973.

Katz, Amron H. *Verification and SALT: The State of the Art and the Art of the State.* Washington, DC: Heritage Foundation, 1979.

Kegley, Charles W., Jr., and Eugene R. Wittkopf, eds. *American Foreign Policy: Pattern and Process.* 3d ed. New York: St. Martin's Press, 1987.

———. *The Domestic Sources of American Foreign Policy: Insights and Evidence.* New York: St. Martin's Press, 1988.

Kemp, Jack F. "Congressional Expectations of SALT II." *Strategic Review* 7 (Winter 1979): 16–25.

Kennedy, Edward M. "SALT II: A Lever for Security." *Arms Control Today* (March 1979).

Kincade, William H., and Jeffrey D. Porro, eds. *Negotiating Security: An Arms Control Reader.* Washington, DC: Carnegie Endowment for International Peace, 1979.

Kissinger, Henry A. *For the Record: Selected Statements, 1977–1980.* Boston: Little, Brown, 1981.

———. *White House Years.* Boston: Little, Brown, 1979.

———. *A World Restored: The Politics of Conservatism in a Revolutionary Age.* Boston: Houghton Mifflin, 1957.

————. *Years of Upheaval.* Boston: Little, Brown, 1982.

Kistiakowsky, George B. "False Alarm: The Story Behind SALT II." *New York Review of Books* 26 (March 22, 1979): 33–38.

Kohler, Foy D. *SALT II: How Not to Negotiate with the Russians.* Coral Gables, Fla.: Advanced International Studies Institute, University of Miami, 1979.

Kreiberg, Louis, and Ross Klein. "Changes in Public Support for U.S. Military Spending." *Journal of Conflict Resolution* 24 (March 1980): 79–110.

Krepon, Michael. *Arms Control Verification and Compliance.* New York: Foreign Policy Association, 1984.

————. *Strategic Stalemate: Nuclear Weapons and Arms Control in American Politics.* New York: St. Martin's, 1984.

Kruzel, Joseph. "SALT II: The Search for a Follow-on Agreement." *Orbis* 17, no. 2 (Summer 1973): 334–63.

Labedz, Leopold. "The Illusions of SALT." *Commentary,* September 1979, 54–65.

Labrie, Roger P., ed. *SALT Handbook: Key Documents and Issues 1972–1979.* Washington, DC: American Enterprise Institute, 1979.

Ladd, Everett Carll. "The Freeze Framework." *Public Opinion* (August–September 1982): 20, 41.

Laird, Melvin R. "SALT II: The Senate's Momentous Decision." *Reader's Digest,* October 1979, 101–5.

Laurance, Edward J. "The Changing Role of Congress in Defense Policy-Making." *Journal of Conflict Resolution* 20, no. 4 (June 1976): 213–53.

————. "The Congressional Role in Defense Policy-Making: The Evolution of the Literature." *Armed Forces and Society* 6, no. 3 (Spring 1980): 431–54.

Legvold, Robert. "Strategic 'Doctrine' and SALT: Soviet and American Views." *Survival* 21 (January–February 1979): 8–13.

Lehman, John F. "SALT: The Radical Change from Ford to Carter." *Commonsense* 1, no.2 (Fall 1978): 1–14.

————, and Seymour Weiss. *Beyond the SALT II Failure.* New York: Praeger, 1981.

Lepper, Mary. *Foreign Policy Formulation: A Case Study of the Nuclear Test Ban Treaty of 1963.* Columbus, Ohio: Bobbs Merrill, 1971.

Levering, Ralph B. *The Public and American Foreign Policy, 1918–1978.* New York: William Morrow, 1978.

Lodal, Jan. "Assuring Strategic Stability: An Alternative View." *Foreign Affairs* 54, no. 3 (April 1976): 462–81.

————. "SALT II and American Security." *Foreign Affairs* 57, no. 2 (Winter 1978–79): 245–68.

————. "Verifying SALT." *Foreign Policy,* no. 24 (Fall 1976): 40–64.

Loeb, Benjamin S. "Amend the Constitution's Treaty Provision." *Bulletin of the Atomic Scientists* (October 1987): 38–41.

Luttwak, Edward. "Ten Questions About SALT II." *Commentary* (August 1979): 21–32.

———. "Why Arms Control Has Failed." *Commentary* (January 1978): 19–28.

McLellan, David S. *Cyrus Vance.* Totowa, N.J.: Rowman and Allanheld, 1985.

Mandelbaum, Michael. "In Defense of SALT." *Bulletin of the Atomic Scientists* (January 1979): 15–21.

———, and William Schneider. "The New Internationalisms: Public Opinion and American Foreign Policy." In *Eagle Entangled: U.S. Foreign Policy in a Complex World,* edited by Kenneth A. Oye, Donald Rothchild, and Robert J. Lieber, 34–90. New York: Longman, 1979.

Marshall, Charles Burton. *Looking for Eggs in a Cuckoo Clock: Observations on SALT II.* Washington, DC: Committee on the Present Danger, January 1979.

Milbrath, Lester W. *The Washington Lobbyists.* Chicago: Rand McNally, 1963.

Milburn, Thomas W., and Kenneth H. Watman. *SALT II Verification.* Mershon Center Quarterly Report, no. 4. Columbus: Mershon Center, Ohio State University, Summer 1979.

Miller, Steven E. "Politics over Promise: Domestic Impediments to Arms Control." *International Security* 8, no. 4 (Spring 1984): 67–90.

Milshetyn, M. A., and L. S. Semeyko. "SALT II: A Soviet View." *Survival* 14 (March–April 1974): 63–70.

Moffett, George D. III. *The Limits of Victory: The Ratification of the Panama Canal Treaties.* Ithaca, N.Y.: Cornell University Press, 1985.

Moore, David W. "The Public Is Uncertain." *Foreign Policy,* no. 35 (Summer 1979): 69–73.

———. "SALT: A Question of Trust." *Public Opinion* (January–February 1979): 49–51.

Moynihan, Daniel Patrick. "The SALT Process." *The New Yorker,* November 19, 1979.

Muravchik, Joshua. *The Senate and National Security: A New Mood.* The Washington Papers, vol. 8, no. 80. Lanham, Md.: University Press of America, 1980.

Muskie, Edmund S., Kenneth Rush, and Kenneth W. Thompson. *The President, the Congress and Foreign Policy: A Joint Project of the Association of Former Members of Congress and the Atlantic Council of the United States.* Lanham, Md.: University Press of America, 1986.

Neuman, W. Russell. *The Paradox of Mass Politics: Knowledge and Opinion in the American Electorate.* Cambridge: Harvard University Press, 1986.

Neustadt, Richard E., and Ernest R. May. *Thinking in Time: The Uses of History for Decision Makers.* New York: The Free Press, 1986.

Newhouse, John. *Cold Dawn: The Story of SALT.* New York: Holt, Rinehart and Winston, 1973.

———. "Reflections: The SALT Debate." *The New Yorker,* December 17, 1979.

———. *War and Peace in the Nuclear Age.* New York: Alfred A. Knopf, 1989.

Newsom, David D. *The Soviet Brigade in Cuba: A Study in Political Diplomacy.* Bloomington: Indiana University Press, 1987.

Nincic, Miroslav. "The United States, the Soviet Union, and the Politics of Opposites." *World Politics* 40, no. 4 (July 1988): 452–75.

Nitze, Paul H. "Assuring Strategic Stability in an Age of Equivalence." *Foreign Affairs* 54, no. 2 (January 1976): 207–32.

———. "Deterring Our Deterrent." *Foreign Policy,* no. 25 (Winter 1976–77): 195–210.

———. *Is SALT II a Fair Deal for the United States?* Washington, DC: Commitee on the Present Danger, May 1979.

———. "SALT II and American Strategic Considerations." *Comparative Strategy* 1 (1980): 9–34.

———. "The Strategic Balance: Between Hope and Skepticism." *Foreign Policy,* no. 17 (Winter 1974–75): 136–56.

———. "The Vladivostock Accord and SALT II." *The Review of Politics* 37, no. 2 (April 1975): 147–60.

———, James E. Dougherty, and Francis X. Kane. *The Fateful Ends and Shades of SALT.* New York: Crane, Russak and Company, 1979.

———, with Ann M. Smith and Steven L. Rearden. *From Hiroshima to Glasnost: At the Center of Decision.* New York: Grove Weidenfeld, 1989.

Nixon, Richard M. *The Real War.* New York: Warner Books, 1980.

———. *RN: The Memoirs of Richard Nixon.* New York: Grosset and Dunlap, 1978.

Nye, Joseph S., Jr., ed. *The Making of America's Soviet Policy.* New Haven: Yale University Press, 1984.

O'Neill, Thomas P., Jr., with William Novak. *Man of the House: The Life and Political Memoirs of Speaker Tip O'Neill.* New York: Random House, 1987.

"Opinion Roundup: Americans Assess the Nuclear Option." *Public Opinion* (August–September 1982): 33–40.

"Opinion Roundup: The Realities of U.S./U.S.S.R. Intentions and Position." *Public Opinion* (August–September 1982): 36.

Ornstein, Norman J., and Shirley Elder. *Interest Groups, Lobbying and Policy-Making.* Washington, DC: Congressional Quarterly Press, 1978.

Oye, Kenneth A., Donald Rothchild, and Robert J. Lieber, eds. *Eagle Entangled: U.S. Foreign Policy in a Complex World.* New York: Longman, 1979.

Panofsky, W. K. H. *Arms Control and SALT II.* Seattle: University of Washington Press, 1979.

"Pass the SALT: An Interview with Paul Warnke." *New York Review of Books* (June 14, 1979).

Pavel, Barry. "JCS Involvement in Nuclear Arms Control." IDA Paper P–2037. Alexandria, Va.: Institute for Defense Analysis, September 1988.

Payne, Samuel B. *The Soviet Union and SALT.* Cambridge: MIT Press, 1980.

Percy, Charles. "The Partisan Gap." *Foreign Policy,* no. 45 (Winter 1981–82): 3–15.

Perle, Richard. "Echoes of the 1930s." *Strategic Review* 7 (Winter 1979): 11–15.

Pfaltzgraff, Robert L., Jr., ed. *Contrasting Approaches to Strategic Arms Control.* Lexington, Mass.: Lexington Books, 1974.

Pipes, Richard. "Why the Soviet Union Thinks It Could Fight and Win a Nuclear War." *Commentary* (July 1977): 21–34.

———. *Why the Soviet Union Wants SALT II.* Washington, DC: Committee on the Present Danger, September 1979.

Platt, Alan. "The Politics of Arms Control and the Strategic Balance." In *Rethinking the U.S. Strategic Posture,* edited by Barry M. Blechman, 155–78. Cambridge: Ballinger, 1982.

———. *The U.S. Senate and Strategic Arms Policy, 1969–1977.* Boulder, Colo.: Westview Press, 1978.

———, and Lawrence D. Weiler, eds. *The Congress and Arms Control.* Boulder, Colo.: Westview Press, 1978.

Podhoretz, Norman. "The Present Danger." *Commentary* 69, no. 3 (March 1980): 27–40.

Potter, William C., ed. *Verification and Arms Control.* Lexington, Mass.: Lexington Books, 1985.

———, ed. *Verification and SALT: The Challenge of Strategic Deception.* Boulder, Colo.: Westview Press, 1980.

Powell, Jody. *The Other Side of the Story.* New York: William Morrow, 1984.

Purvis, Hoyt, and Steven J. Baker, eds. *Legislating Foreign Policy.* Boulder, Colo.: Westview Press, 1984.

Quandt, William B. *Camp David: Peacemaking and Politics.* Washington, DC: Brookings Institution, 1986.

Ranger, Robin. "SALT II's Political Failure: The U.S. Senate Debate." *RUSI: Journal of the Royal United Services Institute for Defence Studies,* no. 617 (June 1980): 49–56.

Rielly, John E., ed. *American Public Opinion and U.S. Foreign Policy, 1983.* Chicago: Chicago Council on Foreign Relations, 1983.

Robinson, Clarence A., Jr., ed. *Aviation Week and Space Technology on SALT.* New York: McGraw-Hill, 1979.

Rosenau, James N., ed. *Domestic Sources of Foreign Policy.* New York: Free Press, 1967.

Rostow, Eugene. "The Case Against SALT II." *Commentary* 67, no. 2 (February 1979): 23–32.

———. "SALT II: A Soft Bargain, a Hard Sell—An Assessment of SALT in Historical Perspective." *Policy Review*, no. 6 (Fall 1978): 41–57.

Rothmyer, Karen. "Citizen Scaife." *Columbia Journalism Review*. (July–August 1981): 41.

Rourke, John. *Congress and the Presidency in U.S. Foreign Policymaking: A Study of Interaction and Influence, 1945–1982*. Boulder, Colo.: Westview Press, 1983.

Rowny, Edward L. "Negotiating with the Soviets." *Washington Quarterly* 3 (Winter 1980): 58–66.

Rubinstein, Alvin Z. *Soviet Policy toward Turkey, Iran, and Afghanistan: The Dynamics of Influence*. New York: Praeger, 1982.

Russett, Bruce. "Democracy, Public Opinion, and Nuclear Weapons." In *Behavior, Society, and Nuclear War*, edited by Philip E. Tetlock, Jo L. Husbands, Robert Jervis, Paul C. Stern, and Charles Tilly, 174–208. New York: Oxford University Press, 1989.

———, and Thomas W. Graham. "Public Opinion and National Security Policy: Relationship and Impacts." In *Handbook of War Studies*, edited by Manus Midlarsky. London: Allen and Unwin, 1989.

Sanders, Jerry W. *Peddlers of Crisis: The Committee on the Present Danger and the Politics of Containment*. Boston: South End Press, 1983.

Saunders, Harold H. "Diplomacy and Pressure, November 1979–May 1980." In *Americans Hostage in Iran: The Conduct of a Crisis*, edited by Warren Christopher, 72–143. New Haven: Yale University Press, 1985.

Schambra, William. "More Bucks for the Bang: New Public Attitudes toward Foreign Policy." *Public Opinion* (January–February 1979): 47–48.

Schattschneider, E. E. *Party Government*. New York: Rinehart and Company, 1942.

Scheer, Robert. *With Enough Shovels: Reagan, Bush and Nuclear War*. New York: Random House, 1984.

Schelling, Thomas C., and Morton H. Halperin. *Strategy and Arms Control*. New York: Twentieth Century Fund, 1961.

Schlesinger, James R., ed. *Defending America: Toward a New Role in the Post-Détente World*. New York: Basic Books, 1977.

Schneider, William. "Conservatism, Not Interventionism: Trends in Foreign Policy Opinion, 1974–1982." In *Eagle Defiant: United States Foreign Policy in the 1980s*, edited by Kenneth A. Oye, Robert J. Lieber, and Donald Rothchild, 33–64. Boston: Little, Brown, 1983.

———. "Public Opinion." In *The Making of America's Soviet Policy*, edited by Joseph Nye. New Haven: Yale University Press, 1984.

———. "'Rambo' and Reality: Having It Both Ways." In *Eagle Resurgent? The Reagan*

Era in American Foreign Policy, edited by Kenneth A. Oye, Robert J. Lieber, and Donald Rothchild, 41–74. Boston: Little, Brown, 1987.

Scott, Alexander. "Strategic Reconnaissance and the Verification of the SALT II Agreement." *Armed Forces Journal International* (June 1979).

Scoville, Herbert, Jr. *MX: Prescription for Disaster.* Cambridge: MIT Press, 1981.

———. "The SALT Negotiations." *Scientific American* (August 1977): 24–31.

———. "SALT Verification and Iran." *Arms Control Today* (February 1979).

Seignious, George M. II. "Introduction: The Recent History of American-Soviet Arms Control Negotiations." In *Arms Control and Nuclear Weapons,* edited by W. Gary Nichols and Milton L. Boykin, 1–6. Westport, Conn.: Greenwood Press, 1987.

Shogan, Robert. *Promises to Keep: Carter's First Hundred Days.* New York: Crowell, 1977.

Shulman, Marshall. *Beyond the Cold War.* New Haven: Yale University Press, 1965.

Sick, Gary. *All Fall Down: America's Tragic Encounter with Iran.* New York: Penguin Books, 1986.

Sienkiewicz, Stanley. "SALT and Soviet Nuclear Doctrine." *International Security* 2, no. 4 (Spring 1978): 84–100.

Slocombe, Walter. "Learning from Experience: Verification Guidelines for SALT II." *Arms Control Today* 6, no. 2 (February 1976).

———. "A SALT Debate: Hard but Fair Bargaining." *Strategic Review* (Fall 1979).

Smith, Gaddis. *Morality, Reason, and Power: American Diplomacy in the Carter Years.* New York: Hill and Wang, 1986.

Smith, Gerard C. *Doubletalk: The Story of the First Strategic Arms Limitation Talks.* Garden City, N.Y.: Doubleday, 1980.

———. "Negotiating with the Soviets." *New York Times Magazine,* February 27, 1977.

———. "SALT after Vladivostok." *Journal of International Affairs* 29, no. 1 (Spring 1975): 7–18.

———. "There Is No Other Way." *Arms Control Today* 11, no. 1 (January 1981): 1, 5–8.

Sullivan, David S. *The Bitter Fruit of SALT: A Record of Soviet Duplicity.* Houston: Texas Policy Institute, 1982.

———. "The Legacy of SALT I: Soviet Deception and U.S. Retreat." *Strategic Review* 7 (Winter 1979): 26–41.

———. "Lessons Learned from SALT I and SALT II: New Objectives for SALT III." *International Security Review* 6 (Fall 1981): 355–86.

Sullivan, William H. *Mission to Iran: The Last U.S. Ambassador.* New York: W. W. Norton, 1981.

Talbott, Strobe. *Deadly Gambits: The Reagan Administration and the Stalemate in Nuclear Arms Control.* New York: Alfred A. Knopf, 1984.

———. *Endgame: The Inside Story of SALT II.* New York: Harper and Row, 1979.

———. *The Master of the Game: Paul Nitze and the Nuclear Peace.* New York: Alfred A. Knopf, 1988.

———. "Scrambling and Spying in SALT II." *International Security* 4, no. 2 (Fall 1979): 3–21.

Thompson, W. Scott, ed. *National Security in the 1980s: From Weakness to Strength.* San Francisco: Institute for Contemporary Studies, 1980.

Tonelson, Alan. "Nitze's World." *Foreign Policy,* no. 35 (Summer 1979): 74–90.

Tower, John. "Congress versus the President: The Formulation and Implementation of American Foreign Policy." *Foreign Affairs* 60, no. 2 (Winter 1981–82): 229–46.

Trofimenko, Henry. "SALT II: A Fair Bargain." *Bulletin of the Atomic Scientist* (June 1979): 30–34.

Truman, David B. *The Governmental Process: Political Interests and Public Opinion.* 2d ed. New York: Knopf, 1971.

Turner, Robert F. "Legal Implications of Deferring Ratification of SALT II." *Virginia Journal of International Law* 21 (Summer 1981): 747–84.

Turner, Stansfield. *Secrecy and Democracy: The CIA in Transition.* New York: Harper and Row, 1985.

Tyroler, Charles II, ed. *Alerting America: The Papers of the Committee on the Present Danger.* New York: Pergamon-Brassy's, 1984.

The United States and Latin America: Next Steps. A Second Report by the Commission on United States–Latin American Relations. New York: Center for Inter-American Relations, 1976.

Vance, Cyrus. *Hard Choices: Critical Years in America's Foreign Policy.* New York: Simon and Schuster, 1983.

Van Cleave, William, and W. Scott Thompson, eds. *Strategic Options for the Early Eighties: What Can Be Done?* New York: National Strategy Information Center, 1979.

Vartian, Armen R. "Approval of SALT Agreements by Joint Resolution of Congress." *Harvard International Law Journal* 21, no. 2 (Summer 1980): 421–66.

Viorst, Milton. "How to Build Public Support." *Public Opinion* (November–December 1978): 41–46.

Vogelsang, Sandy. *American Dream, Global Nightmare: The Dilemma of U.S. Human Rights Policy.* New York: W. W. Norton, 1980.

Warnke, Paul. "Apes on a Treadmill." *Foreign Policy,* no. 18 (Spring 1975): 12–29.

———. "Salt II and NATO Security." *NATO Review* (August 1979).

Watson, Thomas J., Jr., and Peter Petre. *Father, Son and Company: My Life at IBM and Beyond.* New York: Bantam, 1990.

Wayman, Frank Waylon. "Arms Control and Strategic Arms Voting in the U.S. Senate: Patterns of Change, 1967–1983." *Journal of Conflict Resolution* 29, no. 2 (June 1985): 225–51.

Wells, Samuel F., Jr. "The United States and the Present Danger." *The Journal of Strategic Studies* 4 (March 1981).

Widenor, William C. *Henry Cabot Lodge and the Search for an American Foreign Policy.* Berkeley: University of California Press, 1980.

Willrich, Mason, and John B. Rhinelander, eds. *SALT: The Moscow Agreements and Beyond.* New York: Free Press, 1974.

Wittkopf, Eugene R. "Elites and Masses: Another Look at Attitudes toward America's World Role." *International Studies Quarterly* 31, no.2 (June 1987): 131–60.

Wohlstetter, Albert. "Is There a Strategic Arms Race?" *Foreign Policy*, no. 15 (Summer 1974): 3–20.

———. "Optimal Ways to Confuse Ourselves." *Foreign Policy*, no. 20 (Fall 1975): 170–98.

———. "Rivals, But No 'Race'." *Foreign Policy*, no. 16 (Fall 1974): 48–81.

Wolfe, Thomas. *The SALT Experience.* Cambridge: Ballinger, 1979.

Yankelovich, Daniel. "Cautious Internationalism: A Changing Mood toward U.S. Foreign Policy." *Public Opinion* 1, no. 1 (March–April 1978).

———, Robert Kingston, and Gerald Garvey, eds. *Voter Options on Nuclear Arms Policy: A Briefing for the 1984 Elections.* New York: The Public Agenda Foundation and the Center for Foreign Policy Development, 1984.

Yost, David. "Beyond SALT II: European Security and the Prospects for SALT III." *Orbis* 24 (Fall 1980).

Ziegler, L. Harmon. *Interest Groups in American Society.* Englewood Cliffs, N.J.: Prentice-Hall, 1964.

———, and Michael Baer. *Lobbying.* Belmont, Calif.: Wadsworth, 1969.

III. U.S. GOVERNMENT DOCUMENTS

(All of these documents were published by the U.S. Government Printing Office in Washington, DC, unless otherwise noted.)

Bell, Robert G. "U.S. and Soviet Strategic Weapons Permitted under the Tentative SALT II Accord." Congressional Research Service, January 4, 1979.

———, and Mark Lowenthal. "SALT II: The Major Issues." Report no. 78–249F. Congressional Research Service, 1978.

Bellmon, Henry. "SALT II." *Congressional Record–Senate*, June 21, 1979, S 8244.

———. "SALT II and U.S. Interests." *Congressional Record–Senate*, October 1, 1979, S 13772.

———. "SALT II Treaty." *Congressional Record–Senate*, April 4, 1979, S 3941–42.

Bentsen, Lloyd. ""Détente in Jeopardy." *Congressional Record–Senate*, June 28, 1978, S 9952–53.

Brown, Harold. "SALT II and National Defense." Speech to the Council on Foreign Relations and the Foreign Policy Association, New York. Current Policy, no. 62. Washington, DC: Department of State, April 1979.

Brzezinski, Zbigniew. "American Power and Global Challenge." Current Policy, no. 81. Washington, DC: Department of State, August 1979.

————. "SALT II and National Security." Current Policy, no. 62. Washington, DC: Department of State, April 1979.

Byrd, Robert C. "Proliferation of Nuclear Weapons." *Congressional Record–Senate*, October 31, 1979, S 15487.

————. "Strategic Arms Limitation Treaty II." *Congressional Record–Senate*, October 25, 1979, S 15213–17.

Carter, Jimmy. "America's Role in a Turbulent World." Current Policy, no. 57. Speech at Georgia Institute of Technology. Washington, DC: Department of State, March 1979.

————. "SALT II: The Path of Security and Peace." Current Policy, no. 66. Speech to the American Newspaper Publishers Association. Washington, DC: Department of State, April 1979.

————. "Soviet Troops in Cuba." Current Policy, no. 92. Address to the Nation. Washington, DC: Department of State, October 1, 1979.

Cohen, William S. "Senator Cohen's Remarks to the North Atlantic Assembly." *Congressional Record–Senate*, October 31, 1979, S 15544–45.

DeConcini, Dennis. "SALT II." *Congressional Record–Senate*, September 10, 1979, S 12316.

————. "The SALT II Treaty Is Flawed." *Congressional Record–Senate*, December 3, 1979, S 17663–65.

————. "Senate Resolution 229—Submission of a Resolution on Soviet Troops in Cuba." *Congressional Record–Senate*, September 6, 1979, S 12006.

Dole, Robert. "Senate Resolution 228—Submission of a Resolution on Soviet Troops in Cuba." *Congressional Record–Senate*, September 6, 1979, S 12003–6.

————. "The Vienna Summit." *Congressional Record–Senate*, June 18, 1979, S 7909–10.

Duncan, Charles W., Jr. "SALT and the US-Soviet Military Balance." Current Policy, no. 58. Washington, DC: Department of State, March 1979.

Ford, Gerald. "Gerald Ford Takes His Stand on SALT." *Congressional Record–Senate*, September 26, 1979, S 13448–50.

————. "Soviet Troops in Cuba." *Congressional Record–Senate*, September 10, 1979, S 12243.

Garn, Jake. "Examining SALT Violations and the Problems of Verification." *Congressional Record–Senate*, August 17, 1978, S 13668–73.

Gelb, Leslie. "The Facts of SALT II." Current Policy, no. 65. Washington, DC: Department of State, April 1979.

Gellner, Charles R., and David D'Agostino. *SALT II: Some Verification Issues.* Issue Brief no. 79006. Congressional Research Service, 1979.

Glenn, John. "Remarks of Senator John Glenn." *Congressional Record–Senate,* November 18, 1981, S 13664–66.

———. "SALT II." *Congressional Record–Senate,* March 12, 1979, S 2548.

Hatfield, Mark O. "Interview." *Congressional Record–Senate,* June 18, 1979, S 7929.

———. "SALT II and the Arms Race." *Congressional Record–Senate,* March 5, 1979, S 2042–43.

———. "Signing SALT II Won't End the Arms Race." *Congressional Record–Senate,* May 3, 1979, S 5269–70.

Lowenthal, Mark M. *SALT II Verification: Outstanding Issues.* Issue Brief no. IB 79096. Congressional Research Service, 1979.

———. *SALT Verification.* Report no. 78–142F. Congressional Research Service, July 1978, revised April 1979.

McGovern, George. "Arms Control or Arms Race—President Carter Must Choose." *Congressional Record–Senate,* March 5, 1979, S 2041.

———. "The SALT Paradox." *Congressional Record–Senate,* June 26, 1979, S 8567–68.

———. "Senator McGovern on 'Face the Nation.'" *Congressional Record–Senate,* March 15, 1979, S 2848–49.

Morgan, Robert. "SALT II." *Congressional Record–Senate,* October 29, 1979, S 15228.

Moynihan, Daniel Patrick. "SALT II Treaty." *Congressional Record–Senate,* October 31, 1979, S 15490–93.

———. "SALT II Treaty." *Congressional Record–Senate,* November 1, 1979, S 15620–22.

Nimetz, Matthew. "American Security and SALT." Current Policy, no. 50. Washington, DC: Department of State, December 1978.

———. "U.S. Foreign Policy Achievements." Current Policy, no. 102. Speech to the American Bankers Association. Washington, DC: Department of State, October 24, 1978.

Nunn, Sam. "Placing SALT II in Perspective." *Congressional Record–Senate,* June 21, 1977, S 10337.

———. "Response to President Carter's Statement on Cuban Situation." *Congressional Record–Senate,* October 2, 1979, S 13843–44.

———. "SALT and National Security: Where Do We Go from Here?" *Congressional Record–Senate,* November 2, 1979, S 15733–37.

————. "SALT II and Defense Spending." *Congressional Record–Senate*, September 7, 1979, S 12167–71.

Proxmire, William. "SALT II—Too High a Price." *Congressional Record–Senate*, March 5, 1979, S 2043–46.

"*The SALT Syndrome*: Charges and Facts: Analysis of an Anti-SALT 'Documentary.'" *Congressional Record–Senate*, July 30, 1980, S 10366–71.

Seignious, George M. "Special Briefing on SALT Two." Current Policy, no. 51. Washington, DC: Department of State, December 1978.

Smith, Gerald C. "SALT II: The Sense of Horror Is Missing." Current Policy, no. 82. Washington, DC: Department of State, July 1979.

Tinajero, A. A. *U.S./U.S.S.R. Strategic Offensive Weapons: Projected Inventories Based on Carter Policies*. Congressional Research Service, 1981.

Toon, Malcolm. "SALT and U.S.-Soviet Relations." Current Policy, no. 76. Testimony to the Senate Foreign Relations Committee. Washington, DC: Department of State, July 1979.

U.S. Arms Control and Disarmament Agency. *Annual Report*. 1972–1980.

————. *Arms Control and Disarmament Agreements: Text and Histories of Negotiations*. 1980.

————. *SALT II: Glossary of Terms*. Publication 99. n.d.

————. *SALT II Treaty: Index to Hearings before the Committee on Foreign Relations United States Senate and the Committee on Armed Services United States Senate*. n.d.

U.S. Congress. Congressional Budget Office. *SALT II and the Costs of Modernizing U.S. Strategic Forces*. Staff Working Paper, September 1, 1979.

U.S. Congress. House. Committee on Armed Services. *SALT II: An Interim Assessment*. Report, 95th Cong., 2d sess., 1978.

U.S. Congress. House. Committee on International Relations. *Strategic Arms Limitation Talks: Hearings and Briefings*. 95th Cong., 2d sess., 1978.

————. *The Vladivostok Accord: Implications to U.S. Security, Arms Control, and World Peace*. Hearings, 94th Cong., 1st sess., 1975.

U.S. Congress. Library of Congress. *Treaties and Other International Agreements: The Role of the United States Senate*. Washington, DC: Congressional Research Service, 1984.

U.S. Congress. Office of Technology Assessment. *The Effects of Nuclear War*. 1979.

————. *MX Missile and Multiple Protective Structure Basing: Long-term Budgetary Implications*. 1979.

U.S. Congress. Senate. Committee on Armed Services. *Consideration of Mr. Paul C. Warnke to Be Director of the U.S. Arms Control and Disarmament Agency and Ambassador*. Hearings, 95th Cong., 1st sess., 1977.

————. *Military Implications of the Proposed SALT II Treaty Relating to the National Defense*. Report, 96th Cong., 2d sess., 1980.

———. *Military Implications of the Treaty on the Limitation of Strategic Offensive Arms and Protocol Thereto (SALT II Treaty).* Hearings, 96th Cong., 1st sess., 4 parts, 1979.

U.S. Congress. Senate. Committee on Foreign Relations. *Briefing on SALT Negotiations.* 95th Cong., 2d sess., 1978.

———. *Hearings and Markup on the Panama Canal Treaties.* 95th Cong., 2d sess., 1978.

———. *The SALT II Treaty.* Hearings, 96th Cong., 1st sess., 6 parts, 1979.

———. *The SALT II Treaty.* Report, 96th Cong., 1st sess., 1979.

———. *SALT II Treaty: Background Documents.* 96th Cong., 1st sess., 1979.

———. *Senate Delegation Report on SALT Discussions in the Soviet Union, August 25–30, 1979.* Report, 95th Cong., 2d sess., 1979.

———. *Warnke Nomination.* Hearings, 95th Cong., 1st sess., 1977.

U.S. Congress. Senate. Judiciary Committee. *Treaty Ratification Process and Separation of Powers.* Hearings, 97th Cong., 2d sess., 1982.

U.S. Congress. Senate. Select Committee on Intelligence. *Principal Findings by the Senate Select Committee on Intelligence on the Capabilities of the United States to Monitor the SALT II Treaty.* Report, 96th Cong., 1st sess., 1979.

U.S. Department of Defense. *Annual Report of the Secretary of Defense.* 1972–1980.

U.S. Department of State. *Administration Strategy toward Congress on Three Nuclear Arms Issues (Limited Test Ban Treaty, Nonproliferation Treaty, Salt I Agreements).* Research Project no. 1189, March 1978.

———. *Compliance with SALT I Agreements.* Special Report, no. 55. Washington, DC: Department of State, July 1979.

———. *SALT and American Security.* November 1978.

———. *SALT II Agreement.* Selected Documents, no. 12A. June 1979.

———. *SALT II: The Agreement in Brief.* Brochure, n.d.

———. *SALT II Basic Guide.* Publication 8974. General Foreign Policy Series 311, May 1979.

———. *SALT II: The Reasons Why.* Publication 8978. General Foreign Policy Series 312, May 1979.

———. *SALT II Senate Testimony.* Current Policy, no. 72A. July 1979.

——— *Salt One: Compliance. Salt Two: Verification.* Selected Documents, no. 7. February 1978.

———. *The SALT Process.* Publication 8947. General Foreign Policy Series 306, June 1978.

———. *SALT Public Speakers Handbook.* June 1978.

———. *The Strategic Arms Limitation Talks.* Special Report, no. 46. May 1979.

————. *Verification of SALT II Agreement.* Special Report, no. 56. August 1979.

————. *Vienna Summit.* Selected Documents, no. 13. June 1979.

U.S. General Accounting Office. International Division. Letter from J. K. Fasick to Senator Barry Goldwater. ID–79–24. March 16, 1979.

————. Letter from J. K. Fasick to Senator Barry Goldwater. ID–79–50. August 27, 1979.

U.S. Library of Congress. Congressional Research Service. *Foreign Perceptions of SALT.* 1979.

U.S. Office of the Federal Register. *Public Papers of the Presidents of the United States.* 1972–80.

————. *Weekly Compilation of Presidential Documents.* 1972–80.

U.S. White House. Press Office. Office of Media Liaison. *SALT II—In Perspective.* Background Report. May 1979.

————. *SALT II: The Strategic Arms Limitation Talks.* July 1979.

Vance, Cyrus. "Arms Control and National Security." Speech to the American Society of Newspaper Editors. Washington, DC: Department of State, April 10, 1978.

————. "Limiting the Strategic Arms Race." Current Policy, no. 73. Washington, DC: Department of State, July 1979.

————. "SALT II: Armed Services Testimony." Current Policy, no. 78. Washington, DC: Department of State, July 1979.

————. "SALT II: The Choice." Current Policy, no. 79. Washington, DC: Department of State, August 1979.

————. "SALT II: Summation." Current Policy, no. 96. Statement to the Senate Foreign Relations Committee. Washington, DC: Department of State, October 10, 1979.

————. "SALT II: Where We Stand." Current Policy, no. 101. Washington. DC: Department of State, October 1979.

Warnke, Paul. "Arms Control: A Global Imperative." 1978 Gabriel Silver Memorial Lecture, Columbia University. Washington, DC: U.S. Arms Control and Disarmament Agency, April 3, 1978.

————. "SALT: Its Contribution to U.S. Security and World Peace." Current Policy, no. 27. Washington, DC: Department of State, August 1978.

————. "The SALT Process." Speech to National Foreign Policy Conference for Editors and Broadcasters. Washington, DC: Department of State, January 19, 1978.

————. "SALT II: A More Secure World." Speech to the Overseas Writers Club. Washington, DC: U.S. Arms Control and Disarmament Agency, January 6, 1978.

Wrenn, Harry L. *SALT II: Major Policy Issues.* Issue Brief no. IB 79074. Washington, DC: Congressional Research Service, July 19, 1979, revised December 10, 1980.

IV. UNPUBLISHED DOCUMENTS

Americans for SALT. "Comment on the Report of the Coalition for Peace through Strength." Washington, DC: SALT Education Fund Speakers Bureau, April 19, 1979

————. "SALT II Campaign." Washington, DC: SALT Education Fund Speakers Bureau, n.d.

————. "SALT II Point Papers." Washington, DC: SALT Education Fund Speakers Bureau, n.d.

Atwood, J. Brian. "The SALT II Treaty: A Victim of Self-Inflicted Linkage." Speech to the Harvard Club of Boston, Massachusetts, December 17, 1980.

Baker, Howard. Speech to National Press Club. June 6, 1979.

————. "Statement by Senate Republican Leader on the Salt II Treaty." June 27, 1979.

Carter, Jimmy. "The United States and the Soviet Union." Commencement address delivered at the U.S. Naval Academy, June 7, 1978. U.S. Department of State Publication no. 8948, General Foreign Policy Series 307.

Coalition for Peace through Strength. *The SALT Syndrome*, unpublished script. Boston, Va.: American Security Council Educational Foundation, n.d.

Dole, Robert. "Interview on 'Face the Nation.'" Washington, DC: CBS News, August 12, 1979.

Duffy, Gloria Charmian. "Crisis Politics: The Carter Administration and Soviet Troops in Cuba, 1979." Ph.D. diss., Columbia University, 1985.

Earle, Ralph II. Manuscripts on SALT II, 1982, 1983.

Flanagan, Stephen Joseph. "Congress and the Evolution of U.S. Strategic Arms Limitation Policy: A Study of the Legislature's Role in National Security Affairs." Ph.D. diss., Fletcher School of Law and Diplomacy, Tufts University, 1979.

————. "Safeguarding Arms Control." Paper prepared for the Verification Project. Washington, DC: Carnegie Endowment for International Peace, May 5, 1987.

Glenn, John. "No Breakthrough in Carter's SALT II Speech." Press release, June 19, 1979.

————. "SALT—A Congressional Perspective." Speech to the American Defense Preparedness Association, May 17, 1979.

————. "Transcript of John Glenn's Statement on CBS." Press release, June 28, 1979.

Graham, Thomas W. "The Politics of Failure: Strategic Nuclear Arms Control, Public Opinion, and Domestic Politics in the United States, 1945–1985." Ph.D. diss., Massachusetts Institute of Technology, 1989.

Gromoll, Robert L. "Political and Perceptual Aspects of SALT II Verification." Ph.D. diss., American University, 1982.

Hallenberg, Jan. "The Image of the Soviet Union in American Politics: The Role of Public Interest Groups." Paper presented at the Annual Meeting of the International Studies Association, St. Louis, March 29–April 2, 1988.

Hart, Gary. "A Consensus on Defense Policy for the 1980's and 1990's." Press release, August 2, 1979.

———. "Hart Says SALT II Improves National Security." Press release, July 27, 1979.

Heinz, John. Speech to the Philadelphia World Affairs Council. June 22, 1979.

Hollings, Fritz. "Understanding SALT II." *The Fritz Hollings Report.* March 1979.

"Interview with Cyrus Vance." U.S. Department of State, Bureau of Public Affairs, press release. February 3, 1977.

"Interview with President Carter." U.S. Department of State, Bureau of Public Affairs, press release. December 28, 1977.

Jackson, Henry. "The Signs of the Times." Speech to the Coalition for a Democratic Majority, June 12, 1979.

Koontz, Theodore James. "The SALT II Debate: An Analysis of Senatorial Decision Making." Ph.D. diss., Harvard University, 1985.

Kupperman, Charles Martin. "The SALT II Debate." Ph.D. diss., University of Southern California, 1980.

Kurkowski, David Carl. "The Role of Interest Groups in the Domestic Debate on SALT II." Ph.D. diss., Temple University, 1982.

Lugar, Richard. "Statement of Senator Dick Lugar on the SALT II Treaty." *Dick Lugar News.* July 3, 1979.

Moynihan, Daniel Patrick. "Interview on 'Face the Nation.'" Washington, DC: CBS News, June 17, 1979.

Nitze, Paul. "Current SALT II Negotiating Posture." Unpublished paper. Washington, DC: Committee on the Present Danger, April 23, 1979.

Nunn, Sam. "SALT II." Speech to the Air Force Association, July 17, 1978.

Republican National Committee, Research Division. "SALT II: The Best We Can Do?" March 1979.

———. "SALT II: Strategic Arms Limitation Treaty Digest." 1979.

Tarbell, Gregory C. "Congress, Counterforce, and the Genesis of the MX, 1974–1976." Master's thesis, Brown University, 1983.

Vance, Cyrus. "Interview on 'Face the Nation.'" Washington, DC: CBS News, April 30, 1979.

Index